Shakespearean Tragedy
and the Common Law

Studies in Shakespeare

Robert F. Willson, Jr.
General Editor

Vol. 7

PETER LANG
New York • Washington, D.C./Baltimore • Boston
Bern • Frankfurt am Main • Berlin • Vienna • Paris

William M. Hawley

Shakespearean Tragedy and the Common Law

The Art of Punishment

PETER LANG
New York • Washington, D.C./Baltimore • Boston
Bern • Frankfurt am Main • Berlin • Vienna • Paris

Library of Congress Cataloging-in-Publication Data

Hawley, William M.
Shakespearean tragedy and the common law:
the art of punishment / William M. Hawley.
p. cm. — (Studies in Shakespeare; v. 7)
Includes bibliographical references and index.
1. Shakespeare, William, 1564–1616—Tragedies. 2. Shakespeare, William,
1564–1616—Knowledge—Law. 3. Law—Great Britain—History—16th century.
4. Punishment in literature. 5. Law in literature.
I. Title. II. Series: Studies in Shakespeare; vol. 7.
PR2983.H39   822.3'3—dc21   97-15417
ISBN 0-8204-3857-X
ISSN 1067-0823

Die Deutsche Bibliothek-CIP-Einheitsaufnahme

Hawley, William M.:
Shakespearean tragedy and the common law: the art of punishment / William M. Hawley
–New York; Washington, D.C./Baltimore; Boston; Bern;
Frankfurt am Main; Berlin; Vienna; Paris: Lang.
(Studies in Shakespeare; Vol. 7)
ISBN 0-8204-3857-X

Cover design by James F. Brisson.

The paper in this book meets the guidelines for permanence and durability
of the Committee on Production Guidelines for Book Longevity
of the Council of Library Resources.

Printed in the United States of America.

to my wife, BJ

ACKNOWLEDGMENTS

I would like to express my appreciation to the faculty and staff of Loyola Law School, Los Angeles, whose dedication to instruction in the law was a primary inspiration for this book.

Librarians and staff of the Law Library and Research Library at UCLA, the Davidson Library at UC Santa Barbara, and the Huntington Library in San Marino, CA, were most helpful in this project.

Series editor Robert F. Willson, Jr., made invaluable suggestions, as did the talented staff at Peter Lang Publishing.

While this book was being completed, I noted with sadness the passing of my former teacher, John Harrop, professor of Dramatic Art at UC Santa Barbara, in 1995. His professionalism and verve remain unforgettable.

TABLE OF CONTENTS

INTRODUCTION

Hard cases make bad law, according to an old legal maxim, but for Shakespeare they produce great tragedies. His conceptual use of the law is equaled in dramatic scope only by the classical Greek tragedians. Shakespearean punishment, the sine qua non of his tragedies, is often grossly disproportionate in its distribution and execution. To this extent, Shakespearean tragedy expands the philosophy and practice of English Renaissance common law, particularly as it was enunciated by the great jurist of the age, Sir Edward Coke. Coke's legal rationale is sufficiently distinct from our own to suggest that a reasonable spectator in Renaissance England would interpret the art and theory of punishment in Shakespeare's tragedies differently than we do today.

Few known dramatists of the Renaissance were bold enough to represent contemporary cases realistically. To do so was to court the disfavor of influential patrons and the legal system. An innocent evocation of Sir John Oldcastle's name led Shakespeare to add a disclaimer to the epilogue of *2 Henry IV*. This precautionary step was taken either out of common courtesy or to forestall a slander suit, which was a routine matter at the bar. An untoward remark could put at risk his personal and professional freedom as well as endanger his company. More importantly, Shakespeare enters an imaginative sphere removed from the literal representation of common law practice in order to address great metaphysical issues in the tragedies.

The imposition of punishment brings the full weight of legal procedure and dramaturgy to bear upon the individual. Law and Shakespearean tragedy most nearly intersect at the moment the subject is put upon the rack, however disparate the manner in which cases are brought and resolved by the two professions. Coke made plain his wish that the populace might be deterred from crime, but once the legal machinery was set in motion against an offender, he regarded punishment as a necessity in most cases: "For it is a sure Rule, . . . to bring errors to their first, is to see their last" (4 *Institutes* 365). Punishment is equally thorough in Shakespeare; none of the eponymous heroes of his tragedies survives his ordeal.

Shakespearean tragedy builds upon the general schema of punishment theory propounded by the common law over time. The law takes four basic approaches to punishment, though it must be emphasized that few legal scholars hold strictly to one category at the expense of all others. The first and most widely held paradigm is that of retribution, or just deserts retaliation against an offender conscious of his guilt. Immanuel Kant is the main proponent of this plan, which is said to be backward-looking in that it seeks to requite a wrong already committed. The second model is restitution, which demands that reparations be made by the offender in order to preserve social cohesion and progress. Emile Durkheim, the champion of restitution theory, is regarded as forward-looking because he would heal social wounds rather than dwell upon righting past injustices.

A third model is reform, or rehabilitation, the notion that offenders ought somehow to be led to a better path. H. L. A. Hart is a highly skeptical defender of this theory in that he mixes retribution and deterrence by endorsing indeterminate sentencing guidelines while protecting the rights of the accused. He is under no illusions about the prospect of exhorting hardened criminals to mend their ways but sees weaknesses in the other approaches that lead him to adopt this mixed model. Rehabilitation is currently in disfavor because educating recidivists is deemed a hopeless cause, but the influence of this theory is pervasive in the legal system via graded sentencing and consideration of public policy questions in prosecuting offenders. In fact, an aspect of reform theory that Hart himself regards as illogical would be considered a virtue by many today. Hart believes that focusing inordinate attention on a relatively small group—hardened criminals—while ignoring the much larger population of prospective criminals is an inherently flawed outlook. Many today justifiably believe that curtailing recidivism would drastically reduce the incidence of serious crime.

The fourth pattern is that of deterrence, best expounded by Jeremy Bentham, who views punishment to be useful when society can realize a net gain in its enforcement. For Bentham, the criminal's apprehension of pain must outweigh the pleasure of committing the delict.

Unwanted acts can thereby be prevented. Bentham is downgraded by current theorists for crediting criminals with far too great a capacity for intricate cost-benefit analyses. Coke would be most fairly placed in the retribution and deterrence camps, though without the subtleties marking Bentham's utilitarian perspective. That is, Coke would favor deterrence seen largely as threatened punishment, not as an economy of preferences.

Shakespeare expands upon the four punishment categories owing to the greater intellectual and creative freedom afforded him as a dramatist. The model of retribution can be retained almost intact, for it operates with a vengeance in most Renaissance tragedies. I treat *Othello, Macbeth, Titus Andronicus*, and *Hamlet* in this vein. Durkheim's sense of restitution can be expanded until it becomes an emancipatory model in *Coriolanus* and *Romeo and Juliet*, where society is freed from ancient quarrels and blind rage, though at a terrible price. In place of reform or rehabilitation I would propose Shakespearean redemption, given the link between metaphysical issues and subjectivity which *King Lear* and *Antony and Cleopatra* explore. Hegel's philosophy is instrumental in defining this category, which can extend almost endlessly into the vast spiritual universes of these two plays. Finally, as an outgrowth of deterrence I would suggest aesthetics as an omnibus term encompassing works like *Timon of Athens* and *Julius Caesar*, which for different reasons elude more traditional categories. I justify the use of this non-legal expression in part because Bentham's theory can produce strange results. For instance, one could envisage a case in which a cabal of unscrupulous authorities punish an innocent victim in order to prevent an unsuspecting public from committing the alleged unwanted act. This revised model has the advantage of including modern tragedies like *Waiting for Godot*, where illegality seems not to be an issue at all and in which the only punishment inflicted appears to be that of forcing the characters to remain on stage indefinitely. None of Shakespeare's plays falls exclusively into any one of these amended categories; thus, the model is useful conceptually only if the elements are seen to be part of a continuum:

Common Law Punishment		*Shakespearean Punishment*
retribution	—	retribution
restitution	—	emancipation
reform	—	redemption
deterrence	—	aesthetics

Examining Shakespeare's tragedies through the lens of Renaissance common law affords perspectives we moderns might not implicitly understand. Two examples may serve to make my point. U.S. Supreme Court Justice Anthony Kennedy occasionally presides over moot court trials of Hamlet on the question of whether the insanity defense holds in the killing of Polonius. These panels, stocked with the brightest medical and legal minds, generally evolve into humorous debates over whether the currently popular "excuse of abuse" can be invoked to secure Hamlet's release. Defendant Hamlet and his temporary insanity defense fare equally badly in these mock trials, with one "jury" suggesting that the prince should be arraigned forthwith for facilitating Ophelia's suicide. Were Hamlet to be tried fairly under English Renaissance law, he would not need to excuse or defend his killing of Polonius. Well-known laws then in currency made intruders secreting themselves in royal chambers strictly liable for whatever fate befell them. Hamlet could honestly claim that he was defending a member of his royal family from an unknown and, from his perspective, unknowable threat. Legally, his mental state would be a complete non-issue.[1] Of course, Shakespeare complicates the scene by informing us beforehand of Hamlet's divided intentions, but insofar as the law was concerned, Polonius has no legal ground to stand on—or lie on, in his case—no matter what may have been going on in Hamlet's mind at the time he thrust his sword through the arras.

A second example, though not from the tragedies, would complicate Daniel J. Kornstein's interpretation of Portia's judgment against Shylock in *The Merchant of Venice*. Kornstein disagrees profoundly with what he regards as Shakespeare's ruling that Shylock face the possibility of renouncing his religious beliefs. Quoting Richard H. Weisberg's *Poethics* (95), Kornstein fair-mindedly proffers what he believes to be the best possible explanation for this lapse in Shakespeare's high ethical and moral standards: "One theory holds that Shakespeare may have been demonstrating the cruelty of English law and its necessary mitigation by the new courts of equity" (*Kill* 73). In *The Institutes of the Laws of England*, however, Coke reveals that a bureau of the Chancery, the "*domus Conversorum*," existed in Renaissance London to convert Jews to Christianity (4 *Institutes* 95). This bureau outlived another department, "The Court of the Justices assigned for the Government of the Jewes" (4 *Institutes* 254), which had ceased its operations once laws had been enacted banishing outright the Jewish faith from England. Is the ironic distance created by a possible reference to these well-established courts sufficient to dispel Kornstein's objections to Shylock's treatment? Perhaps not, nor should it be, since varying interpretations of Shakespeare's plays are justifiable, but the presence of this court in London adds a layer of complexity that at the very least can be said to distance the playwright's perspective from that of his characters. My point is that seeing the plays in the context of English Renaissance law becomes a useful, if not indispensable, practice.

Though punishment in Shakespearean tragedy is often brutal, such severity is not essential to tragedy per se. The Greek tragedians had a conception of justice as cosmic in its own way as Shakespeare's, but they often let their heroes off scot-free depending upon the capricious judgments of the gods. In Euripides's delightful tragedy, *Helen*, the heroine, with the assistance of Menelaus, concocts an amusing trick to elude her captor, the Egyptian king, Theoklymenos. Punishment in this play is limited to the requirement that Theoklymenos contain his lust for Helen and rethink his hatred of all Greeks. This change of perspective forced upon the Egyptian king is a kind of rehabilitative punishment, while Helen receives emancipation from the captivity and unwanted attention she had endured during her sanctuary before Proteus's altar. Euripides relishes contriving surprise endings for his audiences in which lives are not merely spared but permitted to flourish. Punishment in Shakespeare is far more relentless because his characters violate laws which, from the point of view of English Renaissance reasonableness, would demand satisfaction by some legal agency, whose powers while not god-like are nevertheless ineluctable.

Still, retribution is not the sole punitive measure adopted by Shakespeare or Coke. Acknowledging that mere frequency or intensity of punishment cannot ultimately eliminate criminal acts, Coke suggests that alternative solutions be found: "Now seeing *justitia est duplex*, viz., *severè puniens, et verè præveniens*; that is justice severely punishing, whereof we have spoken, and truly preventing, or preventing justice" (3 *Institutes* 243–44). He argues that educational measures ought to be an essential component of prevention, along with strict law enforcement and the granting of few pardons. Thus, the Renaissance conception of punishment as it is expressed by its leading thinker admits elements of reform and deterrence along with retribution. Shakespeare similarly expands his view of punishment theory beyond mere retribution, but his tragic figures invariably violate some law which leads to their own demise as well as that of innocent bystanders.

Knowing that the reforms he proposes could only be enacted at a glacial pace, Coke is dismayed by the harsh punishment characterizing his age:

> For example, what a lamentable case it is to see so many Christian men and women strangled on that cursed tree of the gallows, insomuch as if in a large field a man might see together all the Christians, that but in one year, throughout England, come to that untimely and ignominious death, if there were any spark of grace, or charity in him, it would make his heart to bleed for pity and compassion.   (3 *Institutes* 244)

One need only witness Lear's reaction to the death of Cordelia to sense Shakespeare's compassion for victims in a quasi-juridical setting, brutalized by torture and utter despair, but the tragedies offer a counter-movement toward metaphysical heights that is remarkably uncynical.

My examination of Renaissance punishment necessarily leads me to emphasize criminal law cases. I spend far less time on matters comprising the first two volumes of Coke's *Institutes*, those which he elegantly describes as "two great pronouns, *meum* and *tuum*" (3 *Institutes* 1). That is, with a few important exceptions I leave aside questions of property, ownership, and inheritance (viz., what is mine, what is yours), along with matters pertaining to procedure and administration of justice. I find the common law case tradition, with its conflict and resolution of ideas, to more nearly parallel the action of Shakespearean drama than parliamentary or ecclesiastical edicts. Each common law case is exceptional, often humorous, in much the same way that Shakespeare's tragedies present unique personal and subjective views in concert with complicated philosophical dilemmas.

My sole radical departure from the Renaissance time-frame arises in my treatment of *Julius Caesar*, which I view in the context of the terrible events surrounding World War II, the greatest tragedy of our century, and the trial of the Nazi war criminals who orchestrated them. The connection is not so remote as one might imagine, and not only because of the resemblance between the play's conspirators and the German High Command. In creating the very first war crimes tribunal, the prosecution team lead by U.S. Justice Robert Jackson, Sir Hartley Shawcross, and Sir David Maxwell-Fyfe reviewed the common law for guidance in its innovations. Justice Jackson revealed a particularly strong understanding of Coke and quoted Shakespeare to great effect at crucial moments during the proceedings. Jackson was the most powerful orator of the prosecution staff, besides being the most open-minded—some would say lenient—as to punishment. His opening and closing statements to the Tribunal are masterpieces of legal and humanistic argument which ought to be more widely read today. Remarkably, Jackson had no formal legal training, but it is clear that by sheer talent and study he gained a great deal by mastering the cases of his day and absorbing the wisdom of Coke and Shakespeare.[2]

In the broadest philosophical sense, the relationship between law and art can be seen as a debate between Kant and Hegel. Kant, a pure retributionist, is doctrinaire on the enforcement of punishment. For his part, Hegel finds legal details to be rather prosaic, but his dialectical theory concerning the subject's role in the state opens up profound personal and spiritual questions surrounding the unified, interactive process between art and law in the formation of the tragic sensibility. Even though their influence is felt more immediately in Continental law, I cite Kant and Hegel because of their vast philosophical output and its effect, directly or indirectly, on common law and art. Broadly speaking, Kant's influence on the common law has been greater than Hegel's, while the two have had a relatively equivalent impact on aesthetic theory.

A brief word about the limitations of these two philosophers might be in order first before noting their contributions. Kant's assertion that apprentices, servants, and women "lack civil personality" and his uncharitable remarks about other cultures seem provincial today (*Elements* 79). Similarly, few today would sincerely approve his dictum: "It is the people's duty to endure even the most intolerable abuse of supreme authority" (*Elements* 86). Kant's theory of retribution appears surprisingly antiquated, though it has the virtue of consistency. He makes no exceptions regarding the death penalty: "If, however, he has committed murder, he must die" (*Elements* 102). Besides making no distinction between a mercy killing and a drive-by shooting, Kant justifies his absolutist view on the grounds that retribution would expiate the "blood guilt" attached to the citizenry (*Elements* 102). Kant's extreme position faces stiff criticism from many theorists today, though he has staunch support particularly among prosecutors, who naturally find it useful to quote him whenever it helps their case.

H. L. A. Hart, who is sympathetic to retribution theory, suggests one weakness in Kantian punishment: "It would be paradoxical to look upon the law as designed not to discourage murder at all . . . but simply to extract the penalty from the murderer" (*Punishment* 8).

Kant extends his law of retribution strictly, one might say automatically, from the categorical imperative of the moral law, which is the "synthetical proposition *a priori*" (*Metaphysics* 1871, 33). While Kant insists that punishment be dispensed by a court of law, the result seems little different than if revenge were exacted in the public square. Nevertheless, Kant articulates the retributionist position in its most austere form, a position assumed by most English Renaissance tragedians as well as by more of us today than we might imagine.

Hegel cannot be said to be a symmetrically opposing voice to Kant. Both share a strong patriotic attachment to their nation and are dismissive to some extent of those who are not fortunately placed on the economic or political ladder. Both seek to define an ideal realm, or a touchstone of truth, the consciousness of which they would impress upon their readers, but Hegel goes about his task in a much different way. He is not enthusiastic about the prospect of punishment; instead, he sees it and other legal matters as necessities, if not necessary evils. If the punishment to be enacted against offenders derives from immutable laws for Kant, in Hegel the growth toward consciousness of the Ideal can be reconciliatory and emancipatory: "For in human Art we are not merely dealing with playthings . . . but with the liberation of the human spirit from the substance and forms of finite condition" (*Fine Art* 4: 349). Hegel's view of art cannot be separated from his position on the law or any other substantive human enterprise, including religion.

Rather than referencing objective, *a priori* categories, Hegel sees a dynamic link between individual subjectivity and external, objective conditions. Dramatic art, for example, embodies the progress of human civilization: "The drama converts the ideal claim of human action into an objective presence" (*Fine Art* 4: 144). Hegel rates Shakespeare as unsurpassed in his creation of characters like Hamlet, though he generally points to the structure of Greek tragedy as most representative of his dialectical conception:

> The heroes of ancient tragedy discover circumstances under which they, so long as they irrefragably adhere to the *one* ethical state of pathos . . . must inevitably come into conflict with an ethical Power which opposes them and possesses an equal claim to recognition.   (*Fine Art* 4: 335)

Hegel finds Sophocles's *Antigone* to be a fundamental instance of ethical conflict between the family and state, while *Oedipus at Colonus* is for him the example par excellence of growth toward self-knowledge. Both tragedies fit nicely into Hegel's dialectical conception of art. Shakespeare, he would maintain, explores more brilliantly than anyone else the subjective realm of characterization that would reach its full flowering, for better or worse, in the age of Romanticism. Hegel admits subjectivity and individuality into his philosophy in a way quite unlike Kant and thus at least provisionally establishes the philosophical grounds for a debate that will be carried on by others in this book.

Finally, in the interest of full disclosure, while I claim expertise on Shakespeare and related theories, I cannot at all say the same of my legal background. I attended Loyola Law School, Los Angeles, very briefly until an illness of some duration forced me to withdraw, much to my regret. During my short stay in law school, however, I was deeply impressed by the absolute integrity of the legal professionals and instructors with whom I came into contact. I was further impressed by their admiration and understanding of literature. Regrettably, modern society does always see fit to return the favor. Lawyers and the legal profession are held up to ridicule daily—until, of course, the jesters require their assistance.

Legal professionals will undoubtedly find my analysis wanting at times. I believe this to be unavoidable. Law and literary theory have developed highly specialized lexicons for communicating in their respective fields. Only a very few are truly fluent in both arenas, each of which takes a lifetime of study to master. For this reason I have chosen to buttress my discussion of the law with references to specific common law cases that bear upon the plays in some relevant fashion. I have also referred to cases that pre- and post-date the plays so that the reader can have some assurance that the opinions expressed therein were reasonably well settled. Some cases are more inherently significant than others, though my intent is not to present abstracts of the most important cases of the English Renaissance. *Calvin's Case* and a few others are undoubtedly extremely important in common law history, but my purpose is to discuss cases that bring key issues in the tragedies into greater relief. If my book encourages the reader to pursue further lines of inquiry into common law cases, I will account my work a success.

This book is written in part to demonstrate that legal considerations play a positive conceptual role in understanding Shakespearean tragedy because there exists a convergence of human interests between them. If it is true, as John Harrop told me in the wings of a proscenium theatre, that dramatic action is "the fundamental human issue presented in a given theatrical space and time," those same fundamental human issues presented in Shakespearean tragedy involve the law but are ultimately resolved by means belonging equally to the creativity of the theatre.

CHAPTER 1

OTHELLO: COMPLICITY AND TRAGIC RETRIBUTION

Othello blurs legal and ethical distinctions by referring to himself as an "honorable murderer."[1] Such paradoxes recur in Shakespeare, though Iago and Desdemona would seem to disprove the hypothesis that the tragedies portray no unmitigated villains or innocent victims of any dramatic significance. Shakespeare goes out of his way in *Othello* to muddy issues of legal complicity and intent regarding a domestic murder-suicide, regrettable cases which for the most part occupy the back pages of our daily newspapers. From such a potentially mundane crime the playwright fashions a profound exploration of legal and metaphysical dilemmas. Complicity here yields tragic retribution transcending the revenge pattern so popular throughout the English Renaissance.

I propose to treat complicity by examining the settled opinions of two Renaissance common law cases. I will then define where law and tragedy part company over questions of complicity and retribution. This remains a tragedy, like the others, not the case of *Rex v. Othello.* I will examine in particular Shakespeare's separation of mens rea, the guilty mind, and the actus reus, the guilty act, as the basis for the play's vision of tragic retribution.

I. COMPLICITY AND MENS REA

Othello commits more than one crime but is not initially motivated by vengeance. This represents a shift from Shakespeare's first tragedy, *Titus Andronicus*, which plainly operates on the tribal level of blood revenge. Perhaps for this reason, the earlier play is generally viewed as one of the playwright's lesser achievements despite its successful debut and significant modern restagings. Thereafter, Shakespeare's relative emphasis on the revenge formula gradually diminishes. To be sure, the warring families in *Romeo and Juliet* fit the revenge motif, as does Antony's rabble-rousing speech against the conspirators in *Julius Caesar*. But by *Hamlet,* the hero's interest in revenge becomes reified into artistic ornaments like the play-within-the-play entitled *The Mousetrap*. Thus, I agree with Judge Posner that *Hamlet* is "not really about revenge," though I am less certain that the "theme of maturing" bears heavily on the plot (*Law* 67).[2] My point is that revenge becomes less and less insistent in Shakespearean tragedy until in *Timon of Athens* the hero does no bloodletting at all. *Othello* is among those mature tragedies transcending vengeance even while representing brutal retribution. Othello commits rash deeds that precipitate the tragedy in a way that the revenge formula cannot comprehend, however bloody the results—and they are indeed bloody.

All of the central characters in *Othello* are complicit in the tragic action, though it is not my intent to excuse Iago or besmirch Desdemona, whose extra-legal complicity can be understood only after Iago and Othello have been properly arraigned. Sir David Maxwell-Fyfe, prosecutor at the War Crimes Tribunal [IMT], defines the common law position on conspiracy as "entering into an agreement to commit an illegal act or a legal act by illegal means" (*IMT* 8: 219). Some critics would pardon Othello for having committed a crime of passion, of having "lov'd not wisely but too well" (5.2.344). Most legal scholars, rightly I think, would have little difficulty convicting Othello under the Model Penal Code on the lesser offense of manslaughter "committed under the influence of extreme mental or emotional disturbance for which there is reasonable explanation or excuse" (§210.3, 1b). Sanford Kadish, for example, finds Othello "guilty of culpable homicide, but perhaps only of manslaughter in view of the circumstances" (*Blame* 182). Coke makes similar distinctions:

> For if A. be appealed, or indicted of murther, *viz.* that he of malice prepensed killed I. A. pleadeth that he is not guilty *modo & forma*, yet the Jury may find the defendant guilty of Man-slaughter without malice prepensed, because the killing of I. is the matter, and the malice prepensed is but a circumstance.
>
> (1 *Institutes* 282)

Legal theorists have more trouble with Iago because complicity is harder to establish without clear knowledge of the principal's mens rea; however, even a determination of delayed complicity makes the actor worthy of criminal sanction, as Sir David Maxwell-Fyfe describes using a theatrical analogy: "The fact that a character does not come in until Act 3 does not mean that he is any the less carrying out the design of the author of the play to present the whole picture which the play embraces" (*IMT* 8: 219).

Othello's mens rea complicates our legal judgment of him just as it undoubtedly did his audience in the English Renaissance. The law then was similar to ours in considering the mental element, though we allow much broader mens rea excuses and would regard their punishments as barbaric. Coke's emphasis on the mental element of murder nevertheless confirms some development in the common law because killing by accident or self-defense would formerly have resulted in an execution even if the deed was unintended: "As if a man had cast a stone over an house, or shot at a mark, and by the fall of a stone, or glance of the arrow a man was slain, the party should suffer death . . . so tender a regard had the Law to the preservation of the life of man" (2 *Institutes* 148). While the play complicates gradations of punishment, it still responds to harshly retributivist tones. Shakespeare explores the protagonist's mens rea sympathetically but obeys the dictates of Renaissance tragedy and law by refusing to let Othello off the hook. In this sense, Shakespeare acts as Othello's defender and prosecutor by making him appear both innocent and guilty. I am not suggesting that Shakespeare had legal training, even though legal metaphors and references to nonsuits, proof, remedy, and summons dot the play.[3] Whether Shakespeare overheard cases at the Middle Temple in his free time is not our concern. Defining Othello's mens rea is essential, because upon Iago's suggestion that he murder Desdemona in bed, Othello replies: "Good, good; the justice of it pleases; very good" (4.1.209–10). Shakespeare leaves us torn between blaming Othello for premeditated murder and excusing the mental state that led to the crime.

One may logically consider Othello to be the innocent agent of Iago's machinations. Othello would have never acted as he did but for Iago's lies. Murder prompted by charges of adultery, particularly if caught in flagrante delicto, would have been greeted sympathetically by an English court, but Shakespeare works against Othello by showing him plotting the deed:

> *Oth.* I would not kill thy unprepared spirit,
>   No, [heaven] forefend! I would not kill thy soul.
> *Des.* Talk you of killing?
> *Oth.*   Ay, I do.   (5.2.32–34)

Othello's blood has time to cool as the play lovingly expands scenes of his criminal preparations while racing through other narrative events. Note, for instance, the velocity of the sinking of the Turkish fleet and the drunken revelry in act two, which speeds the play from ten o'clock at night to the following dawn in a mere fifteen minutes of stage time. By contrast, we see the murder evolve as if in slow motion, a trick of plotting that indicts Othello all the more. Similar temporal strategies are common enough in court today. In the 1993 Reginald Denny beating trial of *Ca. v. Williams*, defense attorney Edi M. O. Faal repeatedly showed videotape of a brutal assault expressly to "desensitize the jurors" ("Faal" 18). Lacking videotape, Shakespeare did the next best thing for the opposite purpose of incriminating Othello. He draws out the central crime to evoke pity and diminish the defense of hot-blooded revenge.

The shock elicited by Desdemona's murder has the additional effect of obscuring Othello's complicity in the attempted murder of Cassio. Lodovico, the official representative of Venice, reminds Othello of that crime as he tallies the carnage surrounding the marriage bed. Even by today's standards, a conspiracy charge draws everyone involved into the most serious element of the group offense, including, for example, the getaway driver of a botched robbery in which a life is taken. Soon thereafter, Othello will compound his problems by making an attempt on Iago's life. Naturally, Lodovico cannot understand Othello's mental state as we do, but his investigation suggests that Othello cannot be excused by any objective standard.

The play defends Othello by exploiting the dramatic potential of his mens rea, for he displays no vicious will. Sir Edward Coke freely admits mens rea considerations in his assessment of homicide statutes:

> Murder is when one is slaine with a man's will, and with malice prepensed or fore-thought; Homicide as it is legally taken, is when one is slaine with a man's will, but not with malice prepensed.   (1 *Institutes* 287b)

Othello's involuntary fainting spells indicate his descent into near-madness, just as his abrupt greeting of Lodovico reveals the depth of his preoccupation: "You are welcome, sir, to Cyprus.—Goats and monkeys!" (4.1.263). Othello's madness is not a tactic to conceal ulterior motives as it is with Titus Andronicus or Hamlet. Shakespeare is ahead of his time in giving Othello's genuine mental stress quasi-legal and tragic substance.

Othello's drift from his mental moorings reflects the substantive nature of his position as a foreigner in Venetian society. We are introduced to him largely though a Senate trial instigated by Iago's hue and cry calling Othello's racial and marital rights into question.[4] The marriage is eventually sanctioned by the Senate based on Desdemona's testimony, but only against the wishes of her father, who more or less adopts Iago's intolerant view of Othello. This Senate trial takes place before an English audience so clannish that James had to enact the 1604 Stabbing Statute to restrain his fellow Scots and the entrenched English nobility from murdering each other at court. Thus, the extent to which Shakespeare allows Othello to find acceptance in Venetian society is rather remarkable. Lodovico's view of Othello is unbiased, and, in a more comic vein, Emilia sees Othello as utterly typical of all men, which is to say fickle, self-absorbed, and domineering: "They are all but stomachs, and we all but food; / They eat us hungerly, and when they are full / They belch us" (3.4.104–06). Nevertheless, *Othello* presents varying perspectives of a racially mixed marriage to establish the hero's outsider status as a possible mitigating excuse.

Such psychological and social factors remain ineffectual defenses before the law, for certain facts argue otherwise. The murder is an anti-ceremony of cleansing that Othello treats as a moral imperative: "It is the cause, it is the cause, my soul; / Let me not name it to you, you chaste stars, / It is the cause" (5.2.1–3). Othello pleads non-culpability for the act he is about to commit, yet by Renaissance legal procedure in murder, battery, and lesser offenses he cannot exonerate himself, according to Coke:

> But regularly by the Common Law, if the Defendant hath cause of justification or excuse, then can he not plead not guilty, for then upon the evidence it shall be found against him, for that he confesseth the battery, and upon the issue cannot justifie it, but he must plead the special matter [i.e., extenuating circumstances], and confesse and justifie the battery.   (1 *Institutes* 282a)

Othello is both an honorable man who commits murder and a murderer who defends honor. His philosophical occupation is honor, however much of his stage time is occupied with murder. The hurricane that sinks the Turkish invaders robs him of the opportunity to prove his heroism, but we see his nobility reflected in his poetic diction, his aristocratic bearing, and his intense reaction to any affront to honor. He descends from such lofty heights to think like a mere revenger against Desdemona by reversing his earlier decision not to spill her blood: "Thy bed, lust-stain'd, shall with lust's blood be spotted" (5.1.36). The motif of revenge is introduced tellingly in Othello's retributive path from murder to suicide as an irreversible error.

Othello's attempted murder of Iago is not entirely divorced from the higher law to which he clings. Othello seeks to murder Iago with metaphysical immunity: "If that thou be'st a devil, I cannot kill thee" (5.2.287). He would test Iago's diabolical status, and from a public policy perspective he could claim he was merely attempting to save Venice the trouble of processing Iago through the legal system. Demanding an explanation for what seems to him but one more transgression in a murderous rampage, Lodovico receives this rhetorical defense: "Will you, I pray, demand that demi-devil / Why he hath thus ensnar'd my soul and body?" (5.2.301–02). That Iago lives is proof to Othello of his inhumanity, but by now Othello is communing with the tragic destiny that awaits him. He has one foot on earth and another in that realm where tragic heroes go, stretched as he is between juridical and metaphysical law. The visual emblem of this extreme position is perhaps nowhere better staged than in *Hamlet* when the prince stands astride the grave contemplating the skulls of two distinctly opposed social types: one belonging to the serious role player of a lawyer, the other to a clown—Hamlet's old friend, Yorick. Still, Othello's imagistic speech accomplishes precisely the same dramatic function.

Lodovico is left to distribute blame. He reminds us that all of Othello's crimes count even if they pale in comparison to the murder of Desdemona. Shakespeare's absolute self-confidence in his craft shows itself here because he knows how deeply we feel the passion of the moment. We wish to see Othello much as he sees himself—a character out of an epic poem, an Odysseus managing hair's breadth escapes and impossible deeds. Instead, his fate is to be cast in a tragedy, where his acts are viewed as those of a desperate and degraded man. Evident here is Shakespeare's signature as a tragic playwright to distance the hero from the quotidian reality of human experience. Iago is a base revenger, but the play is about Othello, who has higher concerns.

Unlike condign retribution, Iago's vengeance levels all distinctions between culpability and punishment. Coleridge's interpretation of Iago's "motiveless malignity" ignores the ensign's stated motives: he is angry at being passed over for promotion and suspects that he has been cuckolded. His motives are as unreasonable as his feeble justifications for the murders he plots, but his method to instill his motive in Othello is the means by which mens rea is pulled apart from the actus reus because Othello translates Iago's motives into his own terms. Direct links in the chain of vengeance thereby become disjoined. This technique increases suspense, of course, but suspense is not the sole purpose of the technique.

Just as Hamlet elects not to kill Claudius at prayer, Othello will not kill Desdemona without giving her an opportunity to pray. By distributing the revenge motive between Iago as the cause and Othello as the agent, Shakespeare has made mens rea and the actus reus infinitely complicated and thus ideal for the exploration of tragic retribution. Iago's guilt of murder and conspiracy becomes clear at a point in the play quite distinct from the moment of Desdemona's death. The issue raised by this off-timing is nicely expressed in a different context by Maxwell-Fyfe:

> The other aspect of the law is as to how far those who act in consort to commit a crime are responsible for each other's acts, that is, irrespective of the substantive offense of conspiracy. If one may take an example . . . assume that you had a conspiracy on the part of road operators to wreck railway trains, and a number of road operators agreed in December to wreck a train on the 1st of January and to wreck a further train on the 1st of February. Between the 1st of January and the 1st of February, another road operator joins the conspiracy. . . . Then there is, as far as I can see, some doubt as to whether that road operator would be liable for a murder committed in the wrecking that took place on the first of January.   (*IMT* 8: 219)

We must constantly reassess the nature of Iago's offenses as the play develops.

English Renaissance law found the issue of complicity as thorny as we do today, particularly when the guilt of an accomplice is greater than that of the principal. Coke defines accessories as "those that incite, procure, set on, or stir up any other to doe the fact, and are not yet present when the act is done" (2 *Institutes* 182). If we excuse Othello of murder on the basis of his intent, his innocence extends to Iago, for no accessory can be charged at a higher level than the principal under Renaissance law. Illustrative of this point are two complicity cases that bookend the staging of the play: the 1575 (18 Eliz.) case of *Queen v. Saunders & Archer* and the 1678 (30 Charles II) case of *Rex v. Cornwallis*, which cites the ruling in *Saunders* favorably. Neither case would be satisfactorily resolved by our standards. Saunders intended to kill his wife by giving her poisoned apples but stood silently by as she fed them to their daughter, who subsequently died. Saunders's manifest guilt resulted in his prompt execution, but the accomplice's culpability as procurer of the poison was considered problematic. Archer was ultimately deemed not guilty as "accessory to the said offense of murder, for that he did not assent that the daughter should be poisoned, but only that the wife should be poisoned" (2 *Plowden's* 475). Archer was judged free to purchase his liberty because English Renaissance law required strict proof of an unbroken chain of progression between intent and the actus reus.

This reasoning still held true in *Cornwallis*, in which a nobleman and his servant threatened the life of a sentinel in a drunken rage that ended with the servant killing an innocent young passer-by. The guilt of Cornwallis as accessory was in question:

> If sundry persons be together, aiding and assisting to an action, wherein a man-slaughter doth ensue, as in the case of a sudden business without malice prepensed, they are equally guilty with the manslaughter, as they are in the case of murder prepensed.[5]

The aristocrat Cornwallis was acquitted by a jury composed of 29 of his peers on a verdict split two-thirds in favor of total innocence and one-third for manslaughter. Though his behavior bordered on mayhem, Cornwallis was found not to have plotted the murder of the victim. Shakespeare exploits this issue of direct causation by making Iago's involvement in Desdemona's murder indirect by all outward appearances and therefore difficult to convict by Renaissance standards. Iago's smarmy denials make him additionally blameworthy in our eyes, but he is pursuing his best defense by hiding the ball as the play ends.

II. COMPLICITY AND RETRIBUTION

We can easily throw the book at Iago from the safety of our seats in the audience, for if anyone can be said to embody mens rea, it is he. A man of his ambition placed in a Venetian setting was by Renaissance dramatic convention the essence of tragic intrigue. He begins his stage life by aligning himself with "the justice of the state" as he informs Brabantio of Desdemona's wedding (1.1.139). He ends by refusing to converse or cooperate with the Venetian authorities. This development is reminiscent of an old saying invoked by Justice Jackson: "No thief e'er felt the halter draw with good opinion of the law" (*IMT* 19: 398). Still, proving his legal culpability in Desdemona's death would not be pro forma. Nor is there extant proof that he killed Roderigo. He stabs Emilia not for her alleged adultery but because she indicts him as Othello's accomplice. All this would serve to confuse the average Jacobean's sense of justice. We suspect Iago will die horribly for his misdeeds; his tortured motives and imminent physical torture are thus metaphorically linked. Even so, Iago's vengeance is of no compelling interest in itself; rather, it is his capacity to kill honor in the persons of Desdemona and Othello that lends him stature as a dramatic antagonist.

If Iago is honor's false friend, honor is the self-sufficient, self-validating bond between Desdemona and Othello. She argues as much during her interrogation before the Senate: "I saw Othello's visage in his mind, / And to his honors and his valiant parts / Did I my soul and fortunes consecrate" (1.3.252–54). This bond does not exclude their mutually felt physical attraction, which some productions and films emphasize more than others. It is fair to say that honor works for them on both a martial and marital level. Honor is not opposed to desire as it is in such neoclassical tragedies as Corneille's *Le Cid*. In choosing Othello, Desdemona molds her destiny by defying her father's will, a considerable risk for the time. She thereby gains an equal claim to honor, a right denied her in her role as Brabantio's daughter. Indeed, she is complicit in Othello's sense of nobility, for she is now able to behave like a soldier, to swagger a bit and exchange coarse jokes with Iago. She becomes a soldier of honor, too, so by showing Desdemona being pulled apart from Othello the play stages honor being divided from itself.

Desdemona modifies the revenge motif by trying to salvage Othello's reputation with her dying breath and thereby elevate him:

> *Des.* A guiltless death I die.
> *Emil.* O, who hath done this deed?
> *Des.* Nobody; I myself. Farewell!
>   Commend me to my kind lord. O, farewell!   (5.2.122–25)

Honor means more to Desdemona than revenge, one reason cases do not come before the bar even today. Through Desdemona we enter the extra-legal aspect of Shakespearean tragedy, which raises issues that cannot be resolved in court. Her elongated death scene is a *coup de théâtre* that has vexed literal-minded critics for centuries, some of whom have produced medical evidence suggesting a physiological cause for her brief, unexpected revival. Shakespeare revisits the tactic of raising, then dashing, prayers that an innocent victim might be spared. King Lear hopes beyond hope that he sees Cordelia's breath on the glass he holds before her. Romeo kills himself in the belief that the drugged Juliet has died, whereupon she stabs herself as she discovers Romeo's body. Desdemona regains consciousness to pardon Othello because she is the metaphysical voice of forgiveness denying the efficacy of revenge while revalidating honor. She is, in effect, the non-Iago principle in a tragic world where simple revenge has had its day. Cyril Tourneur pens a Jacobean version of retribution theory in his *Revenger's Tragedy* of 1608 through his character, Vindice: "When the bad bleeds, then is the tragedy good" (3.5.199). In Shakespearean tragedy, the good too often bleed as well. Such is the difference between *Othello* and tragedies of lesser metaphysico-legal scope.

Desdemona is complicit in denying Othello's crime against her while remaining utterly faithful to their code of honor. She completes the play's tripartite scheme of tragic complicity. Othello is a contradiction in being a perpetrator and a victim, the ultimate sacrifice in the retributive bias of the tragic world. Iago is a perpetrator and catalytic agent in the play's disproportionately harsh retribution. Desdemona is a victim but a thorough non-retributivist whose world view makes the pain of Othello's demise all the greater.

English Renaissance tragedy is noted for wretched excess in punishment. The theory of *lex talionis* retribution has made a comeback in the last decade, though only rarely today are executions laced with the kind of carnival atmosphere and puerile jocularity evident in the public process of hanging, drawing, and quartering from earlier centuries. Iago's punishment satisfies our retributionist urges, for I am aware of few if any critics who protest his imminent torture as unfair.[6] Punishment in the play is excessive but not gratuitous because even Othello fumbles his opportunity to slay his antagonist. Perhaps Brabantio's death reveals the fullness of tragic justice here. He appears only in the first act but is reported at the play's end to have died heartbroken. We recall that it was Brabantio who disowned Desdemona with the ominous public warning: "Look to her, Moor, if thou hast eyes to see; / She has deceiv'd her father, and may thee" (1.3.292–93). Brabantio is not legally accountable for his cruel statement, but his fate suggests the thoroughness of the play's retributive arc.

Any facile link between legal and moral blame is complicated by the death toll.[7] Four of the six main characters die outright; one, Cassio, is maimed for life; and Iago's fate is one few of us would wish to entertain. No one of any dramatic stature remains. The other mature tragedies allow us a sense of sober if unspectacular continuity because we come to know surviving characters like Horatio, Edgar, and Macduff reasonably well. Not so here. Lodovico is little more than a faceless, if fair-minded, agent of the state. We cannot leave the theatre feeling that harsh retribution is inherently good, or if we do we cannot reach that conclusion easily.

III. TRAGIC RETRIBUTION

Othello has been interpreted in numerous ways: by psychoanalytical critics as a failure of Oedipal development; by moralists as a quasi-biblical warning against jealousy; by existentialists as a tragedy of angst; by cultural critics as a representation of racial oppression or sexual tension, or both; by Marxists as a tale of improper ownership; by neoclassicists as an imprecise and excessive instance of poetic justice; and by Romantics as an example of Shakespeare's pure imaginative powers. There is undoubtedly some legitimate basis for all these views and more given the breadth of Shakespeare's imagination.

Sir Laurence Olivier observed that the energy required to play Othello far surpassed that needed for Lear, a part many believe to be more than sufficiently fatiguing. Olivier trained himself to move differently: "I should walk like a soft black leopard. Sensuous. . . . Straight-backed, straight-necked, relaxed as a lion. Kill with beauty" (*Acting* 158–59). He employs the imagery of the lion to describe a role combining physical prowess with some of Shakespeare's most magnificent verse. In short, the part requires the actor to expend all of his gifts so that the audience can sense the loss of a towering stage presence. Othello has no true confidant in Iago and loses a perceived ally in Desdemona for the better part of the action. He has no Kent, Mercutio, Horatio, nor Cordelia with whom he can commiserate. The audience witnesses his destruction based on questions of complicity that it knows remain unsettled. His self-slaughter opens up a minor apocalypse, or what Jacques Derrida would call an "apocalypse *without* apocalypse," at the heart of nobility.[8]

Olivier describes Othello as a lion who kills beautifully. If so, Desdemona may be said to die beautifully while teaching Othello to do the same. That is the aesthetic side of tragedy which the law can never and should never countenance.

CHAPTER 2

MACBETH AND THE REASONABLENESS STANDARD IN LAW

Macbeth's antagonists have the theatrically unenviable task of employing only "modest wisdom" to halt his murderous reign (4.3.119). Meanwhile, Macbeth responds to supernatural soliciting by the Weïrd Sisters with soliloquies of great theatrical intensity inspired by the nether world. This conflict between metaphysics and human reason constitutes the play's dialectic. Shakespeare could draw upon his own imagination and theatrical milieu to stage demons, but his references to reasonableness standards involved a legal controversy with immense repercussions in Renaissance England.

I will first present two cases demonstrating the supremacy of Coke's common law reason over the power of the king. Next, I explore why Macbeth signs a metaphysical pact compelling him to outrun reason. Finally, I will assess how *Macbeth* could safely be misinterpreted by royalists, including of course James I, due to an unreasonable ideological blindness.

I. CASE LAW

Despite James's belief in absolute regal power, the legal profession led by Sir Edward Coke successfully opposed him, much to the king's displeasure. Formerly solicitor-general and speaker of the House of Commons, Coke became Chief Justice of the Court of Common Pleas in 1606. With the backing of the entire legal hierarchy, Coke told his king that royal power was subservient to English common law. In his "*Prohibitions del Roy*," Coke informed James of this reality "in the presence, and with the clear consent of all the Judges of England, and Barons of the Exchequer" (*Coke's Reports* 6: 281). Coke's standard of legal reason undercut James's claim of divinely sanctioned authority:

> The King said, that he thought the law was founded upon reason, and that he and others had reason, as well as the Judges: to which it was answered by me, that true it was, that God had endowed his Majesty with excellent science, and great endowments of nature; but His Majesty was not learned in the laws of his realm of England, and causes which concern the life, or inheritance, or goods, or fortunes of his subjects, are not to be decided by natural reason but by the artificial reason and judgment of law, which law is an act which requires long study and experience, before that a man can attain to the cognizance of it: and that the law was the golden met-wand and measure to try the causes of the subjects; and which protected his Majesty in safety and peace: with which the King was greatly offended, and said, that then he should be under the law, which was treason to affirm, as he said; to which I said, that Bracton saith, *quod Rex non debet esse sub homine, sed sub Deo et lege.*
>
> (*Coke's Reports* 6: 282)

With characteristically dry humor, Coke set limits on James's authority even at the risk of a treason charge.

James's broad interpretation of the divine right of kings had long before been undermined by the evolution of English common law. Two landmark cases that frame the presentation of *Macbeth* on the early Jacobean stage establish the force of legal reason over the absolute authority of the king. *Reniger v. Fogossa* of 1552 (4 Edw. VI) and *Calvin's Case* of 1608 (6 Jac.) define the legal and theoretical limits of regal power in the process of deciding relatively minor property rights issues.[1] This is not to suggest that the attorney-general was indifferent to the king's prerogatives or that he favored a democratic England. His relentless prosecution of Sir Walter Raleigh indicates how seriously he regarded allegations of treason as well as, perhaps, revealing his contempt for overweening aristocrats with whom he had to vie for influence. Coke's demeanor at Raleigh's trial was at times beneath him:

Att.	Thou art the most vile and execrable traitor that ever lived.
Raleigh.	You speak indiscreetly, barbarously, and uncivilly.
Att.	I want words sufficient to express thy viperous treasons.
Raleigh.	I think you want words, indeed, for you have spoken one thing half a dozen times.
Att.	Thou art an odious fellow. Thy name is hateful to all the realm of England for thy pride.
Raleigh.	It will go hard to prove a measuring cast between you and me, Mr. Attorney.

Att.   Well I will now make it appear that there never lived a viler viper
              upon the face of the earth than thou.   (*St. Tr.* 2: 26–27)

Coke made good on his promise to convict Raleigh on evidence so
tainted that the case would have been thrown out of court under normal circumstances. Coke could act forcefully on James's behalf; however, he never permitted the law to become subservient to the crown.

Arguments over reason's place in the law were a source of conflict
prior to James's unfortunate introduction to the debate as Coke framed
it. The case of *Reniger v. Fogossa* during the reign of Edward VI
pitted the king's interests against those of the Barons of the Exchequer over the seemingly innocent confiscation of a foreign merchant's
property by an English customs officer. Oral arguments in the case
concerning the reasonable property rights of foreigners in England
took on immoderate tones out of all proportion to the value of the
cargo seized. The rationale of the victors in the debate indicates the
strength of Coke's legal position when he reprimanded James some
fifty years later. Coke alters the definition of natural reason in cases
like *Reniger* to mean reason as it is established by legal tradition:

> For reason is the life of the Law, nay the common Law it self is nothing else
> but reason, which is to be understood of an artificial perfection of reason,
> gotten by long study, observation, and experience, & not of every mans natu-
> ral reason.   (1 *Institutes* 97a)

James could never outmaneuver his attorney-general or the legal profession to garner absolute power because his authority had already
been circumscribed by the common law.

Reniger limits Edward's authority on the grounds of natural reason, which on the surface seems to accord with James's position. The
king's customs officer, Reniger, seized 1693 quintals of green wood
from a Portuguese merchant, Fogossa, after his ship docked at
Southampton. This amount was the surplus of wood on board over
and above the 2,000 quintals declared on Fogossa's customs papers.
There was good reason for Fogossa's inaccurate declaration, according to the merchant's skilled lawyers from the Barons of the Exchequer, who fought vigorously on their client's behalf. While traversing
the English channel, the merchant's heavily laden vessel was buffeted
by a tempest. Fogossa threw an unknown quantity of wood overboard
to save his ship before arriving safely in port. He agreed with Reniger
that his remaining cargo should be estimated at roughly 2,000 quintals, with the duty for any excess wood to be paid once the load could

be weighed precisely at the port's dockside scales. The cargo was weighed and found to be in excess of the agreed-upon amount. In a surprise move, Reniger seized the excess wood instead of allowing Fogossa to pay the duty surcharge. The king's attorneys justified Reniger's confiscatory practice as simple obedience to the strict letter of the law applied to any merchant caught attempting to evade payment of customs duties. They argued that Fogossa bore strict liability for violating what even they admitted was a legal technicality permitting the king to seize improperly declared cargo despite any prior oral agreement. For, they claimed, the letter of the law is the law, especially where the interests of the king are concerned.

Fogossa's attorneys would have none of this argument. One would like to suppose that the Barons of the Exchequer sided with Fogossa out of a cosmopolitan sense of fair play, though it is far more likely that they wished to avoid inciting a trade war with cooperative nations like Portugal owing to some high-handed application of arcane English regulations. The Barons insisted that the merchant had no means of weighing the cargo on board his ship following the tempest and that, furthermore, Fogossa had struck an oral agreement with Reniger to proceed as he did. The confiscation of Fogossa's wood was therefore said to be an unreasonable act that they would oppose in the higher courts of law as an unwarranted violation of normal business practices. The case proceeded over two sessions with lengthy oral arguments, many of which dealt with issues beside the point of legal reasonableness. These included questions as to the validity of the oral contract between the two principals, whether the agreement was properly witnessed, whether an executory agreement for action in the future constitutes a valid contract, and whether Fogossa should have been able to estimate the quantity of the cargo more accurately. We can pass over these mainly technical legal disputes because they were raised to short-circuit the weightier issue of reasonableness at the heart of this case. Only the question of contractual validity will bear heavily on the action of *Macbeth*, to which I will return later.

Two major points in *Reniger* are worth underlining as they relate to the reasonableness standard in *Macbeth*. First, the court rejected outright Reniger's argument that statutes "shall be construed most strongly for the Benefit of the King" (1 *Plowden's* 11):

> And as to the Construction of the Statute, it seems to me that it shall be taken and construed beneficially for *Fogossa* being a Stranger, for in the same Statute there is a Request, *that all Merchants, as well Denizens as Strangers,*

> coming into this Realm, be well and honestly treated and demeaned, as
> they were in the Times of the King's Progenitors, without Oppression,
> &c., which Words prove that it was the Intent of the Makers of the Statute,
> that it should be construed favourably for Strangers.   (1 Plowden's 12)

Remarkably, the court would lend no support to a fine point of law
which simply gave the benefit of doubt to the king. Thus, the principle
of royal absolutism found diminished respect in the English legal system well prior to James's accession.

The second, more far-reaching debate centered on the king's ability
to prosecute alleged crimes by the letter of the law despite mitigating
circumstances. Exchequer attorneys argued that to punish Fogossa
for an honest miscalculation was unreasonable because "if the Law
should punish a Man for an Accident, which by no Foresight, Dili-
gence, or Possibility, could be avoided, it would be utterly against Reason" (1 *Plowden's* 9). This opinion is consonant with one of Coke's
maxims: "That wheresoever there is the like reason, there is the like
Law" (1 *Institutes* 192). Fogossa's attorneys claimed that the reasonableness standard underlying the law excused breaches of the strict
letter of the law:

> And so we see that some Cases shall be construed contrary to Statutes, con-
> trary to Customs, and contrary to the ordinary Course of the Common Law,
> and this for the Necessity of the Matter, and therefore Reason maintains that
> such Persons as do so shall not be wrong-Doers.   (1 Plowden's 9–9a)

If reasonable mitigating circumstances can supersede the king's own
black-letter laws, the distance between the crown and his subjects is
narrowed considerably before the bar. Reason dictates, then, that a
"Man may break the Words of the Law, and yet not break the Law
itself" (1 *Plowden's* 18), for reason is the highest text behind the text
of the statutes. As Coke put it, common law is the "absolute perfec-
tion of reason" (2 *Institutes* 179).

The king capitulated in the face of these arguments when it became
clear that neither Fogossa nor the Barons of the Exchequer would
back down. Furthermore, the judicial panel hearing the case was felt
to be leaning strongly in favor of Fogossa. The crown vacated the
action faced with the certainty that it would lose, for the case would
have revealed the limitations of the king's powers as it worked its way
up through the legal system. Fogossa was granted the right to trade
his cargo with local merchants. The king cut his losses with a hollow,
face-saving threat of renewed action against the merchant at some

unspecified future date. Strict constraints on regal power were thus well fixed by 1552, granting the court latitude to evaluate the reasonableness of excuses for technical breaches of the law. The lawyers and law students who heard Shakespeare's plays at the Globe or Blackfriars were fully aware of these cases circumscribing the king's prerogative by giving discretion to the court over the most mundane economic transactions.

Nor can James be said to have consolidated his power to a greater extent than Edward, for Coke continued to refine the definition of the law to the benefit of the legal profession. This held true in *Calvin's Case*, or *Calvin v. Smith & Smith*, which tested the rights of Scottish subjects *postnati* to James's 1603 accession. While seeming to expand the king's reach, the legal community actually reasserted control over his authority in this case according to the tradition of the common law. In *Calvin*, a child born in Scotland after the accession was deprived of his London Southwark property. Young Calvin and his backers sought relief in a London court, with the defendants objecting on the grounds that the child's status as an alien afforded him no jurisdiction in England. The case, regarded as the "weightiest" legal discussion of the time (77 *Eng. Rep.* 381), attracted the leading figures of English jurisprudence. Coke himself participated heavily in oral arguments along with Eggerton, Lord Chancellor of England. Most of the legal firepower took Calvin's side. In the process of deciding whether the young Scot could plead his cause in English courts, old issues surrounding the priority of legal reason as well as the balance of power between the king and Parliament were revisited in a way consistent with the ruling in *Reniger*.[2]

The subordination of the king to the common law was restated in *Calvin* during the course of oral arguments: "But if a King hath a kingdom by title of descent, there seeing by the laws of that kingdom he doth inherit the kingdom, he cannot change those laws of himself, without consent of Parliament" (77 *Eng. Rep.* 398). While in *Reniger* necessity was deemed by natural reason to invalidate an unyieldingly strict construction of the law, here it is legal reason that holds sway:

> If the said imaginative rule be rightly and legally understood, it may stand for truth: for if you intend *ratio* for the legal and profound reason of such as by diligent study and long experience and observation are so learned in the laws of this realm, as out of the reason of the same they can rule the case in question, in that sense the said rule is true: but if it be intended of the reason of the wisest man that professeth not the laws of England, then (I say) the rule absurd and dangerous.   (77 *Eng. Rep.* 400)

Coke's sentiments in *Calvin* duplicate those he set forth in the *Prohibitions*. The Chief Justice shifts the grounds of the debate over the royal prerogative very neatly, for where James had argued that his natural reason alone should prevail, Coke maintains that reason and law taken together must rule the court's opinion. Thus, while speaking on the king's behalf in *Calvin*, Coke employs arguments whose underlying assumptions negate the rationale by which James sought to augment his power.

The overwhelmingly favorable decision in *Calvin* on behalf of the king was from James's perspective roughly equivalent to winning the battle while losing the war. It was decided that Calvin had legal standing in England despite having been born in Scotland. The decision virtually assured Calvin of winning back his property. The rationale was based on the now familiar concept of the king's two bodies. Coke expanded the power of the legal profession where the king's political body was concerned. On the other hand, he would severely prosecute an alleged crime of treason, as he did in Raleigh's case, which jeopardized the king's natural body. Subjects swore allegiance not to the king's political body but instead to his natural, mortal body:

> Whosoever are born under one natural ligeance and obedience due by the law of nature to one sovereign are natural-born subjects: but Calvin was born under one natural ligeance and obedience, due by law of nature to one sovereign; *ergo*, he is a natural-born Subject.   (77 *Eng. Rep.* 407)

Though Calvin's parents would have no similar legal standing, their child was affirmed to have the full protection of English common law and was deemed capable of suing for his rights of inheritance and other economic protections: "And whosoever is born within the fee of the King of England, though it be in another kingdom, is a natural-born subject, and capable and inheritable of lands in England" (77 *Eng. Rep.* 403). So if the court extended the king's geographical reach, it did not grant any new powers to James that were not already well under control of the courts of law and Parliament. Coke's opinion as to the supremacy of legal reason in *Calvin's Case* was a matter of public record preventing James from claiming those powers which he regularly promulgated in his public utterances and expository writings concerning his status as a "child and servant of God" and the "Lord's anointed" (*Newes* 29). English common law, not James, was the ultimate power in the land, for it could determine the parameters of the king's authority.

The reasonable person standard is one of the most powerful theoretical concepts in the law, though the term per se was not adopted until much later and with numerous variants. The 1837 case of *Vaughn v. Menlove* is considered the first to apply a reasonable person standard, though it uses the expression "prudent man" (132 *Eng. Rep.* 490). *Vaughn* is a negligence case in which a defendant carelessly permitted combustibles on his land to raze the property of his neighbor. Unanswered questions arise from this case as to the meaning of objective or subjective prudence, ordinary or extraordinary prudence, and a myriad of other possibilities involving the difference between "reasonable" and "prudent." It took centuries to formulate the current American Law Institute definition of a reasonable person having "those qualities of attention, knowledge, and judgment which society requires of its members for the protection of their own interests and the interests of others . . . taking into account the fallibility of human beings" (*Restatement* 12). Legal reason in its broadest sense permeates the common law from the start, but some cases were decided during the English Renaissance in a manner that would strike us today as unreasonable. The landmark 1616 tort law case of *Weaver v. Ward* applied strict liability for damages against a defendant whose gun accidentally discharged and injured the plaintiff during practice military maneuvers (80 *Eng. Rep.* 284). This decision demonstrates that the reasonableness standard was a subject of debate both within the legal profession and in the conflict between the crown and its legal representatives. Reasonable characters like Banquo, Malcolm, and Macduff would not have been as uninteresting to a Jacobean audience as they appear to some contemporary critics and theatergoers.

Given the contested quality of reason in Shakespeare's age, it is not outlandish to suggest that what is at stake in *Macbeth* is the protagonist's theatrically vital errancy from the course of reason, for James continually asserted his right to overstep the law on those very grounds. Some new historicists like Stephen Orgel overstate James's power in assessing the Stuart masque, for example, as an expression of "the developing movement toward autocracy" (*Illusion* 51). As we have seen in *Reniger, Calvin,* and the "*Prohibitions del Roy,*" the law continually solidified its hold on ultimate authority in the land. When Orgel argues that the Jacobean masques "expressed the strongest Renaissance beliefs about the nature of kingship, the obligations and perquisites of royalty" (*Illusion* 38), he could not have been referring to the legal profession or even to *Macbeth*.

II. PSYCHO-BABEL, CONTRACTS, AND THE REASONABLE PERSON

Reason, unreason, and supernatural voices compete for our attention with widely varying degrees of success in the play. Tragedy and madness intersect profoundly in *King Lear*, as we shall see, but Lady Macbeth suffers from mental trauma in the course of her sleepwalking induced logically by her complicity in murder. Shakespeare's conception is in accord with the analysis of Foucault, for whom "dreams, madness, and the unreasonable" interact in the formation of the Renaissance imagination (*Madness* 19). The refrain of "man" leads some critics to find Oedipal patterns in the play along with related issues concerning phallocentrism and male anxiety about female power. The question of reasonableness is raised at the outset when Banquo asks the Sisters: "Live you? or are you aught / That man may question?" (1.3.42–43). As I treat the issue, Banquo is referring to a shared human reasoning capacity, not so much to gender oppositions or variations on Oedipal conflicts.

The play raises the issue of the reasonable person standard when Banquo questions the reality of the Sisters' presence: "Were such things here as we do speak about? / Or have we eaten on the insane root / That takes the reason prisoner?" (1.3.83–85). Macbeth is most adept at shading the differences between rational and irrational thought. He lets slip his most problematic character trait when he invents a convenient excuse for killing the grooms: "Th' expedition of my violent love / Outrun the pauser, reason" (2.3.110–11). Macbeth's stage life is dedicated to outrunning any pauser, reasonable or otherwise. Lady Macduff refers to this standard in chiding her absent husband for having fled to England: "All is the fear, and nothing is the love; / As little is the wisdom, where the flight / So runs against all reason" (4.2.12–14). In recounting Banquo's alleged wrongdoing to his hired assassins, Macbeth abuses the reasonable person standard by arguing that only a lunatic would disagree with him.

Macbeth remains at bottom most reasonable in his unreasonableness. He retains his capacity for moral discrimination, contrary to the view of G. Wilson Knight that Macbeth has no "ethical code" and that the play represents the "apocalypse of evil" (*Wheel* 158). Macbeth initially posits reason as the basis for secure human existence. If, as he says, man is a happy microcosm of good government, to commit crimes is to be inhuman: "I dare do all that may become a man; / Who dares [do] more is none" (1.7.46–47). Later, steeped in blood guilt and clinging desperately to his sanity, he regards Banquo's ghost as an indomitable foe. Here, the battle between reason and demonic unreason has been joined. With the departure of Banquo's ghost, he can say: "I am a man again" (3.4.107), primarily as to the issue of human self-governance, though matters concerning the patriarchal order are undoubtedly present as well.

"Man" is also used as a gender insult, to be emphasized by whatever vocal interpretation the actor or actress wishes to place on the word. Lady Macbeth employs the term in a derogatory fashion, calling Macbeth's "green and pale" hesitation effeminate: "When you durst do it, then you were a man" (1.7.37, 49). Malcolm's sense of masculinity is gender-traditional when he urges Macduff to mourn the loss of his wife and children patiently: "Dispute it like a man" (4.3.220). Macduff's response: "I shall do so; / But I must also feel it as a man" (4.3.220–21), only modestly redefines the customary sense of how a man should play his role. Macbeth associates cowardice with effeminacy by admitting that Macduff's disclosure of his birth-delivery has "cow'd my better part of man!" (5.8.18). This sense continues with Ross's relation of Young Siward's battlefield comportment: "But like a man he died" (5.9.9). Shakespeare's variations on the meaning of masculinity range from banal insults to the most complex issues of reason and unreason, of the human and demonic. Ultimately, both sexes are shown to have equal access to unreason if only because Macbeth and Lady Macbeth end up losing their heads in disparate ways.

The play's quasi-Gothic horror suggests forces at work beyond the healing power of psychoanalysis. Appealing to "murth'ring ministers," Lady Macbeth asks that they "unsex me here, / And fill me from the crown to the toe top-full / Of direst cruelty!" (1.5.48, 41–43). Many psychoanalytical critics see Oedipal patterns in the play by following Freud's contention that Lady Macbeth and Macbeth are "disunited parts of a single psychical individuality" (SE 14: 324). These critics treat the murder of the amiable Duncan as patricide and matricide. In Janet Adelman's terms, we see "the failure of the androgynous parent to protect his son, and the final victory of a masculine order in which mothers no longer threaten because they no longer exist" ("Born" 111). Perhaps Macbeth's description of Duncan of having "borne his faculties so meek" is suggestive to some of femininity taken in traditional terms (1.7.17), but meekness here refers less to the man than to the manner of his rule. Duncan is a wise general and good ruler, though suspicions of his maternal characteristics and androgyny run through Freudian criticism.[3] Harry Berger, Jr., sees the murder of Duncan as a "group project" borne out of Scottish political practice ("Text" 65), but generally psychoanalytical critics view the men as striking out against their parents in an incoherent Oedipal rage.

For the familial relationships in Macbeth to fit the Oedipal pattern, good father figures like Banquo must be seen to die at the hands of bad symbolic sons, and mother figures like Lady Macduff must die unmourned because they are women. Adelman, for example, sees Lady Macbeth as "more terrifying" to men than the Weïrd Sisters, who are an "odd mixture of the terrifying and the near-comic" ("Born" 99). Yet Lady Macbeth dies in control neither of her own faculties nor of others, while no hereditary sons like Fleance actually kill their fathers. Psychoanalytical critics transform Macbeth from a bad symbolic son to a bad symbolic father, but he is in one sense superior to the virtuous Macduff, who appears less than noble in deserting his family. If we follow Lacan's view that "in the psyche, there is nothing by which the subject may situate himself as a male or female" (Four 204), gender differences become fundamentally irrelevant in a world where fair is foul and foul is fair. Macbeth and Lady Macbeth are already half in the world of spirits before the audience's seats are warm, much less before the cosmic messengers address them.

The play quickly identifies what can logically but not finally shake the reasonable person standard: a Babel of metaphysical voices. The dissonant chorus infects Macbeth immediately, though Shakespeare follows Holinshed's Chronicles in permitting Banquo to resist their spell: "Banquo would call Makbeth in jest, king of Scotland, and Makbeth againe would call him in sport likewise, the father of manie kings" (5: 268). Macbeth is repeatedly referred to as "rapt" upon hearing the prophecy (1.3.57), his suggestibility facilitated by the fury of the battle from which he has just arrived. Fighting like a man already possessed on the battlefield, he wades through blood to find the rebel leader, Macdonwald, "Till he unseam'd him from the nave to th' chops" (1.2.22). Entering the stage from this Golgotha, Macbeth offers only a brief, ambiguous remark: "So foul and fair a day I have not seen" (1.3.38). Banquo is far more voluble, particularly in his interrogatories to the Sisters, suggesting that his mind is not fertile ground for their prophecies. Macbeth asks that the Sisters reveal their identities, but rather than answer him directly, they lay the snare that will entrap him. He is to proceed from Thane of Glamis, to Cawdor, and eventually to the crown itself. He is their ideal victim, leaning as he is ever so slightly toward willingness to perform the requisite acts. Leaping ahead at all occasions faster than those around him, Macbeth outruns reason and the law but never outpaces his audience, which remains perfectly attuned to his dramatic progress.

The contrast afforded by Banquo reveals Macbeth's incapacity to live within the bounds of reason, a characteristic he refers to as "ambition," for lack of a better word. He accepts the gratuitous verbal contract offered by the Sisters, which promises him the world while remaining vague as to his means of procuring it. The metaphysical pact that the Sisters devise is shunned by the common law. Theirs is *nudum pactum*, a promise of good fortune or advantage without consideration of a corresponding exchange or return obligation. Such contracts are illegal because there is no reciprocity of benefit and cost. The reasonable social progress that the law seeks to preserve depends upon the validity of contracts. We recall that the king's lawyers in *Reniger* sought to win their case on a technicality involving just such a dispute over the verbal agreement struck between the customs officer and Fogossa. The king's gambit did not succeed because his lawyers misapplied the rule, but the concept of a contract involving consideration is as old as the law itself based on its reasonableness. Macbeth, being partly unreasonable, hears the one-sided contract and imaginatively fills in the performance clause that the Sisters illegally leave blank: "If chance will have me king, why, chance may crown me / Without my stir" (1.3.143–44). Implicit is Macbeth's understanding that a benefit requires a corresponding debt, but this contract is, after all, not a reasonable one between people; rather, it originates from metaphysical spirits with "strange intelligence" (1.3.76). Perhaps the rules for such a pact do indeed differ, for when Macbeth becomes Thane of Cawdor the Sisters' initial prediction seems to have been borne out. Shakespeare delights in presenting fatal misinterpretations in the dialogue between the law and metaphysics. Like the devilish contract in *Doctor Faustus*, *Macbeth* has a dramatic premise based on a contract without any tangible consideration.

Defective contracts encouraging metaphysical equivocation become a constant source of dramatic tension and humor. Lady Macbeth shows a willingness to sign such contracts beyond even the minimal caution voiced by her husband. She makes him believe he had flatly promised to carry out Duncan's murder though he had said nothing final on that point, having merely stated that greatness was promised her at some time. Still, Macbeth comes to resemble the Porter's equivocator—without the servant's earthier concerns. Macbeth knows enough to be stayed by the force of law: "This even-handed justice / Commends th' ingredience of our poison'd chalice / To our own lips" (1.7.10–12). He tentatively concludes that the benefits of treason cannot outweigh the loss of good opinion he would suffer by breaking the social contract requiring him to act as a good host toward Duncan. Nevertheless, he is pushed along by the many voices influencing him as well as by the mistaken hope that his special metaphysical contract negates the rational one by which the rest of the human race abides.

Macbeth and *Doctor Faustus* are tragedies sharing the comic underpinning of a fatally flawed contract working against the protagonist in unusual and entertaining ways, though Faustus seems impelled by little more than intellectual boredom. Far from being a dark, solemn play, *Macbeth* too has a great deal of wry and understated comedy, with some broad humor coming from the Porter and Macduff's precocious son. Rich dramatic irony laces comments by the Doctor of Physic as he diagnoses Lady Macbeth: "Go to, go to; you have known what you should not" (5.1.46–47). Though Macbeth's sympathy for his wife's degenerating mental condition is admirable, his request for a cure is, as he knows, hopelessly tardy:

> Canst thou not minister to a mind diseas'd,
> Pluck from the memory a rooted sorrow,
> Raze out the written troubles of the brain,
> And with some sweet oblivious antidote
> Cleanse the stuff'd bosom of that perilous stuff
> Which weighs upon the heart? (5.3.40–44)

Macbeth can thrill like Tarquin at the prospect of horror, but only a residually reasonable person could recount spiritual anguish for us so effectively because the opinions of an insane individual would count for nothing in law. Macbeth's bargain with us is that he should brilliantly describe in various registers the fear he institutes in the land. He comes to live in a world apart from his subjects. His common law position is accurately reflected in Hart's rationale for the reasonableness theory: "Further difficulties of proof may cause a legal system to limit its inquiry into the agent's 'subjective condition' by asking what a 'reasonable man' would in the circumstances have known or foreseen" (*Punishment* 33). That is, the reasonableness standard acts as a brake on society's imposition of its values on the individual with the proviso that it may enforce a responsibility upon him to live reasonably within

certain objective circumstances. The difference between the percep-
tions of Macbeth and his antagonists is theatricalized in the banquet
scene, where his guests gape at him in bemusement while he alone is
transfixed by the spectacle of Banquo's ghost. The ghost's glaring,
unseeing eyes are part of the metaphysical riddling that confounds
Macbeth, who seeks definitive responses to unanswerable questions
at every turn.

III. MACBETH VERSUS THE COURT

Macbeth is the willing dupe of an immense and somewhat terrifying
metaphysical joke played by the Weïrd Sisters. His development forces
his antagonists to question their own rational faculties, for he has the
effect of making reason seem strange. The scenes involving the Sisters are in a sense anti-masques akin to those Ben Jonson and Inigo
Jones presented at court, though without the unreasonable flattery
that those masques conveyed and to which Shakespeare apparently
never succumbed.

If James heard the play at court, he could no doubt regard himself
as the *deus ex auditorium* of the performance. He imagined himself
capable of curing scrofula, or "the Evil" (4.3.146), a dreaded lym-
phatic disorder resembling the Black Death. We can place this illusory
skill alongside James's claim of absolute political power, which was
equally chimerical before the law, according to Coke:

> There be three things as here it appeareth, whereby every subject is protected
> . . . the King, the Law, and the Kings Writ. The Law is the rule, but it is mute:
> The King judgeth by his Judges, and they are the speaking law, *Lex loquens*:
> The process and the execution, which is the life of the Law, consisteth in the
> Kings Writs. (1 *Institutes* 130)

Shakespeare adopts Coke's defense of legal reason while taking certain liberties with this serious subject given the metaphysical horse-
play in *Macbeth* surrounding contracts and other legal matters. Reasonableness is a standard no playwright can afford to ignore, or if he
does, he does so at his peril.

Coke's common law priorities cast doubt on the new historicist
contention that the social and literary dynamics of the English Renaissance enabled the crown to consolidate and project its power. New
historicism occupies a place in literary theory roughly akin to Critical
Legal Studies (CLS) in the law as to its subject matter, for CLS would
include sociological factors in the juridical decision-making process.

With all its talk of power, containment, and subversion, however, old-line new historicism borrows the cold war concepts of neo-conservative foreign affairs analysis, in contradistinction to the political affinity of CLS. For Stephen Greenblatt, Shakespeare's work reflects an ultimately servile posture "concerned with the production and containment of subversion and disorder" ("Invisible" 292). Orgel stops only slightly short of Greenblatt's position by suggesting that the legal profession was merely "uncomfortable about royal prerogatives, and unsympathetic to the crucial principle of divine right" (*Illusion* 79). Neither Coke nor his colleagues were willing to have their rights contained; instead, they boldly put the king in his place. Naturally, Shakespeare could not be so open in his criticism of the king, but the play comes down much nearer to Coke's position than to James's.

It is reasonable that Macbeth should respond as he does to the news of his wife's passing: "She should have died hereafter" (5.5.17). He equivocates on both the inevitability and untimeliness of her death. His hastily conceived eulogy, not incidentally the most inward-looking of them all, concerns his life as an actor who "struts and frets his hour upon the stage" (5.5.25). The definition-seeking Macbeth sees himself through the eyes of another—an actor—when he refers to his life as a "tale / Told by an idiot, full of sound and fury, / Signifying nothing" (5.5.26–28). Signifying nothing is logically and literally impossible. It is certainly up to the audience to signify what it wishes, but signify it will. Like being told not to imagine a pink elephant, an audience would find it cognitively impossible not to signify something, if only Macbeth's presentational greatness as a tragic protagonist. The audience can act as his judge and jury, unlike its courtroom counterpart, for which a division of labor was strictly enforced in Coke's age: "For matters in Law are decided by the Judges, and matters in fact by Juries" (1 *Institutes* 71a).[4] Macbeth fights with renewed but hopeless vigor until he is dispatched offstage in a silence mirroring the one ushering him onto the boards at the start of the play.

Shakespeare's England would continue to live with the Stuart kings as long as they stayed within the reasonable limits of the law. James's successors were unfortunately even less rational than he, which visited disastrous consequences on the Stuart legacy. But whatever powers he might claim, James remained absolute king only of the Cockpit at Court. *Macbeth* is neither a warning to unreasonable tyrants nor an encomium to the king, but if James perceived it as the latter, it was but an illusion.

CHAPTER 3

HAMLET AND THE WAGER OF LAW

Much of what seems imperfect in Hamlet arises from his inability to expose the perfect crime. His investigation is so amateurish as to leave him open to Claudius's countermeasures. Hamlet's key witness could never appear in court because his testimony would be inadmissible as hearsay. Imagine the difficulties involved in hauling the Ghost to the witness chair—presumably for a pre-dawn hearing—and swearing him in either as King Hamlet or his surrogate. Forced to take extra-legal means to reveal the facts, Hamlet ruminates on "the law's delay" while playing the procrastinator himself (3.1.71). He ultimately dispenses justice through an ancient legal ritual, the wager of battle, that Claudius hoped would mean his quietus.

I leave aside rich areas of psychological analysis in this most psychoanalyzed of all literary figures.[1] In so doing, I am heartened by Sir John Gielgud's remarks on Hamlet because his numerous performances in the role constitute some of the finest in theatre history:

> In spite of all its complicated problems of psychology, I believe Hamlet is what we actors call a 'straight' part. The man who essays it must obviously be equipped with certain essential qualities—grace of person and princely bearing, youth, energy, humour, and sensitivity. . . . Hamlet must impress us with his loneliness and agonies of soul without seeming portentous or self-pitying.
> (*Stage* 59)

In part I, I consider legal issues surrounding treason trials, which, politically charged as they were, inevitably involved hearsay testimony and other unfair legal procedures. The cases examined are those of Sir Nicholas Throckmorton in 1554, Robert, Earl of Essex, in 1600, and Sir Walter Raleigh in 1603. The latter two trials bracket the staging of the play and have stakes as high and convoluted as any earthly trial could in relationship to Hamlet's dilemma. Apart from his metaphysical sensibilities and supernatural connections, the young prince resembles these Renaissance aristocrats forced to endure the rigors of a treason trial. In part II, I treat the tragic and legal elements of the play itself. Mens rea is separated from the actus reus in *Othello*, but here the actus reus becomes stretched apart from punishment. In dramatic terms, the spectacle of Hamlet becoming a player in the wager of law undergirds his elevation as a nonpareil tragic hero.

I. State Trials

The treason trials of Throckmorton, Essex, and Raleigh are notable for the intelligence of the defendants, the ferocity of the prosecution, and the unethical or illegal elements in the proceedings. The political coloration of the trials led to divergent results. In a remarkable verdict given the circumstances, Throckmorton was acquitted, then went abroad before making a political comeback during Elizabeth's reign. Essex received the death sentence but remained a hero to many, even receiving posthumous praise from his prosecutor, Sir Edward Coke. Raleigh met his end after more than a decade in confinement and one ill-fated voyage to the Americas. Shakespeare could not have been indifferent to Essex's trial, particularly since his former patron, Southampton, was a co-defendant convicted for his part in the uprising. Though some of the same legal issues pervade Shakespeare's tragedy, *Hamlet* is anything but a representation of a treason trial. Hamlet's pursuit of a remedy for a monstrous crime based on evidence provided by supernatural intervention forms the basis of the play's central complication.

A high treason conviction invoked extraordinarily harsh punishment on the offender and his lineage, associates, and property:

> Implied in this judgement is, first, the forfeiture of all his mannors, lands, tenements, and hereditaments in fee-simple, or fee-tail of whomsoever they be holden. Secondly, his wife to lose her dower. Thirdly, he shall lose his children (for they become base and ignoble.) Fourthly, he shall lose his posterity, for his blood is stained and corrupted, and they cannot inherit to him or any other auncestor. Fifthly, all his goods and chattels, &c. And reason is, that his body, lands, goods, posterity, &c. shall be torn, pulled asunder, and destroyed, that intended to tear, and destroy the majesty of government. And all these severall punishments are found for treason in holy scripture.
>
> (3 *Institutes* 210a)

Deals could be struck to reduce the scope of punishment, but the beheading of the offender was an ineluctable outcome. Treason trials provoked the most intense legal scrutiny of any criminal case. Unlike the intricate details of, say, an inheritance dispute, the results of a treason trial would be widely disseminated because the crime went against God, society, and nature. Treason was so elemental a crime that Coke could chart its parameters:

By compassing	King	and declaring the
or imagining }	Queene, }	same by some
the death of the	Prince,	overt deed. (3 *Institutes* 3)

Essex's participation in a revolt through the streets of London constituted the most overtly treasonous offense of the three cases, for such evidence did not exist against Throckmorton and Raleigh.

The common law procedure allowing a defendant to be confronted by two or more witnesses was denied in these latter cases, though witnesses were readily available:[2]

> When a trial is by witnesses, regularly the affirmative ought to be proved by two or three witnesses, as to prove a summons of the Tenant, or the challenge of a Juror, or the like. But when the trial is by verdict of 12. men, there the judgement is not given upon witnesses, or other kind of evidence, but upon the verdict; and upon such evidence as is given to the Jury they give their verdict.   (1 *Institutes* 6a)

Parliamentary courts composed of twenty to thirty juror-peers generally heard the evidence but had to rely on hearsay of the most suspect kind. All conspiracy trials require some degree of second-hand testimony from an informant, but these cases were unusual due to the court's unwillingness to permit cross-examination of the witnesses. Throckmorton's prosecution by attorney-general Edward Griffin was simply corrupt from the start. In Raleigh's case, Coke introduced flimsy evidence by distinguishing accusers from witnesses, and indictments from trials, to reach the requisite standard of proof. Absent here was the deliberative process Coke demanded of common law trials: "After all the evidence given for the king, and the prisoners answers, and proofs at large, and with patience heard" (3 *Institutes* 29). Coke had regarded accusation by hearsay as a "strange conceit" concocted during Mary's reign (3 *Institutes* 26), so his own use of hearsay and improbable testimony caused understandable confusion in otherwise intelligent men of political affairs like Raleigh who had neither the health nor training to defend themselves against Coke's hairsplitting rhetoric.

Throckmorton's treason trial of 17 April 1554 exemplifies how legal procedure could be manipulated for political ends by Mary's attorneys. In what was standard operating procedure for such defendants, Throckmorton stood trial weakened by ill-health due to prolonged incarceration. The irregularities in his case were wide-ranging, with the court failing to specify charges, using perjured testimony, and refusing to admit exculpatory evidence and testimony. Furthermore, Mary had introduced a statute permitting single accusers in treason trials instead of the old standard of two or more. Coke regarded this innovation as a dangerous throwback to ancient common law where one accuser could induce a trial by combat in much the way that Edgar forces Edmund into a wager of battle in *King Lear*. Mary's statute was quickly reversed under Elizabeth's reign.

For all these reasons, Throckmorton was correct to remark that he was permitted only "the form and image of the law" (*St.Tr.* 1: 888). Despite the odds, he proved to be an excellent advocate on his own behalf, able somewhat miraculously to recall to his advantage relevant points of treason law which had been debated years earlier during his tenure in Parliament. Among his recollections was the basic common law doctrine involving criminal accusations: "That no penal Statute may, ought, or should be construed, expounded, extended, or wrested, otherwise than the simple words and nude letter of the same Statute doth warrant and signify" (*St.Tr.* 1: 891). Throckmorton's feats of memory were disconcerting to his accusers, who grudgingly came to acknowledge his forensic skills.

Throckmorton scored most heavily in recalling the specific requirement that treason be an "open deed" or an "overt act" (*St.Tr.* 1: 889). This should have effectively demolished the accusation against him of being merely knowledgeable of Wyatt's treasonous intentions. The court, however, was driven to arrive at a guilty verdict. Three out-of-court confessions were admitted from prosecution witnesses Winters, Arnold, and Vaughn, but only Vaughn appeared because he seemed the most likely of the three to adhere to his deposition. Aid for Throckmorton might have come from defense witness Croftes, who languished in the courtroom until being dismissed before he could give testimony damaging to Mary's case. Another potential ally, Fitzwilliams, was similarly refused the right to testify. Even Wyatt's deathbed recantation concerning Throckmorton's complicity in the uprising was excluded. Ultimately, Throckmorton stood accused of being an adherent, deviser, and procurer of treason merely because he may have known of Wyatt's whereabouts during the unrest. The mere possibility that he heard Wyatt rail against the Spanish was deemed sufficient to convict him, though any conversations between them were acknowledged to be in all probability free of political overtones. The prosecution used the common law analogy in complicity cases of defrauding one through the agency of another to press home their accusations of treason. The gambit was skillfully rebutted by Throckmorton:

> I do and must cleave to my innocency, for I procured no man to commit Treason; but yet for my learning I desire to hear some case so ruled; when the law was as it is now. I do confess it, that at such time there were Statutes provided for the procurer, counsellor, aider, abettor, and such like, as there were in king Henry 8th's time, you might lawfully make this cruel construction, and bring the procurer within the compass of the law. But these Statutes being repealed, you ought not now so to do; and as to the principal procurer in felony and murder, it is not like as in Treason, for the principal and accessories in felony and murder be triable and punishable by the common law; and so in those cases the Judges may use their equity, extending the determination of the fault as they think good: but in Treason it is otherwise, the same being limited by Statute Law, which I say and avow is restrained from any Judge's construction by the Maxim that I recited.   (*St. Tr.* 1: 891–92)

Throckmorton's analysis left his accusers nonplused. He effectively answered the charge making suspicion of another's wrongdoing criminal under treason law by citing the new statute's narrower scope. Judges at common law had some latitude in applying the law, but Throckmorton's reasoning here was sound.

In a stunning act of integrity, the jury sided with Throckmorton by finding him innocent. The court imprisoned the jury for its temerity and fined the individual members severely, but Throckmorton was set free to leave for France, where he stayed until Elizabeth took the throne. Upon hearing the verdict, Mary, it is said, took to her bed in despair for three days. Because Throckmorton engaged in no overt act of rebellion, the court found it necessary to trump up conspiracy charges against him to convict him as much in the court of public opinion as that of the law. Mens rea need not be established in treason trials when the act itself demonstrates criminal intent, but to the extent that these trials were political, such evidence carried with it considerable weight.

Mens rea was less an issue in Essex's trial because he was the leader of the rabble. He had the additional disadvantage of facing Coke in court. Coke proved merciless in prosecuting the treason statute in defense of the crown even if he regarded the legal profession as the preeminent power in the land. Southampton was convicted as well, but because the Earl repented during the trial, he was forgiven. I therefore leave aside Southampton's case in favor of addressing that of Essex.

Though a mens rea finding was not strictly required, the prosecution felt obligated to evaluate whether Essex raised a revolt out of private ambition or, as he claimed, in response to a law of nature allowing him to defend the Queen from some nebulous Spanish threat. Essex admitted that he put the Queen's council under house arrest but argued rather incredibly: "It was done in charity, and without disloyalty, but intending only to save them, lest they should take hurt; considering the people abroad in the streets" (*St. Tr.* 1: 1340). Policy differences between the defendant and the faction led by Cobham, Cecil, and Raleigh probably incited Essex to rebel in view of accusations of treason hurled between these opponents midway through the trial. Essex may have been sincere in his protestations of innocence surrounding his intent to defend the Queen's safety, but his participation in a mob action through the streets of London with weapons raised against the government was prima facie evidence for conviction. Even Southampton conceded that the failure to disband their followers was a "foolish action" (*St. Tr.* 1: 1350). The overt act of rebellion left Essex with no defense at all.

Despite several overheated remarks by Coke during the trial, it proceeded reasonably given the rigid authoritarian structure of Renaissance politics. Essex was unable to credibly refute two essential points against him: first, that the level of force raised on the streets could not readily be suppressed by Elizabeth's troops; and second, that the uprising in itself threatened Elizabeth's safety whatever his intent. Unlike Southampton, Essex could not bring himself to repent, which would have involved a tacit admission that his political foes constituted no danger to the state. Despite his loyalty to the crown, he was convicted and executed, though mourned upon his passing. The pardon of Southampton indicates that the sentence imposed took the political effects of such trials into consideration.

There was a measure of personal malice evident in Coke's demeanor toward Essex during the proceedings, though he operated within the bounds of the law because he could point to the Earl's manifest rebellion. The same cannot be said of his treatment of Raleigh in 1603. Coke publicly vilified him: "Nay, I will prove all: thou art a monster;

thou hast an English face, but a Spanish heart" (St. Tr. 2: 7). No credible witness was presented; instead, Coke introduced evidence that Raleigh may have known persons involved in various unsavory affairs but not that he worked on their behalf. Coke did not permit the main prosecution witness to testify, the oft-impeached Cobham, though he was available for cross-examination.

Coke found a loophole in the treason statutes allowing him to ignore the common law tradition requiring cross-examination of multiple witnesses against the defendant. In the course of his defense, Raleigh referred to this tradition stemming from biblical law: "Good my lords, let it be proved, either by the laws of the land, or the laws of God, that there ought to be two Witnesses appointed" (St. Tr. 2: 15). Recent changes in the law, however, permitted sworn testimony to replace viva voce testimony, as Lord Chief Justice Anderson informed the chagrined defendant:

> You have offered Questions on diverse Statutes, all which mention two accusers in case of Indictments: you have deceived yourself, for the laws of 25 Edw. 3d, and 5 Edw. 6th are repealed. It sufficeth now if there be Proofs made either under hand, or by testimony of Witnesses, or by oaths; it needs not the Subscription of the party, so there be hands of credible men to testify the Examination. (St. Tr. 2: 15)

Coke initially justified his refusal to allow Cobham to testify by commenting on the difficulties involved in finding reliable eyewitness testimony in conspiracy cases. Later, though, he came nearer the truth by arguing that the damage to a defendant confronted by unreliable witnesses was less important than the potential danger of an alleged conspiracy against the king. Raleigh's fate would be decided politically rather than legally, for Coke would win by the letter but not spirit of his own interpretation of the law: "The proofs of the offence ought to be so clear and manifest, as there can be no defence of it" (3 Institutes 29). Coke's behavior in this case can only be seen as a personal debacle for this lawyer's lawyer, who fiercely defended the law and the legal profession within the English Renaissance political hierarchy.

Raleigh was charged with inciting Cobham to seek assistance and financing from the Austrian ambassador, Aremberg, in order to foment rebellion in England. An indictment of indirect foreign intrigue is one of the least offensive of the six high treason accusations, ranking in importance just above counterfeiting and debasing the king's coin, but well below acting directly to kill the monarch, assault his spouse, or levy war against the realm. Thrown into the mix was a flimsy accusation concerning Raleigh's publication of disparaging remarks about James's accession. Stronger proof existed that Cobham dealt traitorously with foreign ambassadors and spoke contemptuously of the king, but no credible evidence suggested Raleigh to be a traitor in word or deed. Given Cobham's jailhouse confession, Coke was surely being disingenuous when he declared: "The law presumes, a man will not accuse himself to accuse another" (*St. Tr.* 2: 19). A prisoner like Cobham, enfeebled by age, disease, and terror, might well do just such a thing to avoid the executioner's axe. The case turned on Raleigh's word against Cobham's, so the full weight of Coke's rhetorical skills buttressed the accuser to ensure Raleigh's conviction.

Contributing to Raleigh's woes after his arrest was an intemperate letter written to Cobham expressing his contempt for the witness's false accusations against him. The fact that it was written at all added one more tenuous connection between the two, however irrelevant and inadequate it may have been to serve as a basis for proving Raleigh's guilt. That the evidence used to convict Raleigh was so unreliable, particularly given Cobham's later recantation, probably contributed to the suspension of his death sentence until 1614, some eleven years later. As in most treason trials, the law existed for the defendant only insofar as politics allowed; James was a constant presence and note-taker at the trial. Such would have been Hamlet's fate had Claudius proceeded against him, for Hamlet had precious little evidence to present against a king determined to retain his throne.

II. The Wager of Law

Hamlet must reveal what was for Claudius at one stroke a *coup d'état*, a murder, and a marriage. The usurper gambled shrewdly enough that his crime could not have been revealed by any human agency. Secure in his new role, he wisely chooses not to engage in wanton slaughter, unlike such villains as Iago and Richard III. He could not reasonably have predicted that supernatural forces would bring his crime to light. Both Claudius and Hamlet are given reasons to desire the other's elimination, but they are forced to plot and delay until a charge perceived to be sufficiently strong would enable the winner to deliver the *coup de grâce*.

For his part, Hamlet must decide which method of proof might reasonably convince his associates of the Ghost's veracity. Knowing that the Ghost will speak only to him, he senses that his tale might seem unsound even to a close friend like Horatio. Metaphysical displays outside of court would persuade no judge of Claudius's guilt. These difficulties force Hamlet to split his allegiance between the common law and ecclesiastical law, which becomes evident when he wishes that "the Everlasting had not fix'd / His canon 'gainst [self-]slaughter" (1.2.131–32). Torn between the call to revenge and the quasi-legal procedure he undertakes to gather and test the evidence, Hamlet remains uncertain as to which jurisdiction he should direct his appeal. Of course, his strongest relationship is with the audience, but he has two legal avenues available in the context of the common law: "In the secular Courts the Kings Lawes doe sway and decide causes, so in Ecclesiasticall Courts the Lawes of Christ should rule and direct, for which cause the Judges in those Courts are Divines" (2 *Institutes* 488). An implicit jurisdictional split develops between common and ecclesiastical law here that *Romeo and Juliet* introduces but does not explore in any real depth. Simply playing the stock revenger would diminish Hamlet as a tragic hero, not to mention shortening the play by several acts. He makes the harder choice of administering punishment only after uncovering certain proof of Claudius's crimes. His caution carries with it the disadvantage of allowing Claudius to throw potential pursuers off the scent. Suspending revenge in favor of determining the truth, Hamlet respects his conscience, for he insists that the retribution he exacts be proportional to the crime itself.

Shakespeare was wise to leave aside a normal courtroom drama in favor of staging a duel. Illegal if initiated in private circumstances, the "wager of battail," "duellum," or "trial by battel," as it was variously called, was regarded as an anachronistic remedy for cases in which there was an absence or dearth of witnesses or missing evidence, the presumption of law being that "God will give victory to him that right had" (2 *Institutes* 247). Monomachia was another ordeal whereby leaders of opposing armies could duel *solus* to spare their troops harm. Thus, it matters only in narrower ethical terms that the game is rigged against Hamlet as he enters the arena against Laertes. No rules of evidence apply as such in a wager of battle, for God oversees the contest. No behavior is illegal in this most quintessentially providential of all patterns. Hypothetically speaking, while this extra-legal contest arises out of the action that preceded it, terrible results would have come to pass despite the murder of King Hamlet. Had Claudius been a rightful ruler with an odd penchant for trying to win bets underhandedly, and had the intended victim been alerted to an irregularity by witnessing an innocent bystander like Gertrude drinking from a tainted chalice, all the deaths that logically should have occurred would have simply as a result of Hamlet's response to the duel's fraudulent nature. So while there is no absolute retributive connection between the results of the duel and the play's initial four acts, there is a dramatic connection that transforms the final wager of battle into an unforgettable tragic climax.

It makes no difference whether or not Shakespeare studied common law history to resolve Hamlet's case as he did. W. S. Holdsworth's description of this juridical proceeding from early modern Britain was well known in Renaissance England: "They were not rational adjudications upon evidence. They were methods of proof; and the party who went through the form of proof—witness, battle, compurgation, or ordeal—won his case" (*History* 9: 130). Some metaphorical resemblance exists between the audience and a jury hearing the evidence. The audience sees the dramatic action in a given theatrical space and time much like a jury and with similar privations: "By the law of *England* a Jury after their Evidence given upon the issue, ought to be kept together in some convenient place without meat, or drinke, fire or candle, which some Books call imprisonment" (1 *Institutes* 227a). This privation was taken seriously because a juror buying his own meal during deliberations could face a fine. If the plaintiff bought meals for the jurors, the case could be dismissed. *Hamlet* combines three suspenseful elements: an audience made anxious by the protagonist's delay, a complicated treason trial, and a king seeking to win at all costs. Given the inadequacies of a hypothetical treason trial in Denmark, Hamlet's case would involve so much official bias that a wager of battle would have been his best alternative in any event. Too noticeable to be unintentional, the play skirts standard legal procedure expertly by seeming to operate on the margins of the law.

Many critics regard Hamlet's killing of Polonius to be evidence of his unworthiness to be king. Hamlet, they say, shows himself to be a flawed prince with a deteriorating command of his faculties and morals. His sword thrust is seen as partial justification for his death, but by normal standards of Renaissance law, Hamlet could not easily have been convicted of a crime for killing Polonius as he did. The state trials indicate with certainty that one such as Polonius who secrets himself in the Queen's chamber is strictly liable for the act. It is not without reason that Hamlet refers to the old gentleman, and not to himself, as a "wretched, rash, intruding fool" (3.4.31). Though it is he who most alarms Gertrude, Hamlet could rightly argue that Polonius was hidden to "conspire and imagine the death of the Queen's majesty" (*St. Tr.* 1: 870). Merely thinking the death of the Queen would have been fatal to the old courtier, and acting suspiciously in the presence would seal his fate. Had he survived, any claim by Polonius that he was serving as the crown's agent would be irrelevant in a proper proceeding against Hamlet, who was unaware of the ploy. Certainly, Hamlet would have to smooth over the implications of his utterance following the deed: "Is it the King?" (3.4.26). This complication would have more dramatic than legal significance, for it would be easier to denounce Polonius as a threat to the Queen's safety than prove Hamlet to be an incipient assassin. The prince was not guilty of Polonius's murder under the treason statutes, but the act gives Claudius an added excuse to tarnish Hamlet's reputation and banish him to a darker fate abroad. In later referring to the prince as "he that is mad, and sent into England" (5.1.148), the gravediggers have absorbed a cover story for Hamlet's departure not based on alleged criminal wrongdoing.

Were Hamlet to come to trial, he would need a good lawyer because his attention to legal matters constantly wavers. The audience knows he had hoped to kill Claudius, but the law would regard his acts as falling short of the requisite intent:

> Chance-medly or *Per infortunium,* is when one is slaine casually and by misadventure, without the will of him that doth the act, whereupon death ensueth; but of this no Appeal doth lye. (1 *Institutes* 287a)

It is good for English Renaissance drama that it is so, for common law murder involves will and malice aforethought, while homicide involves will but no prior malice. Claudius is therefore forced to devise a means of removing Hamlet other than through a legal process of uncertain outcome because the act could under no circumstances rise higher than accidental homicide. This complication creates more delays and heightens Hamlet's intimations of his own mortality. He reacts to Gertrude's anger over Polonius's murder by implying that she was complicit in the death of her husband: "A bloody deed! almost as bad, good mother, / As kill a king, and marry with his brother" (3.4.28–29). The inequities accumulate as Claudius forgives Laertes of treason. Laertes, "in a riotous head" (4.5.102), holds a sword to the king's breast, a far greater offense than that which sent Essex to the block. Claudius's pardon serves double duty because he uses the occasion to arrange for Hamlet's removal and to reinforce the myth of his rule: "There's such divinity doth hedge a king / That treason can but peep to what it would, / Acts little of his will" (4.5.124–26). Hamlet, on the other hand, resigns himself to the mercy of providence: "There's a divinity that shapes our ends, / Rough-hew them how we will" (5.2. 10–11).

Claudius does not show restraint by allowing Hamlet to live after Polonius's death; rather, he lacks sufficient acceptable evidence to demolish his antagonist as he wishes he could. Hamlet is in an equivalent evidentiary position vis-à-vis Claudius but not for reasons of public appearances. This view runs counter to the moralistic emphasis that many critics following G. Wilson Knight see operating in the play: "Now Claudius is not drawn as wholly evil—far from it. We see the government of Denmark working smoothly. Claudius shows every sign of being an excellent diplomatist and king" (*Wheel* 33). One may question whether a nation embroiled in drunken riots and a general alert is running smoothly, or that buying off minions with "now must your conscience my acquittance seal" constitutes good rule (4.7.1). If Knight is correct, then Hamlet surely does not deserve to be king.

It is an old saying that the common law cannot work a wrong. Neither does Hamlet as he seeks proof, evidence, and valid testimony despite the Ghost's emotional appeals. The Ghost beckons Hamlet into the tragic firmament by demanding that he transcend his political and legal roles. He calls for revenge of a "foul and most unnatural murther" (1.5.25), a plea that would resonate with Coke, who rates death by poison as the most underhanded of all: "And albeit of all felonies, murder is the worst, and of all murders, murder by poyson is the most unavoidable and detestable" (2 *Institutes* 634). The Ghost seeks not justice but only the most primitive of human responses. Were Hamlet a better detective, he might look for hebenon juice in Claudius's pantry or dust the poisoned vial for the king's fingerprints. Instead, he is more interested in wheedling a confession out of Claudius or provoking some public display proving wrongdoing—hence *The Mousetrap*. The Ghost claims that an edict prevents him from revealing all the horrible secrets of hell. How he knows about the details of Claudius's preparations for the murder is uncertain given that King Hamlet was asleep at the time. Perhaps residents of the underworld are privy to the entire book of human history. The Ghost chooses to speak only to Hamlet, not to the Danish constabulary, where his summons would no doubt have been quashed. He wagers his revenge on

Hamlet's shoulders and in so doing sends the prince to his death. The Ghost adopts too many roles to be credible, for not only is he an advocate for immediate revenge, he would adjudicate the punishment of Claudius and Gertrude. Thus, given an opportunity to kill Claudius at prayer—at confession, really—Hamlet refuses to make a premature leap from evidence-gatherer to revenger.

The Ghost offers hearsay evidence because he is King Hamlet's spirit or representative, not the King himself. The Ghost can give excellent testimony concerning the torments of hell, but is it King Hamlet's testimony? He mainly refers to himself as King in the first person but later slips into the third: "If thou didst ever thy dear father love" (1.5.23). The Ghost is only a piece of the father and is therefore not in any position to give first-hand testimony. For unavoidable reasons, part of the true father must remain underground. Additionally, the Ghost presents problems of hearsay that are more conceptual in nature. Laurence Tribe lists the fourfold defects of hearsay testimony: "Ambiguity, insincerity, erroneous memory, and faulty perception" ("Triangulating" 959).[3] The Ghost is neither ambiguous, forgetful, nor unclear about the details of the crime—far from it—but he makes no attempt to disguise his contempt for Claudius. Owing to his present circumstances, his candor is understandable. The fact that the Ghost urges leniency in Hamlet's treatment of Gertrude argues further on his behalf. His bias against Claudius is, however, decisive given Hamlet's eventual choice of tactics. The antic disposition Hamlet adopts is thus far less problematic than centuries of psychology and para-psychology would suggest it is. He remains unconvinced by the Ghost's testimony even given his own prior suspicions of Claudius's guilt. The argument that Hamlet delays because he suspects that the Ghost might entertain diabolical intentions is a secondary though valid concern. Given his intelligence and the stakes involved in the political game, Hamlet must be convinced to a metaphysical certainty, not simply to a reasonable doubt, of Claudius's guilt.

Interfering with Hamlet's quest is political necessity in the form of Fortinbras, who seeks to regain land his father gambled away. Such necessity ravages the already bleak landscape of the play. King Hamlet ruled Denmark as the result of a successful land wager, while Claudius risked all to usurp Hamlet's gain. As for Laertes, he seems unfit to rule because he is easily manipulated, hypocritical in his advice to Ophelia, and cowardly in facing down Claudius. Ophelia, whose venture into a pastoral setting ends with her death, is the gentle spirit broken by Danish politics and the vagaries of love. Shakespeare is interested in her *felo de se* suicide only insofar as it pertains to ecclesiastical law and her budding love interests.[4] The breadth of legal concerns is thus narrower here than in *King Lear*, where property issues play a greater role in the action:

> *Felo de se* is a man, or woman, which being *compos mentis*, of sound memory, and of the age of discretion, killeth himself, which being lawfully found by the oath of twelve men, all the goods and chattels of the party so offending are forfeited.   (3 *Institutes* 54)

Disputes rage as to the cause of her madness and her right to a Christian burial but not over the disposition of her property. The passionate grave-side confrontation between Laertes and Hamlet nicely foreshadows their final encounter with poisoned rapiers. Hamlet's reflections on Yorick's mortal remains supersede the gravediggers' mangling of "crowner's quest law" (5.1.22), or the coroner's inquest, which took Ophelia's mental state into account even if the clowns did not. Here particularly, the metaphysical concerns of the play ultimately outweigh all others.

If the appearance of the Ghost incites Hamlet to action, Osric's entrance signals the play's tragic resolution. That Shakespeare placed so much dramatic weight on so slight a character is but another bold stroke in a play that needs no further praise heaped upon it. If what the Ghost demands of Hamlet is punishment discordant with the law, Osric's baroque overtures send a strong subtextual warning of danger to Hamlet and Horatio. Osric's incompetent diplomacy greatly amuses Hamlet, who is easily diverted by inappropriate words and gestures, as Horatio knows only too well: "I knew you must be edified by the margent ere you had done" (5.2.155–56). Hamlet's interrogatories temporarily divert Osric from his task to announce the duel that will decide the fate of Denmark. This messenger's incapacities are metaphorically those of the ruler he represents. As it turns out, Osric had nothing more to disclose under his lighthearted interrogation than the message Hamlet ultimately extracts from him, but we must note the precautionary step taken. Osric describes a wager, not a legal process, though his tone would at first appear to indicate otherwise: "And it would come to immediate trial, if your lordship would vouchsafe the answer" (5.2.167–69). The trial to which Osric refers is ambiguous, suggesting at once a normal legal proceeding and the older wager of

battle in which strict rules of fair play are cast to the winds of providence.

Hamlet throws Osric off-stride with a seemingly innocent question:
"How if I answer no?" (5.2.170). Playing with a refusal to engage in
what he would do anyway is typical of Hamlet, and it reminds us of
Throckmorton's half-jesting response to the tribunal he faced before
attorney-general Sendall:

Sendall:	How wilt thou be tried?
Throckmorton:	Shall I be tried as I would, or as I should?
Sendall:	You shall be tried as the law will, and therefore you must say, by God and by the country.
Throckmorton:	Is that your law for me? It is not as I would; but since you will have it so, I am pleased with it, and do desire to be tried by faithful just men, which more fear God than the world. (St.Tr. 1: 870–71)

I am not suggesting that Shakespeare cribbed from the court records
of Throckmorton's case to construct Hamlet's scene with Osric, but
situations in which intelligent men are forced to undergo illegal trials
under the pretense of volition evoke remarkably similar human responses. Hamlet's quibbles undercut Osric completely, which in itself
makes the scene worthwhile. He also disparages Laertes's expertise
in arms, raising suspense about the imminent confrontation. Finally,
he lures Osric into revealing any hidden peril lurking behind this apparently sportsmanlike challenge. By attempting to minimize its significance, Osric unwittingly suggests its dire implications. The foreshadowing is heightened by the appearance of a higher-ranking courtier
setting the exact time and place for the match, all of which bodes ill
for Horatio: "If your mind dislike any thing, obey it" (5.2.217). These
punctilious messengers convey Claudius's hidden malice, but Hamlet
is no longer concerned with such details. Metaphysical timing is all-
important to him, just as it was to Claudius when he timed his murder
of King Hamlet. In coming to this understanding, Hamlet answers at
least to his own satisfaction the fundamental metaphysical question
he had raised earlier as to whether he ought to be or not be:

. . . we defy augury. There is special providence in the fall of a sparrow. If it
be [now], 'tis not to come; if it be not to come, it will be now; if it be not now,
yet it [will] come—the readiness is all. Since no man, of aught he leaves,
knows what is't to leave betimes, let be.   (5.2.220–24)

Relying on his improvisational intelligence to see him through, Hamlet has received adequate intelligence as to the danger surrounding the match.

At stake in this most unnatural wager is Hamlet's life and the future direction of the state. The prince opens the contest by claiming that madness altered his past behavior, using rather tortured discourse in a way that has troubled some commentators:

> Was't Hamlet wrong'd Laertes? Never Hamlet!
> If Hamlet from himself be ta'en away,
> And when he's not himself does wrong Laertes,
> Then Hamlet does it not, Hamlet denies it.
> Who does it then? His madness. If't be so,
> Hamlet is of the faction that is wronged,
> His madness is poor Hamlet's enemy. (5.2.233–39)

No judge would accept this excuse, but Hamlet is not in court and he knows it. He insists on casting his relationship with Laertes as fraternal, heightening the irony of the deadly contest and its subsequent carnage. Under English common law, participants in the duel would have to be free of serious moral or criminal taint, hence Laertes's importance as a stand-in for Claudius. Coke regarded such duels as abhorrent in the eyes of God and a diminution of the law as the King's lieutenant, but after punishment has been distributed in the play, Laertes can say of the king: "He is justly served, / It is a poison temper'd by himself" (5.2.327–28). The wager of battle works inequitably against Gertrude and Hamlet, though it is the logical outcome of an unjust process originating with Claudius's brazen crime.

Fortinbras's accession is mild confirmation that Hamlet could not have escaped the fate that befell him, though the prince remains innocent of wrongdoing by any reasonable legal standard. Hamlet's capacity to plan, revise his tactics, and suit his words to his actions gives him the theatrical power of a Machiavel. If his acts seem criminal to some, perhaps it is partly because we generally see the criminal in tragedy scheming along the lines of a Richard III, Aaron, or Iago. Hamlet occupies the Machiavel's theatrical position without having the Machiavellian intent, which is one source of the mystery about him that so intrigues his audiences. Having become a player in the tragedy, he requires Horatio to tell his tale aright after he is gone. Not being a lawyer, Hamlet has no compunctions about asking his friend to use hearsay in the court of public opinion.

CHAPTER 4

KING LEAR AND THE LEGALITY OF MADNESS

> *Nulle terre sans seigneur* [No land without a lord]
> —feudal law maxim

Lear is at once the most extroverted and introverted of Shakespeare's tragic heroes. The divergence between his mental trauma and child-like or childish innocence makes the role supremely difficult to play, as Peter Brook told his actors:

> Brook spoke of the play as a mountain whose summit had never been reached. On the way up one found the shattered bodies of other climbers strewn on every side. "Olivier here, Laughton there; it's frightening."   (Marowitz 135)

This summit has yet to be conquered partly because our knowledge of what is inadequately termed madness has grown as fitfully as our will-ingness to confront it. As to legal issues, Lear's abdication of political and juridical responsibility leads indirectly to a test of his sanity that solicits our redemptive sensibilities.

I begin by treating legal interpretations of madness in the context of the Jacobean era, revealing similarities between Shakespeare's age and our own. In Part II, I compare King James's superstitious and moralistic critique of madness with that of Dr. Edward Jorden, who publicly opposed his monarch's opinions. Part III focuses on the play's complex representation of Lear's mental state, which affects many layers of the social fabric. Lear has the disadvantages of mens rea responsibility without having truly performed the actus reus. When Lear kills, his act is unquestionably defensible. Part IV treats legal issues concerning ownership of the realm and the crown.

I. MADNESS AND RENAISSANCE LAW

English law has changed throughout time as to the degree of madness required to excuse wrongdoing, but since the Middle Ages it has not punished the insane. Only an assault on the king's life rendered a defendant absolutely liable for the deed. I do not mean to suggest that mental illness was humanely addressed in the Jacobean era or that the law took steps to treat it in a positive light. Indeed, within the legal profession at this time, madness was seen to be its own punishment. But while Coke held that an insane defendant is disqualified from having the requisite mens rea to be convicted of a crime, the neoclassical age, for example, adopted such an unreasonably harsh attitude toward the disease that defending individuals deemed insane became extraordinarily difficult. Three insanity cases relating to the performance of *King Lear* on the Jacobean stage show madness to have been as vexing a legal issue then as it is today.

One of the earliest judgments in an insanity case surfaced in 1278 during the reign of Edward I. The king interceded on behalf of a murderer, Hugh de Misyn of Leyton, who evidently experienced intermittent bouts of insanity. Hugh was found to have "hanged his daughter whilst suffering from madness, and not by felony or of malice aforethought" (*Close Rolls* 1: 518). The court had still to determine if Hugh constituted a risk to others before concluding their investigation, but Edward's intervention demonstrates the medieval English common law position that madness negates malice aforethought, the mental element of the illegal act necessary for a murder conviction.

Hugh's case also reveals the historical function of the king to care for his mentally ill subjects. This requirement is part of what Lear comes to understand as his failure to provide alms for the infirm souls populating his realm. When Edgar adopts the disguise of Tom O' Bedlam, he plays a role that inherently ought to persuade the king to rule rightly by traditional standards. Lear awakens to his duties in a central scene involving the mock arraignment of his daughters, but Edgar strikes a sympathetic chord in the protagonist and his audience concerning the evils of poverty and mental distress. Coke explains the king's quasi-legal responsibility:

> And that the King shall have the protection of the goods and chattels of an idiot, as well as of his lands appears . . . where he says, that if an idiot who cannot defend or govern himself, nor order his lands, tenements, goods, and chattels, the King of right ought to have him in his custody, and to protect him and his lands, goods, and chattels.   (*Coke's Reports* 2: 576)

On this point, Coke follows the mid-thirteenth century *Prærogativa regis*, which was of uncertain legality but which helped to maintain the property rights of the insane during their periods of illness.[1] Thus, the appetite for *lex talionis* revenge against mentally unstable offenders was absent even as early as the reign of Edward I. The eighteenth and nineteenth centuries were to be far less understanding regarding this human rights issue.[2]

Rather than oversimplifying madness by making Tom little more than a useless eater, Shakespeare notes the character's loyalty and resourcefulness in the context of Lear's ever-diminishing retinue. Whether Lear's hundred are a chivalrous or roguish lot is difficult to ascertain, though the king seems predisposed to choose men resembling Kent in his coltish moods. Traditionally, the king had a national security right to retain a following: "Knights service *in capite* were for the honor and defense of the Realm; and concerning those that served the King his household, their continual service and attendance upon the Royall person of the King was necessary" (2 *Institutes* 631). Interpretative decisions regarding the behavior of Lear's followers are left to theatre practitioners. Peter Brook's 1962 production characterized them as layabouts capable of erupting into violence at the slightest provocation. The ruling classes in Shakespeare's London had ongoing concerns regarding laws to control sturdy beggars given well-documented prentice riots. In this vein, Robert Burton describes London's decline by 1621:

> Wee have many swarmes of rogues and beggers, theeves, drunkards, and discontented persons (whom *Lycurgus* in *Plutarch* cals *morbos reipub.* the boiles of the common-wealth) many poore people in all oure Townes, *Civitates ignobiles,* as *Polydore* cals them.   (*Anatomy* 1: 76)

The knights whose removal so enrages Lear as a sign of his lost power and prestige are to be distinguished from the portrayal of the insane, whose uncomfortable presence was seen to flatter no one.

Coke's 1603 brief in *Beverley's Case* constitutes in miniature an agenda for the legal treatment of insanity in early Jacobean England. Acting on behalf of Beverley, Coke took care to differentiate his client's behavior from that of a merely irresponsible person. The simple ability of a defendant to distinguish right from wrong was not central to Coke's analysis, though it is undoubtedly assumed in the reasonableness standard of Renaissance law. Instead, Coke was more pragmatic in considering soundness of mind, memory, and harmlessness as tests for sanity. The plaintiff, Snow, sought to have his £1,000 bond upheld against Beverley. Coke, who is nobody's bleeding heart, felt that

Beverley could not comprehend the significance of incurring such a large debt. Coke did not report the medical evidence upon which he based his conclusion, but having convinced the court of his opinion, the attorney-general easily won his case. No contract is valid when one or more of the signatory parties is unable to reason, and so it was with Beverley: "Because at the time of the making of the said bond, he was *non compos mentis*" (*Coke's Reports* 2: 569). Beverley's case is important in English common law because Coke delineated the four mental states by which *non compos mentis* insanity may be established:

> 1. Idiot or fool natural. 2. He who was of good and sound memory, and by the visitation of God has lost it. 3. *Lunaticus qui gaudet lucidis intervallis,* and sometimes of good and sound memory, and sometimes *non compos mentis.* 4. By his own act, as a drunkard . . . yet his drunkenness does not extenuate his act or offense, nor turn to his avail. . . .
>
> (*Coke's Reports* 2: 572–73)

For Coke, reason more than morality is the ultimate basis for determining the validity of an insanity defense.

Just as Beverley was held unanimously to have been *non compos mentis* at the time he agreed to the bond, Shakespeare suggests Lear's madness is temporary. It scarcely needs stating that defining Lear's mental condition in non-medical terms is of great importance to the actor playing the role. One director, Harley Granville-Barker, worked out the problem perhaps too exactingly for his Lear, the unfailingly polite Sir John Gielgud:

> My dear Gielgud. Did we ever agree as to the precise moment at which Lear goes off his head?
>
> I believe that Poor Tom's appearance from the hovel marks it. The 'grumbling' inside, the Fool's scream of terror, the wild figure suddenly appearing— that would be enough to send him over the border-line.   (Gielgud 132)

Though Granville-Barker took Lear's insanity to be a given, one recent production resisted that interpretation with superb results. Peter Brook's landmark 1962 production with the contemplative Paul Scofield in the lead was castigated at the time for failing to "convey the sense of a mind being driven into madness" (Wardle 50). It was still expected in the theatre that Lear's madness be performed within the stock traditions of the play's stage history. Scofield's Lear retained his sanity to emphasize the bestiality of human actions rather than to project the king's damaged mental state onto the universe:

Between the first and last of his experiences there lies a whole lifetime's agony. It is an agony that strikes terror because Scofield's Lear does not strut and fret his hour away in the empty histrionics of stage madness, but in the despair that arises from man's growing self-awareness and from his consciousness of the real calamity involved in the breaking down of the reasoning mind.

(Roberts 53)

Theatrical raging is by no means an inherently empty gesture, but critical assumptions about Lear's insanity raise questions concerning how his madness ought to be presented to the audience. Scofield conveyed anguish and despair under the rubric of existential dismay; nevertheless, audiences generally expect some of the old histrionic magic to impart the fullness of Lear's tragic demeanor.

Shakespeare's play is modern in presenting a Bedlam fool and a king who by some reports goes temporarily mad, item three in Coke's definition. The king's traditional responsibility for the "natural fool" does not extend to one who is only temporarily impaired because, as Coke notes: "The lunatic may recover his memory which he has lost, and therefore in the case of the idiot, the Law says, *Rex habebit custodiam*, but in the case of *non compos mentis, Rex providebit*" (*Coke's Reports* 2: 577). Lear's recovery of his memory and identity near the play's end is a sign of lucidity falling very much within Coke's guidelines, which given the medical ignorance of the age permit a rational evaluation of insanity on a case-by-case basis. Shakespeare forces every actor to evaluate Lear's sanity to his own satisfaction, thereby making madness an issue for each successive theatrical generation.

Arnold's Case of 1724 reveals a drastic shift in the receptivity of the court to insanity defenses. The test required to sustain an insanity defense became excessively rigorous at this time. Penalties grew harsher even for mentally deficient defendants. The insanity question in this case centers on whether the obsessed Arnold bears responsibility for shooting his perceived foe, Lord Onslow. Arnold had convinced himself over time that the aristocrat was intent upon harming him, though the two had never formally met. Lord Onslow had much earlier arranged to send Arnold into naval service along with other young men, an experience that traumatized Arnold, but the evidence suggests that his entire life was troubled. His sister Eleanor described him as having been "distracted for seven years" (*St. Tr.* 16: 725). Another sister, Mary, reported that he had claimed to have been visited by "imps" who "danced in his room all night, and he could not lie in his bed for them, and the devil did tempt him, and the imps stood by his bed" (*St. Tr.* 16: 725). Everyone in the village described Arnold as a morose, distant young man who often talked to himself in public. But if this testimony argued on his behalf, key elements of the crime indicated some premeditation. On the day he encountered Lord Onslow, Arnold went out of his way to purchase shot of an unnecessarily large calibre. Additionally, he appeared to take careful aim before shooting, knocking the aristocrat off his mount with a severe shoulder wound.

In the neoclassical era, harsh retribution masquerading as morality clouded the flexible standard Coke postulated. Not coincidentally, this is the very age that fostered Tate's "happy ending" adaptation of *King Lear,* which held the stage until the mid-nineteenth century. The essence of the prosecutor's argument in *Arnold's Case* reflects a renewed emphasis on *lex talionis* retribution: "Gentlemen, though he acted like a wicked man, void of reason, you will have little reason to think he acted like a madman" (*St. Tr.* 16: 701). Arnold's purchase of extra-large shot proved decisive in vitiating any lingering questions surrounding his mental state. The prosecution made good use of a new statute (9 Geo. 1. c. 22) assigning blame if "any person or persons shall willfully and maliciously shoot at any person in any dwelling or other place" (*St. Tr.* 16: 745). The prosecution seized upon the evidence of premeditation to overwhelm the insanity defense. Judge Tracy outlined the insanity guidelines for Arnold's jury: "If a man be deprived of reason, and consequently of his intention, he cannot be guilty" (*St. Tr.* 16: 764). At the same time, however, he placed extraordinary emphasis on his black-letter interpretation that insanity be "very plain and clear" and that the defendant should appear to be little more than a "brute or wild beast" to secure a favorable verdict (*St. Tr.* 16: 764, 765). Thus, by 1724, insinuations of wickedness and wildness had begun to supplant more reasoned legal definitions surrounding lesser levels of insanity. Far from seeming the raving lunatic in court, Arnold was polite and meek, if immensely confused. He was condemned to death, but through Lord Onslow's intercession his sentence was reduced to life without parole. Arnold was held at Southwark jail for thirty years, where he died of natural causes.

II. Lear and Renaissance Madness

King Lear makes distinctions between "mental illness and the resulting incapacity" that we allow today but which were obscured in Arnold's case (Brooks 111). Arnold's apparent ability to reason his way into purchasing large shot obliterated the argument that he might be insane. Coke, on the other hand, would entertain evidence of prior mental illness as a basis for concluding that the defendant could not behave reasonably. We, like Coke, would probably have dealt with Arnold far less harshly, though any attack by a commoner on an aristocrat in the Renaissance would have worked against the defendant. In Shakespeare's complex psychological understanding, Lear never loses his capacity to act in a dramatic sense even when we might suspect that he has lost touch with his surroundings. Reasonable people can differ as to his mental state, though I would argue that his madness is very brief, which is not to understate the depth of his passion—his hallmark as a tragic protagonist.

Lear's madness does not release him from his dramatic responsibilities, for if it did he would be as uninteresting as the wild beast to which Judge Tracy so confidently refers. Indeed, one of Lear's more emphatic character traits is his desire to suppress madness, even though profound mental disturbances cannot be resisted without medical intervention. Lear's efforts here can be seen as virtuous if "giving in" to madness constitutes a moral failing, as many then and today see it. Lear's force of will is emphasized at least half a dozen times in the opening two acts: "O, let me not be mad, not mad, sweet heaven! / Keep me in temper, I would not be mad!" (1.5.46–47). Suffering from exposure and exhaustion, he seems to drift in and out of madness. So *King Lear* is a tragedy about madness, but only if the mental state is seen to be more than a simple bifurcation between immoral wickedness and pure reason. Neither does the play resort to the opinion that everyone is a little bit mad, which is at the heart of today's victimization theories. Fortunately for the actors who play Lear, there is a vast middle ground between madness and sanity which no profession can yet claim to understand completely.

Coke's reasonable legal approach to madness had powerful foes. King James published tracts asserting melancholy to be aggravated by immoral acts and predispositions. He claimed to see these tendencies in the wretches who were unfortunate enough to undergo his interrogation:

> Further experience daylie proues how loath they are to confesse without torture, which witnesseth their guiltiness; whereby the contrary, the Melancholiques never spares to bewray themselves, by their continuall discourses, feeding thereby their humour in that which they thinke no crime.
>
> (*Dæmonology* 30)

James sought to link the humour theory of psychology to the spiritual crimes over which he had some influence. Robert Burton's lay opinions about humour psychology could have been aimed directly at Lear. Burton held that in the elderly, black choler is "superabundant":

> *After 70 years* (as the Psalmist saith) *all is trouble and sorrow*, and common experience confirmes the truth of it in weake old persons, especially in such as have lived in action all their lives, had great employment, much business, much command, and many servants to oversee, and leave off *ex abrupto*. . . .   (*Anatomy* 1: 204)

King Lear complicates the moralizing with which humour psychology had become associated, for a mentally distraught person refusing to confess to witchcraft under torture was to James all the more a sign of guilt.

Even among physicians there was little public disagreement over the perceived supernatural foundation of mental illness that James propounded, and virtually none at all with humour psychology per se. In 1603, though, the English physician Edward Jorden published a tract denying supernatural causation in hysteria. Jorden defined hysteria as a psychiatric disease properly placed in the hands of medical experts. He naturally had to rely on existing knowledge about humour psychology because scientific evidence to the contrary would not be available for centuries, but his opinion was based on sufficient observation to be called medically sound. This objectivity stands in stark contrast to that of James, his occasional employer, and the Puritan fathers, whose opinions Jorden rejected:

> But disclaiming both hony and gall, I have plainely set down the true doctrine of physicke concerning that disease which gives so great occasion of distraction among many good men: especially such as have not learning sufficient to resolve them of this point, or not that moderation and humilitie of spirit to acknowledge their insufficiencie, and to hearken unto others whom in all reason they might thinke able to direct them better in such a case. (Jorden A2)

Jorden's observation that emotions can master a reasonable, intelligent person anticipates Freud and more modern experts in the field by centuries. Indeed, Jorden diagnosed hysteria as a problem derived from sexual anxiety with various side effects: "For sometimes the instruments of respiration alone doe suffer, sometimes the heart alone, sometimes two or three faculties together, sometimes successively one after another" (Jorden C2). When Lear exclaims: "O how this mother swells up toward my heart! / [Hysterica] passio, down, thy climbing sorrow" (2.4.56–57), Shakespeare gives him physiological reactions that are not so very far afield from those Jorden recorded.

Jorden was ahead of the law courts in his observations on hysteria. Renaissance law could be flexible in judging insanity, but the extent to which it would heed Jorden's testimony was limited. In the notorious 1602 case of fourteen year old Mary Glover, the alleged victim of Elizabeth Jackson's witchcraft, Jorden's testimony on the defendant's behalf ultimately had no effect. Because Jorden could not specify a biological cause and remedy for Mary's rapid decline into blindness, deafness, and various abdominal irregularities, Judge Anderson followed the strict letter of the law in passing his sentence against Jackson:

> Divines, Phisitians, I know they are learned & wise, but to say this is naturall, and tell me neither the cause, nor the Cure of it, I care not for your Judgement: give me a naturall reason, & a naturall remedy, or a rash for your Physicke. (Hunter 75)

Though Judge Anderson could not conceal the mockery in his tone when referring to physicians, he operates within the bounds of his professional code and Renaissance common sense by weighing the evidence as he does. His sympathies clearly lay with those who believed demonic possession was not only real but constituted an active threat to the security of England. He had no doubt of Elizabeth Jackson's guilt: "She must of necessitie be a Prophet, or a Witch" (Bradwell 29). As for Mary, the efforts of physicians to heal her went for naught during the trial, but her health cleared up remarkably upon hearing that Jackson was convicted, a development for which the Puritan fathers took their share of credit. Little support existed for insanity defenses in the Renaissance when charges of witchcraft might be leveled against some unfortunate and usually uneducated victim. Regrettably, there was insufficient evidence at the time to make medical opinion count more heavily in court in order to overturn popular misconceptions about psychological illnesses.[3]

Lear's fragile mental state is used against him cruelly, but the simplicity of the Renaissance understanding of madness actually extends his life span:

> So if the body of a man be taken in execution, and the Plaintiff release all actions, yet he shall remain in Execution; but if he release all debts or duties, he is to be discharged of the Execution, because the debt or duty in itself is discharged. (1 *Institutes* 291)

Legal action is uncertain as to its outcome, but debts and duties are real. Thus, had Lear sought to retain control over the kingdom, he would have been viewed as a threat by his foes. As it is, by renouncing his claims, he is made harmless in the eyes of his antagonists. His rejection of his duties becomes injurious to him later due to his sense of guilt; however, his agony provides the basis for the sublime tragedy that unfolds before us.

III. LEAR'S THEATRICAL INSANITY

Lear's madness occurs in the context of a range of emotions which are natural rather than supernatural in origin. While this statement is not newsworthy by our standards, it places Shakespeare squarely in Jorden's camp rather than in James's. Lear's rage raises questions of justice and social equity without turning the play into a political tract: "O, reason not the need! our basest beggars / Are in the poorest thing superfluous" (2.4.264–65). It is with some justification that Regan refers to Lear's characteristic "rash mood" and Goneril to his "indiscretion" (2.4.169, 196). Lear regards as treasonous his daughters' refusal to sustain him in the manner to which he had become accustomed, but his over-hasty division of the kingdom fosters inevitable aristocratic infighting that leaves Britain exposed to foreign invasion. Coke refers to the dangers of a divided kingdom throughout the *Institutes*, citing the reigns of Gorboduc and Oedipus as cautionary examples (*4 Institutes* 243). The fact that the invaders side with Cordelia and Lear is less incriminating than the king's fundamental dereliction of duty. Of course, whatever justification Goneril and Regan have to curb his profligacy vanishes when they banish him to the storm. Shakespeare tips the play's emotional scales toward Lear by having him play against the very emotions in which he constantly indulges himself against the backdrop of a gathering storm:

> You think I'll weep:
> No, I'll not weep.
> I have full cause of weeping, but this heart
> Shall break into a hundred thousand flaws
> Or ere I'll weep. O Fool, I shall go mad! (2.4.282–86)

Lear's anger leads him toward madness but never to suicide, unlike the much abused Gloucester, who after one attempt dies overwrought with emotion when Edgar reveals his true identity to him. As with

Lear, death arrives not as a benediction but as a lethal dose of intermingled joy and sorrow. The punishment of these two characters is extreme because the very law that grants rights to society to act against an offender must also serve as a buffer which, in Hart's terms, "*protects* the individual against the claims of the rest of society" (*Punishment* 44). Such prophylactic measures disappear under the realm's malignant new leadership.

The storm on the heath is more than Kent or the Fool care to endure, but Lear's pronouncements there are not insane. One Renaissance test of insanity is insensitivity to pain, but Lear remains aware of his surroundings. He merely ranks its effect below that of his emotional suffering: "[This] tempest in my mind / Doth from my senses take all feeling else, / Save what beats there—filial ingratitude!" (3.4.12–14). Lear's madness shows itself as anger which has a limit and direction in wishing to "show the heavens more just" (3.4.36). His capacity to rule evenhandedly is in doubt, but his sense that law should hold sway remains consistent with Coke's views:

> Customes & usages. *Consuetudo* is one of the main triangles of the Laws of England, those Laws being divided into Common Law, Statute Law, and Custome. . . . Of every Custome there be two essential parts, Time and Usage; Time out of mind . . . and continuall and peaceable usage without lawfull interruption.   (1 *Institutes* 110a)

Lear's common-sense reaction to the harmful innovations brought about by his abdication marks progress on his part because he thought so little of violating the bond Cordelia recounted early in the play. Observance of custom is admittedly the weakest of the three legs of the legal triangle to which Coke refers, but it has a place in the history of the common law.

Shakespeare gives madness a human face as part of a boundless tragic experience, no mean feat for his age. If Lear, so politically naive, had a touch of the Machiavel about him, we would cease to care about him instantly. In the mock trial within the hovel, he charges Goneril with abuse and Regan with hard-heartedness; however, their faults at this point are ethical but not criminal, just as his illness is human, not supernatural. Lear adopts the appearance of the Bedlam beggars, but the play remains ambiguous on the question of Lear's madness until he enters "*crowned with weeds and flowers*" (4.6.80). With this appearance, the play refutes Edgar's assertion that the "worst returns to laughter" (4.1.6), as it refutes in advance the neoclassical prescription for poetic justice in tragedy. Moral rearmament cannot reverse the tragic revolution of fortune's wheel in *King Lear*.

Justice and madness intersect because Lear has become entirely concerned with mens rea, or the guilty intent, rather than with the guilty act. He focuses wholly on human motivation, for a tremendous leveling process has taken place in his perception of the actus reus. He castigates flatterers and corrupt beadles with the same energy. So devoted is he to final causes that he takes on the role of justice in a court of last resort: "I pardon that man's life. What was thy cause? / Adultery? / Thou shalt not die. Die for adultery? No" (4.6.109–11). Lear's sanguine reaction to Gloucester's loss of sight is a difficult moment of staging that usually draws an uncomfortable laugh in the theatre, but all outrages have become as one with him as he absolves petty crimes and roars with anger in the same breath. He lives in two extremes simultaneously, unlike Othello, whose path to disaster is singular; unlike Macbeth, who seems single-minded in his pursuits despite his depth of vision; and even unlike Hamlet, in whom metaphysical curiosity predominates. All acts are the same to Lear—until he kills the rogue who hangs Cordelia. His capacity for revenge is never entirely extinguished. At this stage of the tragedy his exaction of rough justice is redemptive, for he believes Cordelia may still be alive.

Lear's retribution is more complicated in terms of tragic action than Edmund's hackneyed stage villainy or the stylized, insane revenge of Heironimo in *The Spanish Tragedy*. The weight of a theatrical tradition nourishing revengers like Iago and Aaron makes Edmund a somewhat more striking role than that of Edgar. Most Edmunds revel in their opening soliloquies making nature their goddess, but they tend to outroar Lear, thereby undercutting the action of the play. Hyperactive Edmunds rarely wear well on the audience and almost never survive a misdirected chuckle from the audience upon hearing news of his fate: "*Messenger*: Edmund is dead, my lord. / *Albany*: That's but a trifle here" (5.3.296). However true it may be, Albany's response cannot sum up our contempt for him. Perhaps it is because his belated recantation seems incredible, reversing his role as a self-libeling villain and thereby spoiling our delight in his discomfiture.[4] That he undergoes a conversion too late for Cordelia suggests an incompetence discordant with true villainy. Underplaying Edmund could be the key to overcoming the difficulty he presents as a major character disconnected from the play's exploration of psychological anguish.

Edgar's theatrical pose is quite effective and humorous, though method-acting Toms who appear to suffer too much by covering themselves in mud, stinging nettles, and thorny crowns detract from the irony inherent in the role. Edgar is a skilled actor who cannot always separate himself from the fictions he creates: "My tears begin to take his part so much, / They mar my counterfeiting" (3.6.59–60). For Edgar to take his role too seriously leads to mawkishness. Many actors playing him merely restate what is transparent on stage: "Why I do trifle thus with his despair / Is done to cure it" (4.6.33–34). His attempt to work miracles is not necessarily sentimental in a work that has people killed for sport, but he must play off the layered ironies arising from Gloucester's tortured perception of the world: "'Tis the time's plague, when madmen lead the blind" (4.1.46). Neither Edgar nor Lear are mad in the sense Gloucester understands it because theatrical irony has colored their world view.

Edmund has no understanding of the filial devotion leading Edgar to save Gloucester from self-slaughter. In a legal context, Edgar's act preserves the family legacy because those shown to have committed *felo de se* suicide must by law lose their possessions to the king. The crown thus had a vested interest in determining as few suicides as possible to have resulted from insanity. Michael MacDonald calculates that 97.7% of suicides between 1600–1609 were deemed to be illegal (29). This absurdly high number is but another consequence of the moralistic interpretation of madness that James's prejudices reflected. Any suggestion that some enlightened self-interest influences Edgar in protecting his father should be discounted because throughout most of the play he is in no position to gain in the event of Gloucester's death.

The duel between Edmund and Edgar resolves a number of outstanding legal issues, many of which, admittedly, would have been settled eventually due to the wars. Edgar is not only initially presumed guilty by Gloucester, his flight makes him guilty as such:

> If a man that is innocent be accused of felony, and for fear flieth the same, albeit he judicially acquitteth himself of the Felony; yet if it be found that he fled for the felony, he shall notwithstanding his innocency forfeit all his goods and chattels, debts and duties; for as the forfeiture of them the Law will admit no proof against the presumption in Law grounded upon his flight.
>
> (1 *Institutes* 373–373a)

By vanquishing his brother, Edgar regains the advantages of lineal descent that had passed to Edmund through various sordid acts. The deaths that follow give him a claim to rights and honors that Regan and Goneril had planned to bestow upon Edmund, about which more must now be said since it follows as a consequence of Lear's madness.

IV. The Land and the Crown

From the most elemental forces of nature to the heights of regal power, *King Lear* invokes the broadest array of legal issues in Shakespearean tragedy. The focus of this chapter is on the insanity element, but some mention must be made of the issues of inheritance and possession surrounding the realm and its rule. At the start, Lear gives possession of the land to Goneril and Regan, a gift for which he receives quite literally no consideration. Such a bequeath is permissible in law but is deemed unwise. By the end, when the scepter is contested, ownership of the land becomes difficult to ascertain and the crown a title no one wishes to claim.

Given the immense scope of the tragic action, to say that *King Lear* is a play about fee-simple, or absolute, ownership and inheritance of land falls a bit flat. Lear undertakes just such a momentous decision, though, in dividing the map of the realm. The crown owns all of the land in a metaphysical sense however it comes to be apportioned by right of ownership or rent: "It is a Principle in Law, that of every land there is a Fee simple, &c. in somebody" (1 *Institutes* 343). Inheritance and ownership issues comprise the better part of the first two books of Coke's *Institutes*, so the importance of fee-simple and related ownership questions cannot be understated in English Renaissance life.

When Lear dispossesses Cordelia, he violates not only familial bonds but the spirit of inheritance law: "It is commonly said, that these things be favoured in Law, Life, Liberty, Dower" (1 *Institutes* 124a). Lear has every right to cut Cordelia out, but a punitive and unreasonable distribution of dowry gifts creates discord, as everyone at the opening assembly understands. It also tends to violate the principle in law that "no man is presumed to do anything against nature" (1 *Institutes* 373), though of course Lear in his blindness believes that it is Cordelia who offends nature. Much of the play is devoted to his painful enlightenment regarding natural relationships.

Lear is not alone in speaking out of turn where inheritance issues are concerned. When Gloucester makes a jest of Edmund's bastardy, he raises legal questions that subject his family to misery and death. Edgar can claim Gloucester's estate on the grounds that he is the eldest legitimate son:

> No man can be heire to a fee simple by the Common Law . . . but he that hath *sanguinem duplicatum*, the whole blood, that is, both of the father, and of the mother, so as the half blood cannot be a compleat heire, for that he hath not the whole and compleat blood.   (1 *Institutes* 14)

Gloucester's public garrulousness regarding Edmund's birth nonetheless puts Edgar at risk because it increases Edmund's rights of inheritance under law. There are admittedly multiple obstacles to Edmund's enfranchisement, including the problem of primogeniture, but Gloucester vitiates some of the arguments against his place in the line of succession: "A bastard having gotten a name by reputation may purchase by his reputed or known name to him and heirs, although he can have no heir but of his body" (1 *Institutes* 36). Once Edmund gets his foot in Gloucester's door, so to speak, he has only Edgar standing in his way. His amorous affiliations with the two landed daughters of Lear make his chances for property ownership that much more real. Were he to marry one or both of them, he would have ownership of a portion of the realm through the wife:

> Also, if I let certain land to a feme sole for term of her life who taketh a husband, & after I confirm the Estate of the husband and wife, to have and to hold for term of their two lives. In this case the husband doth not joyntly with his wife, but holdeth in right of his wife for term of her life. But this confirmation shall enure to the husband for term of his life if he surviveth his wife.
> (1 *Institutes* 299)

Given Edmund's ambitions, it is likely he would survive both Goneril and Regan, though in the play's dazzlingly rapid denouement, the trio are metaphorically married and killed "in an instant" (5.3.230). Coke invokes an old common law term for mixed ownerships of the kind Edmund plots: a "Hotchpot," or "Pudding" (1 *Institute* 176a), an apt description of the mixture of land ownership resulting from hasty and unusual marriages and other associations.

The battle of champions that Edgar arranges with Albany before the battle ensures that if Lear's side loses, the eldest son of Gloucester might still influence the inheritance decision. The letter Edgar captures proves to be a remarkably influential document, for it provides evidence of Goneril's unfaithfulness and the threat to Albany's life. Motivated by a desire to possess the kingdom as well as both of Lear's errant daughters, Edmund accepts the stranger's challenge to his loyalty. The formality of the *duellum* in English law is retained in the play, but Shakespeare's version elevates the tone with musical flourishes while highlighting the charge of treason:

> Captain: [Sound, trumpet!] *A trumpet sounds.*
> Herald: *(Reads.)* If any man of quality or degree within the lists of the army
>   will maintain upon Edmund, supposed Earl of Gloucester, that he is
>   a manifold traitor, let him appear by the third sound of the trumpet.
>   He is bold in his defense.   (5.3.109–114)

Innuendoes of Edmund's brash corruption are particularly delightful when compared to the common law version of the ceremony, which includes rather mundane requirements:

> Heare this you Judges, that I have this day, neither eate, drunke, nor have
> upon me either bone, stone, ne grasse, or any inchauntment, sorcery, or
> witchcraft, where through the power of the word of God might be inleased or
> diminished, and the Devils power increased, and that my appeale is true, so
> help mee God and his Saints, and by this Booke.   (2 *Institutes* 247)

The concern in Coke's version is that the trial ought to return God's verdict of the truth; thus, the combatants should be free of supernatural assistance. Coke cites the biblical injunction on this point: "Vengeance is mine, and I will repay it, saith the Lord" (3 *Institutes* 157). The state's approval of the contest is essential, for otherwise it would become a mere brawl of revenge, which the common law sought to avoid at all costs. Albany seeks revenge, naturally, but retributive sentiments are muted between the combatants, who share final respects and some vital information before Edmund dies.

With Edmund's passing, Goneril becomes the putative ruler given the mortal dose of poison she has administered to her sister. Confronted by Albany with the damning letter, Goneril speaks as one who intends to retain the crown: "Say if I do, the laws are mine, not thine; / Who can arraign me for't?" (5.3.158–59). This assertion is ambiguous, however, signifying not only her intent to rule above the law but also possibly that she may not survive long enough to be arraigned. The latter hypothesis proves true. Once Goneril is dispatched, Albany has the strongest claim to the throne. All these affairs of state are transacted while our attention, unlike Albany's, is diverted offstage to the survival of Lear and Cordelia. Upon Lear's pathetic entrance with the dead Cordelia in his arms, Albany transfers power back to the old king. Lear is unable or unwilling to recognize this honor being restored to him, for he is overwhelmed with grief concerning the loss of his loved one. Upon the death of the king, Albany seeks to revert power to Kent and Edgar. Kent, sensing his own demise, wants no part of the offer. Edgar accepts the title by default mainly because he does not expressly reject it.

Lear's tragic end has diminished the perceived value of the crown and the land. The economy of punishment is so horrific that it overwhelms deterrence and retribution as relevant concepts for, as Hart puts it, deterrence must be "a claim to the *outer* limit of punishment; as fixing a *maximum* beyond which punishment is not justified" (*Punishment* 80). The savagery of punishment here exceeds all bounds, permitting only a vision of redemption between the reunited Lear and Cordelia which does not outlive their ordeal. The problem of representing fully in a single production the play's innocent beauty and utter savagery, its psychological darkness and world-historical implications, will remain for actors playing the defiant, ultimately unbroken, old king at the play's center.

CHAPTER 5

VISIBLE GODS: *ANTONY AND CLEOPATRA*

Two self-mythologizing protagonists rise above the strictures of the common law to redeem themselves in such a way as to become oblivious to their punishment. Antony speaks some of Shakespeare's mightiest lines and behaves in most respects as a hero should, but the play complicates the concept of the tragic subject. Antony dissolves into Cleopatra to the extent that he concedes he "cannot hold this visible shape" (4.14.14). Cleopatra, the last of the Pharaonic rulers, stages her death in the form of a belated marriage ceremony. Unlike Marlovian tragedy, Shakespearean tragic action in its redemptive phase admits passion and heroism as mythical elements with the lovers' phoenix-like renewal.

In Part I, I examine cases that define the rights of wives in the English Renaissance. Antony violates his marital vows, for which there can be no good excuse. Octavius protests too much, I think, the outcome of his sister's marriage, while Octavia fails to press her claim against Antony adequately within the given circumstances of the play. She is not obliged to do so, but given the strength of Cleopatra's interventions, there is a theatrical if not legal imperative for her to object to Antony's wanderings more forcefully.

Part II briefly assesses modern legal efforts to emancipate women by banning indecent representations, of which Cleopatra receives her share from the ambivalent Romans. Shakespeare's play treats gender oppression progressively, for who subjugates whom in the play, Cleopatra, Antony, or Octavius? I focus on two rulings in the U.S. and Canada inspired by Andrea Dworkin and Catharine MacKinnon because their efforts have borne fruit in the courtroom. Despite their good intent, though, the censorship they sponsor has tended to pit one oppressed group against another.

Lastly, I treat the relationship between Cleopatra and Antony as one of Shakespeare's most delicate tragic creations, involving a confluence of traits and cultures. The play reaches tragic heights through a conflict of doubt leading not to the profound despair of Othello or Macbeth but instead toward the regenerative power of love.

I. INDECENCY AND THE WAGER OF LOVE

The premise underlying Shakespeare's treatment of the lovers is that their relationship is perceived to be improper but not illegal, though Dryden refers to their "crimes of love" in *All for Love* (pref. 18). Shakespeare's characters cannot be indicted under law; thus, criminal punishment theory contributes little to the play directly. Absent is a violent antagonist like Aaron, Edmund, or Iago. Octavius's accession to the world throne is opportunistic, but he cannot be placed under arrest for failing to comprehend the lovers' poetic supremacy. This majestic quality was expertly represented in Peter Brook's 1978 production at London's Aldwych Theatre. The dynamic use of Middle Eastern and Indian music and lush amber lighting during the Egyptian scenes signified a world removed from Rome but infinitely richer. Brook's handling of Cleopatra's final moments was a master stroke. The moribund queen, adorned in gold finery and dark-outline makeup, gazed upward as she sat alone center stage on a throne illuminated by an increasingly bright spotlight until an abrupt blackout concluded the performance.

Cleopatra and Antony surmount the greatest military machine in history with a leap of the imagination. Theirs is a triumph over the logic of war, which Octavius implements to great advantage by turning Antony's troops against him and by refusing his challenge to single combat. Roman advancements in the tactics of warfare are shown to be insuperable, yet Octavius's world affords little place for the ethos of heroism and love. Cleopatra and Antony transmute Roman values into their own terms. Loyalty, the single fundamental requirement of the Roman soldier, becomes the central complication in the lovers' relationship until it is ultimately resolved in their favor. Indecent urges are not solely Egyptian, nor is martial ability purely Roman. Shakespeare set himself a formidable dramatic task in eternalizing Egypt's dissolving culture while diminishing the Roman empire. The play builds upon Marlowe's bipolar tragic world of heroism and sensuality, but while Marlowe's heroes might disintegrate, their language remains monumental. Shakespeare provides Cleopatra and Antony the heroism of the Marlovian line while interpolating subtler qualities of versification at appropriate occasions. As a challenge to his own dramatic technique, Shakespeare raises the bar above the poetic and theatrical heights attained in Marlovian tragedy and soars over it.

If this play is rated below the four tragedies discussed above, it is because the tragic end does not involve a near-apocalyptic contest with evil that G. Wilson Knight and others so value in Shakespeare. The lovers have created a world in each other that they regard more highly than the Roman imperial state. They see themselves and their empires evolving metaphorically rather than through force of arms. Thus, Antony can proclaim: "Let Rome in Tiber melt," and Cleopatra: "Melt Egypt into Nile!" (1.1.33, 2.5.78). They violate at least three traditional standards in criticism, a gambit inviting the audience to prejudge the lovers. First, for Cleopatra and Antony to be dismissive of empire-building is antithetical to the broad course of Shakespearean criticism if not the audience's better judgment.[1] Attacks on Antony's military sufficiency relate both to his effectiveness as a leader and his strategic prowess in defending Rome. Antony's talent as a warrior is seriously questioned only after the disastrous Actium retreat, where the distinction between a cowardly retreat and a defeat cannot hold. Second, Antony's alliance with Cleopatra runs afoul of traditional and legal notions of patriarchal dominance.[2] In his revised version of the play, Dryden attributes Antony's downfall almost exclusively to a surplus of passion through the use of multiple debates on the conflict between reason and emotion. Third, Antony's hedonism condemns him in the eyes of some critics of having lost the traditional battle between the spirit and the flesh.[3] Testing his vision on "pain of punishment" (1.1.39), however, Antony finds love not to be wanting.

As commander of his forces, Antony could not easily be tried for desertion or misconduct, while Cleopatra is more forgiving than any military court would be. Since criminality is not an issue here, perhaps Renaissance tort law on malfeasance, or "Malefesans" (1 Croke 285), suggests how a Jacobean audience might view Antony's defects. In cases of malfeasance, liability attaches to the party failing to take positive steps to prevent waste or damage. Edward's Case of 1592 (34 Eliz.) shows the gap between our perception of malfeasance liability and that of the Elizabethan age. In this case, which Sir Edward Coke lost, the plaintiff Edward owned and stored hogsheads of wine in a cellar above which the unnamed defendant maintained wares of considerable dead weight. Owing to the decrepitude of the flooring, the wares fell through, shattering the hogsheads of wine below. The defense claimed that the state of decay of the warehouse was known to all of the parties, including the owner, one J. S., and that the defendant had in fact been storing products of a weight 20% less than previous occupants. Unlike today, J. S. as owner was seen to bear no responsibility for the condition of the warehouse. Though the defendant exhibited neither malicious intent nor callous indifference, he lost because his argument did not address the legal issue at hand: "The Plea was not good for want of a Traverse; for when a *Malefesans* is laid to the Defendants charge, he ought expressly to traverse it, and not to answer it by Argument" (1 *Croke* 285). It was up to the defendant in cases like this to demonstrate that he had taken positive steps to prevent accidents. Antony does not traverse his malfeasance with logical arguments of any kind, legal or otherwise, but instead generally responds with appeals to passion.

Shakespeare airs unsparing criticism of Antony in the Actium scene, including the character's own self-reproach, but there is nothing to suggest that the praise showered upon him even by his detractors as a titan on the battlefield is undeserved. Octavius is not alone in recalling Antony's martial skill and willingness to endure harsh campaigns. Antony approaches war as a painter would his canvas, casting himself as an artisan in a heroic occupation ancestrally affiliated with that of Hercules. Under Antony's stewardship, the Roman empire is secure at the outset of the play despite the internecine military brushfires that Octavius cites with such urgency. Antony diplomatically conceals his contempt for Octavius's lack of military experience. When personal and policy differences within the triumvirate threaten the empire, Antony patches up the disputes with a temporary accord: "And though I make this marriage for my peace, / I' th' East my pleasure lies" (2.3.40–41). Furthermore, Antony remains loyal until Octavia, with some justification, severs their relationship to flee to her brother's side. Apart from the exceptions already noted, Antony sacrifices his personal needs in order to maintain Rome's tactical security. The sole fatally flawed policy decision made early in the play originates with Pompey, who refuses Menas's suggestion to slaughter his rivals at the banquet.

Criticism that Antony fails the patriarchal order evaporates when he is compared to his compatriots in the play. The portrait of Antony's exuberance comes at the moment of the flowering of his relationship with Cleopatra, which even he recognizes as dangerous. Still, Antony's pleasures seem positively wholesome when contrasted with Octavius's rather repressed demeanor. Octavius's attachment to his sister seems excessively emotional, bordering on the incestuous, or so it could easily be played. Octavia's passions are restrained, yet she chooses her brother over Antony following news of Pompey's assault. Octavius's outrage over Antony's renewed Egyptian affair sounds hollow given that he had used Octavia as a pawn for his own political ambitions.

The issue of Antony's personality being overborne by sensuality is a complicated one. We see inside the bedroom of Antony and Cleopatra, as it were, a perspective rarely afforded in Shakespeare. This presents an immediate disadvantage for any critic trying to make a case for Antony's relatively balanced libidinal urges. The preliminaries to the peace accord struck aboard Pompey's galley suggest that sensuality is equally a Roman preoccupation. Enobarbus enchants the Romans with his narration about Cleopatra's sloop, with its "pretty dimpled boys" and "amorous" strokes (2.2.202, 197). These descriptions provoke wonder rather than outrage on the part of the hearers. Romans are guilty as well of surfeiting on spirits. Antony and Pompey can hold their liquor, unlike Octavius and the drunkard Lepidus, whom Antony can ridicule by making commonplace observations about Egypt and her crocodiles seem miraculously strange.

The dramatic action swirls around gaming as a wager of law, life, and love. Antony regards all of his affairs in this vein, including important matters of state; thus, honor and passion obey the same rules for him. The 1615 (12 Jac.) trespass case of assault and battery, *Ward v. Ayre,* is illustrative of the legal theory in games of chance that possession equals right. In the heat of gambling, Ward pushed an uncertain sum of his money into Ayre's pile. Ayre later refused to return any funds to his competitor, whereupon a struggle ensued. The unanimous opinion of the court was that Ward's "own mony cannot be known, and this his intermedling is his own Act, and his own wrong, that by the Law he shall lose all" (2 *Croke* 366). The common law insisted upon a clear distinction between what is one's own and another's; hence, if Ward's loss of money through his own neglect meant that no recovery could lie, then so be it. The law's logic in the instant case is that if Ward prevailed, Ayre might have been forced to hand over some of his own money, thereby becoming "a Trespasser against his will, by the taking of his own goods" (2 *Croke* 366). Disputes in military affairs arise similarly over the distribution of assets.

Antony shows greatness of spirit by breaking the rules of the game in sending Enobarbus's valuables after him following his defection. Antony understands gaming as an element in public and private matters and is dismissive of the rights of partners who are not as frolicsome. As a result, Octavia and Octavius suffer some humiliation at Antony's hands; so too does Cleopatra. A gamester herself, though, she manages to recast the wagering to her benefit.

Antony's view of public affairs resembles Octavius's because both regard the Roman mob as slippery. Antony waits serenely for political impostumes to burst before strapping on his military harness, while Octavius remains constantly on edge about the stability of the kingdom. This nervousness is apparent before their initial greeting, when Antony expounds on military strategy to Ventidius with the confidence of a seasoned veteran, unlike Octavius, who defers such considerations to Agrippa. Thereafter, the principals' subtextual dialogue reveals subtle antagonisms couched in diplomatic niceties: [Caes.] "Welcome to Rome." [Ant.] "Thank you." [Caes.] "Sit." [Ant.] "Sit, sir." [Caes.] "Nay then" (2.2.28). Antony's sense of heroism clouds his reason, if by that we mean self-interest and territorial ambition. A hero by Antony's standards would have accepted the challenge of single combat and with it the judgment of the gods. Octavius's scornful rejection of the offer demonstrates that he is guided by efficiency over heroism and by back-room maneuvering instead of the force of visible personality. Still, the more Antony dates himself in terms of current Roman politics, the more his verse fashions him as a quasi-mythological hero.

In the ultimate wager, Antony takes the Roman road to suicide. What remains is his mirthful comportment, an essential part of his character. Plutarch describes Antony's complexity with imagery from drama: "*Antonius* shewed them a commical face, to wit, a merie countenance: and the ROMANES a tragicall face, to say, a grimme looke" (North 6: 331). Retaining his Roman sense of loyalty even while informing Octavia that he cannot overlook her brother's broken contracts, Antony proves honor to be the unwritten law he observes whether or not it suits his ends. Though Antony wrongly accuses Cleopatra of betraying his forces to Octavius, he is correct to sense that his foe would have logically attempted to broker a treaty with Egypt. Octavius proves a good workaday deal-maker, but he fails in his attempts to lure the biggest prize of all to Rome.

English Renaissance common law was exacting as to the need to complete communicative loops in the matter of contracts. In the 1601

(43 Eliz.) case of *Brashford v. Buckingham and his Wife*, the King's Bench affirmed an Exchequer ruling that the plaintiff had a right to receive a refund of £10 for failure of the wife to cure his wound as promised. Two tests had to survive scrutiny: first, suit had to be brought against both Baron and Feme, which it was; and secondly, it was necessary that the Feme "alledges *in facto*, that she cured it: And for non-performance of this promise, they brought their Action upon the Case" (2 *Croke* 77). The key incriminating element was the wife's expressed claim to have cured what in fact had not been cured. Such an explicitly broken promise was an element missing in the 1587 (29 Eliz.) assumpsit case of *King v. Robinson*. King alleged that Robinson employed flattering words to receive monies from him by fueling his hopes that she would wed him. She garnered payment for her enticements, but the court found that King himself did not overtly "declare of any promise of marriage in *facto*" despite the obvious inference to be drawn from the gifts he lavished upon her (1 *Croke* 79–80). The communicative circle remained incomplete; thus, no contract was said to have existed. Robinson made suggestions and received payments for an implicit offer of marriage, but mere assumptions were not good in the law. Of King's suit, the court remarked tersely: "Failing in part, he fails in all" (1 *Croke* 80).

Such details of contract law do not interest one such as Antony, who is equally at ease with the common soldier or visiting dignitary. Excesses like whipping Octavius's saucy messenger while offering up his own as collateral would cheapen or indict him had he not deemed them matters of honor. Like the equality inherent in his proposed monomachia, the exchange of servants derives from an oversimplified conception of honor given the intricacies of Roman diplomacy. In light of this, the Soothsayer can safely predict that Antony will lose to Octavius Caesar:

> Thy daemon, that thy spirit which keeps thee, is
> Noble, courageous, high unmatchable,
> Where Caesar's is not; but near him, thy angel
> Becomes a fear, as being o'erpow'r'd. (2.3.20–23)

Antony's mythological ancestry and outlook supplant depth psychology as explanations for his personality shifts. His character flaws appear in concert with his metaphysical gambles. He gains and loses kingdoms with equanimity, while Caesar behaves in a cowardly fashion and rules the world. Occupying an uncertain middle ground between the gods and humankind, Antony is deserted by Hercules, accompanied by hautboys under the stage, as well as by Enobarbus, to his own notes of despair.

Antony has legitimate legal grounds for complaint against Octavius, who does not dispute their validity. He admits failing to share Antony's portion of Sicily in order to use it as a bargaining chip to gain similar advantages in Armenia. His silence on the issue of restoring the vessels Antony lent him suggests a dilatory tactic. He agrees with Antony that Lepidus should be rebuked for abuse of power. So Antony remains abreast of the issues facing the triumvirate upon his return from Egypt. While the charge is made that Antony bends his will to a woman's bidding, Enobarbus rightly observes that Octavius's moods swing with those of his sister. There is, fairly speaking, an equivalency of feminine influence over actions undertaken both in Rome and Egypt. One stark contrast remains in the arena of military comportment. Octavius's efficiency is revealed in the advance of the Roman forces toward Actium. Military tacticians receive due respect from historians, but bloodless leaders like Octavius are generally not admired in the theatre. When he promises an era of global peace, which puts an end to universal gamesmanship, he creates dramatic interest inversely proportional to that excited by Antony.

Perjuries abound in the play, but their context and purpose remain all-important. Though we regard perjury as a serious offense, it is rarely prosecuted today. The legal status of perjury was even more confused in the Renaissance, as we see in the 1596 (38 Eliz.) case of *Damport v. Sympson*. Star-Chamber and ecclesiastical courts could punish perjury rather freely, but common law courts faced more restrictions according to the majority in this decision: "For at the Common Law, there was not any Course in Law to punish Perjury" (1 *Croke* 521). The rationale here is that apart from a case of attaint, in which an entire jury brings a corrupt verdict, the effect of a witness's perjured testimony on a jury cannot be adequately measured. The case developed out of a quarrel between Damport, owner of a silver chalice worth £500, and one J. D., who was entrusted to sell the item abroad but who seems to have sold it for himself at an unknown price. In an earlier phase of the case, J. D. called upon Sympson to swear that the chalice was worth no more than £150. Damport sued Sympson for perjury and won £200 in damages. This amount was raised to £300 upon the lower court's confirmation of Sympson's perjury. On appeal, the court stayed the additional assessment because it was felt that the law could not "draw in Question the intent of the Jurors, what greater Dammages they would have given" (1 *Croke* 521). It was felt that the jurors ought to determine the veracity of a witness appearing before them and dispose accordingly whether or not he was later found to be lying under oath. Thus, a wager is inherent in the law even as to those who are proven to be liars, which Octavius, Antony, and Cleopatra are at various stages of the play. The gaming quality of the law is reflected in the play through its representation of wagers in human affairs, including comic and serious scenes concerning whether the intent of lies is merely to procure love or to gain territory.

If Antony and Caesar offer alternative perspectives on a shared Roman ideal, Cleopatra presents another with her "immortal longings" (5.2.281). She evolves from the woman whose thought-processes could be short-circuited by Mardian's erotic suggestions into becoming a rare Egyptian phoenix. Effortlessly and even unintentionally, she seduces all who see her. Childish pranks like hopping breathlessly through a marketplace induce pleasure. If Antony could not leave her, it is because nc Roman could. Cleopatra modulates her seductive capacity for political and personal gain. In seeking attention from her lover, she can adopt a contrarian approach, ordering her messenger to tell Antony that she is sad if he is happy, or happy if he is sad, or even that she has perished. Modern audiences split over approving her obvious vitality: "Age cannot wither her, nor custom stale / Her infinite variety" (2.2.234–35). Antony's threats of physical harm and accusations that she prostituted herself for Caesar might be sufficient to anger members of a modern audience because a woman is seemingly dominated in a sexual context, but the playwright's dramatic action reflects no gender bias.

There is plenty of evidence to indicate the subservient role women were forced to play under English Renaissance law even in good marriages. In *Tayler v. Fisher*, a 1590 (32 Eliz.) trespass case for a break-in, the defendant claimed he was retrieving his weapons from Tayler's house with the consent of the wife. The court allowed Fisher to keep his weapons but left him open to the trespass charge because "the Wifes licence to enter into her husbands house is not good, for she cannot give one Authority to enter into her husbands house" (1 *Croke* 246). Such social restrictions were sustained by law. In the 1611 (9 Jac.) assumpsit case of *Tampion v. Newson and Bridget his Wife*, a promise made by Bridget to Tampion was nullified by a higher court because "a plea of a *Feme* without the *Baron* is no plea at all; and an

Issue being joyned and tried thereupon is idle" (2 *Croke* 288). This lack of legal recourse is reiterated in the 1617 (15 Jac.) case of *Anonymus* (T. D. *v.* J. S. & A. S.), wherein A. S., an enterprising female merchant, was taken to court by T. D. for reasons unclear today. The verdict on appeal was that "the *Feme* without the *Baron* cannot be sued" (2 *Croke* 445). Nor could a wife collect damages without the husband being a party to the action. In some unusual cases, then, a woman's lack of legal standing could redound to her benefit in court, but such rare instances cannot compensate for the general disadvantage women faced as a result of occupying a secondary position in Renaissance English life. Shakespeare's mature perspective on love involves seeing shifting power relationships as a game, often serious, sometimes not, but accruing to the benefit of both *feme* and *baron*. Love, the solace for loss of empire, is here an affirmative force regarded as insufficient by moralists on all sides of the political spectrum.

II. INDECENCY LAW

Official attempts to limit speech on the English stage date approximately from 1534, when the Master of the King's Revels received independent status and found occasional headquarters in what would become Shakespeare's Blackfriars theatre space. The reasons given for the necessity of censorship are manifold, but Cleopatra's sufficiency as a tragic figure is being questioned under a new wave of social critique concerned with decency in representations of gender submissiveness in art and the media. Andrea Dworkin presents one feminist's view among many concerning gender relations: "Rape is the primary heterosexual model for sexual relating" (*Blood* 31). Her view has considerable implicit legal and academic currency today, with the effect of encouraging infringement on expression and due process on the grounds of gender equality. Shakespeare's play already assumes the concept of gender fairness, but Dworkin would limit expression, including possibly the right to stage plays like *Antony and Cleopatra*: "Literature is always the most eloquent expression of cultural values; and pornography articulates the purest distillation of those values" (*Blood* 102). Though literature can also be said to work against a culture's dominant values, I focus on Dworkin's theme of dominance and submission in art because it forms the rationale of an indecency statute enacted briefly in Indianapolis before being struck down by the

7th U.S. District Court of Appeals in 1984, a reversal affirmed by the U.S. Supreme Court in 1986.[4] With rulings due on the transmission of various images over the internet, some artistic, others not, decency restrictions promise to remain a lively topic for years to come.

In order to achieve a policy goal by limiting free speech, Dworkin and MacKinnon briefly created a new category of illegal art distinct from existing laws barring works of prurient interest with no redeeming social value. Indianapolis Code §16–3(q) of April 1984 sought to outlaw the "graphic sexually explicit subordination of women whether in pictures or in words" (771 F.2d at 324). Other groups are mentioned in passing, but the agenda was to repeal representations of subordinated women. Article 6 of the Code is the most relevant to the discussion here: "Women are presented as sexual objects for domination, conquest, violation, exploitation, possession, or use, through postures or positions of servility or submission or display" (771 F.2d at 324). Strict construction of this article could banish *Antony and Cleopatra* from the stage or *Schindler's List* from the cinema. With the use of "or" instead of "and," and with the insertion of vague phrases like "hurt" or "postures of submission," any section of a work of art, including masterpieces, could face censorship. The fact that MacKinnon, a noted law professor, helped draft the ordinance suggests that the vagueness is intentional.

MacKinnon would unnecessarily sacrifice literature on the altar of social reform as she envisions it: "If a woman is subjected, why should it matter that the work has other value?" (*Toward* 202). The U.S. 7th District Court of Appeals disagreed, striking down the Indianapolis statute with a rationale that was in its own way rather conservative: "It is unclear how Indianapolis would treat works from James Joyce's *Ulysses* to Homer's *Iliad*; both depict women as submissive objects for conquest and domination" (771 F.2d at 325). The urge to defend the classics is conjoined with a perceived need to balance rights: "The Constitution forbids the state to declare one perspective right and silence opponents" (771 F.2d at 325). The court chose to distinguish works of art from reality and to avoid picking winners and losers in the marketplace of ideas:

> The description of women's sexual dominance of men in *Lysistrata* was not real dominance. Depictions may affect slavery, war, or sexual roles, but a book about slavery is not itself slavery, or a book about death by poison a murder.   (771 F.2d at 330)

The court did not take up the literary critical debate over the degree to which a work of art dynamically shapes reality. It merely rejected the view that representation in art equals the act itself.

Finally, the court rejected the low-value argument for banishing an entire work of art on the basis of one objectionable scene of perceived domination. Had the court accepted Dworkin's and MacKinnon's view, countless works of art would have been snared in a drift net of pornography law that had heretofore passed the muster of obscenity rulings. The court was unambiguous in its ruling concerning the Indianapolis ordinance: "The definition of 'pornography' is unconstitutional" (771 F.2d at 332). I leave aside other elements of the court's rationale, including its finding that no reasonable evidence had been presented to show that a strict cause and effect relationship exists between indecent materials and violence toward women.

In *R. v. Butler* of 1992, the Canadian Supreme Court ruled favorably on the indecency statute promoted by MacKinnon that had been struck down in the U.S. No fire wall exists between censorship and free expression according to the *Canada Supreme Court Reports*: "Any publication a dominant characteristic of which is the undue exploitation of sex, or of sex and any one or more of . . . crime, horror, cruelty, and violence, shall be deemed to be obscene" (1 *RCS* 453). The key word, "undue," opens a loophole in the law:

> Section 163 of the *Code* is aimed at preventing harm to society, a moral objective that is valid under s.1 of the *Charter* [Charter of Rights and Freedoms]. The avoidance of harm to society is but one instance of a fundamental conception of morality . . . since the harm takes the form of violations of the principles of human equality and dignity.   (1 *RCS* 457)

Canadian Supreme Court Judge John Sopinka interpreted the "undue" harm clause as pertaining to works that place "women (and sometimes men) in positions of subordination, servile submission or humiliation" (1 *RCS* 479). It is difficult to imagine how *Antony and Cleopatra* could elude censorship given the vagueness of this ruling. Indeed, the law of unintended consequences arose almost immediately as works for gays and lesbians became the first to be caught up in the *Butler* ruling. The seizure by Canadian customs officials of gay materials sent to the Glad Day Book Store in Toronto and the store's subsequent prosecution elicited this tortured reaction from MacKinnon: "I am not necessarily at all clear that Glad Day should not be prosecuted" (Toobin 77). In attempting to protect women from what she sees to be a harm, MacKinnon and others have curtailed free expression in Canada, creating a chilling effect in the artistic community.

MacKinnon's role in drafting this legislation is affirmed by Women's Legal Education and Action Fund supporter Karen Busby: "The LEAF factum in *R. v. Butler* was written in three intensive weeks by Kathleen Mahoney, Catharine MacKinnon, and Linda Taylor" ("LEAF" 165). Canada's experience with an indecency law based on MacKinnon's principles is summed up by Toronto law professor Bruce Ryder: "Customs has seized thousands of titles" ("Little Sister" C2). Canadian customs officials have even confiscated works by Andrea Dworkin. MacKinnon dismisses criticism of *Butler* as propaganda from groups that are "being used" by smut peddlers (Toobin 77). For her part, Dworkin now maintains she has opposed laws like *Butler* all along:

> I was consulted and asked my opinion, and I asked them not to support that obscenity law. . . . This is something MacKinnon and I disagreed on. We agree on a lot of things, but not this time. My position on obscenity law is unequivocal. Obscenity law is a total dead end in dealing with the pornography industry. (Toobin 78)

Dworkin neatly shifts the discussion from pornography, her *bête noire*, to obscenity by obscuring the difference between them. By calling *Butler* an obscenity law, Dworkin can distinguish it from the censorship laws she has tried to enact for over a decade. Dworkin cannot be faulted for desiring to elevate humanity: "The innocence we want is the innocence that lets us love. People need dignity to love" (Letter 15). Dignity and love constitute a useful transition point to return to the cases of Cleopatra and Antony. Her life has dignity despite the opprobrium heaped upon her by the Roman world. The Romans come to admit this, as they do less grudgingly of Antony.

III. TRAGIC BOUNTY

Remaining an absolutist on loyalty and heroism, Antony speaks in Marlovian tones upon hearing the false report of Cleopatra's death: "Unarm, Eros, the long day's task is done, / And we must sleep" (4.14.35–36). The first verse evokes Marlowe's mighty line, but the enjambment augments it in Shakespeare's fluid handling of the metre. Meanwhile, Antony elevates his common law marriage by imagining an Ovidian afterlife: "Where souls do couch on flowers, we'll hand in hand, / And with our sprightly port make the ghosts gaze" (4.14.51–

52). This foreshadows a death not of despair but rather of a stoicism buoyed by a life of full accomplishment. The tension between tragedy and melodrama is stretched to the breaking point as Cleopatra hoists Antony up the monument, a slow progress Cleopatra terms "sport" (4.15.32). Their love is memorialized in passion more lasting than the self-serving manuscript Octavius promises to compose, which brings to mind Oscar Wilde's joke about diaries containing the private thoughts of young women and therefore intended for immediate publication.

Shakespeare takes on one of his most difficult cases in granting Cleopatra the status of a tragic hero. She changes visibly as she promises to contemplate her death in the Roman style. Antony speaks of their eternal life in the pantheon of the gods, but it is she who must face the emptiness of a world without Antony. Referring self-consciously to her refusal to witness squeaking boy-actors mimic her glory on the stage, Cleopatra shows a weariness with worldly affairs that is not cynical like Macbeth's. Macbeth's remark that the wine of his life has been drawn reveals a darkly criminal metaphysical perspective that has gripped him throughout most of the play. For Cleopatra to reunite with Antony is to regain their wager: "The odds is gone, / And there is nothing left remarkable / Beneath the visiting moon" (4.15.66–68). The entrance of the Egyptian Clown bearing poisonous medicine involves a comic technique foreshadowing Cleopatra's demise in a more emphatic manner than the devil-porter in *Macbeth*. Her death is an act of love and loyalty as she calls out to Antony as her husband and coos maternally to the poisonous asps suckling at her breast. Shakespeare elevates Cleopatra by reversing the gender stereotypes, for she has now become a mother-figure and common law wife.

However forceful it is as drama, Cleopatra's adoption of Antony as husband would have gone nowhere in English Renaissance law. In the 1601 (43 Eliz.) case of *Ryddlesden v. Cicely Wogan*, the plaintiff was awarded restoration of a debt against Cicely, who claimed she could not be sued because she was *feme* to one John Inglebert, since deceased. The court found through an investigation of spiritual court records that Inglebert had another spouse at the time Cicely claimed him as her mate. This discovery simplified the court's decision on the relationship between Inglebert and Wogan: "It was void *ab initio*, and she always sole" (1 *Croke* 858). Ryddlesden easily won his case based on the illegitimacy of Cicely's marriage claim. Like Cicely, though, Cleopatra uses her guile to promote her interests. The gaming ends when she ponders life without her chosen mate, an intensely tragic prospect with universal human appeal.

The indecency issue as framed by Dworkin and MacKinnon, which was overturned in the U.S. courts, was nullified in advance by Shakespeare. The lovers' relationship is stormy, shifting, mature, monumental, and therefore theatrically compelling. No criminal or civil statute can restrain them as they transcend their worlds, nor does their death alter the existing order.

Shakespeare splits his focus among the three protagonists in accordance with the multifaceted nature of the action, but the play presents Cleopatra as the fully developed female tragic figure Shakespeare is often said to have omitted. Glenda Jackson's 1978 creation was a slightly severe, regal, though warm figure—certainly no dominated woman. The lovers' visible physicality diminishes the play in the eyes of some, though I regard it as Shakespeare's finest achievement in the realm of redemptive tragedy and love, far more complex and mature than its logical predecessor, *Romeo and Juliet*.

CHAPTER 6

ROMEO AND JULIET:
THE FAILURE OF RESTITUTION

If Cleopatra and Antony transcend the law, Juliet and Romeo are imprisoned by it due to their political and familial circumstances. These bonds are a source of both strength and weakness for the play because punishment becomes relatively more grounded in restitution than in full emancipation or redemption. The lovers harbor neither criminal intent nor guile. Technically speaking, Romeo engages in criminal behavior, though these unpremeditated bad acts arise out of civil mutinies extending throughout the entire community. Even if, as the Chorus promises, the lovers' deaths will "bury their parents' strife" (1.0.8), complete restitution remains an impossibility. Shakespearean tragedy holds consistently to such inequality, for while the playwright grants improbable restitutions in the romances, in *Romeo and Juliet* the pain of loss is diminished only marginally through the use of the choric framing device.

Veronese factional strife bears a superficial resemblance to the tragic conflict in *Antigone*, in which two nearly equal legal positions are taken by antagonists in open debate. Antigone defends Polynices's right to a burial, a powerful claim since to leave a decedent exposed to sunlight constituted grounds for the death penalty in Greek law.[1] Haemon acknowledges the validity of her position when he turns against Creon, who argues somewhat convincingly that in order to maintain the security of the state a traitor's corpse ought to remain unsolemnized. Both positions carry weight in Greek law, though the play favors Antigone's position because sacrilegious acts were deemed to be among those most deserving of prosecution. The clear ethical debate seen by Hegel in Greek tragedy between characters who are "entirely and absolutely just that which they will and achieve" is supplanted in the

Renaissance by figures with inconsistent or unstated beliefs (*Fine Art* 4: 320). Furthermore, Shakespeare's tragedy contains a division of labor as dense as any treated by Emile Durkheim in his analysis of modern social structures.

Hegel regards Antigone as being "animated by an ethical principle of equal authority" in seeking to bury her brother (*Fine Art* 1: 293), but he omits to add that hers was a principle already codified in the law. Creon's baldly political edicts diminish his persuasiveness as the play unfolds. Hegel's central thesis regarding the equivalency of ethical values adopted by the antagonists in *Antigone* is therefore susceptible to some dispute, but his point is well taken. *Romeo and Juliet* provides no concordance between equitable and actual restitution, though the gap is partially bridged by what Durkheim would call reasonable "moral links" designed to memorialize the young couple (*Division* 276). Contrary to the Athenian ideal, restitution and equity have not been viewed as coterminous in English common law because of the state's overriding interest in punishing those responsible for disturbing civil order. Blackstone argues that just punishment must be inherently unequal to be fair to the victim:

> And truly, if any measure of punishment is to be taken from damage sustained by the sufferer, the punishment ought rather to exceed than equal the injury: since it seems contrary to reason and equity, that the guilty (if convicted) should suffer no more than the innocent has done before him; especially as the suffering of the innocent is past and irrevocable, that of the guilty is future, contingent, and liable to be escaped or evaded. (4 *Bl. Comm.* 13–14)

While holding out the suggestion that some solace obtains despite the lovers' tragic fate, the play can be said to present a vision more of truncated restitution than of emancipation. Shakespearean tragic figures cannot enjoy the synthesis Hegel so admired in Greek life, the "happy middle sphere of self-conscious and subjective freedom and substantial ethical life" (*Fine Art* 2: 181), due to their relatively extreme self-consciousness which, if not modern, is nevertheless distinct from the classical style.

Shakespeare is not interested in the truth value of the accusations hurled between the families as much as he is in using their arguments to sharpen the conflict. To this extent, Aristotle's limited definition of thought as a well-conceptualized postulate on the human condition generally independent of character and plot does not correspond to Shakespeare's more comprehensive dramaturgical strategy. The playwright emphasizes restitution in only one play because of its curtailed ability to scan the heights of Renaissance tragedy. In Aeschylus's *The Eumenides*, Athena's divine judgment of reconciliation combines reasonableness, equity, and well-placed flattery, but the Shakespearean model differs because his resolutions cannot entirely dispense with common law principles. This chapter will first examine unsettled questions of restitution in common law theory. Second, I treat cases of restitution in English common law and other courts. Next, I assess Durkheim's theory in the context of the tragic action of the play. Finally, I explore the limitations of restitution per se as a theory underpinning Shakespearean tragedy.

I. RESTITUTION AND COMMON LAW THEORY

The lovers regard their marriage as sacred to the extent that it overwhelms the imperatives of all other social relationships and the civil law. Escalus's juridical impulse to enforce peace leaves him blind to the hypothetical the play develops regarding the corrective social implications of the lovers' budding relationship. This hypothetical, vitiated by what are referred to in *Hamlet* as "carnal, bloody, and unnatural acts, / Of accidental judgments" (5.2.381–82), constitutes the sum total of political and psychological forces driving Shakespeare's tragic form here. The play's special emphasis on seeking civil remedies in human relationships contributes to its heightened lyricism in relationship to Shakespeare's other tragedies.

Legal issues in the play ripen as quickly as the young couple's mutual admiration. Romeo's banishment seems fair and reasonable given Tybalt's death and the standing proclamations against public dueling. In the world of *Titus Andronicus*, Romeo would have been executed on the spot, but Escalus wisely refuses the retributivist settlement proposed by Lady Capulet. Even Montague thinks in such terms, though he circumscribes the time frame strictly so that his son might be acquitted outright: "Not Romeo, Prince, he was Mercutio's friend; / His fault concludes but what the law should end, / The life of Tybalt" (3.1.184–86). Escalus rejects these backward-looking proffers; instead, he regards his juridical role as being forward-looking. He sees some justification for Romeo's act, but for good public policy reasons he cannot allow riotous behavior to go unpunished. The explicit rationale for his ruling centers on the deterrent effect of banishment, though his decision to negate his prior ruling imposing the death penalty for public sword-play is fundamentally charitable.

There is neat dramatic irony in having Escalus unwittingly sever a relationship that would have constituted the sort of bonding he hopes might heal Veronese cultural strife. Harsh retribution remains uppermost in the minds of the warring families, who are deeply wounded by the losses they suffer. The young lovers regard Romeo's banishment as a breach of the sanctity of their relationship given the imagery marking their initial encounter. In a moment of lucidity, Friar Lawrence sees the marriage as a curative: "For this alliance may so happy prove / To turn your households' rancor to pure love" (2.3.91–92). Though his verdict is destined to achieve the opposite effect, Escalus places restitution and social cohesion at the fore. The families' rancor turns to despair over the deaths of their loved ones, but they are nevertheless reminded of the primacy of such love.

Romeo's banishment occurs midway through the play, with the remaining acts spinning out its personal and social consequences. The duel with Tybalt is neither climactic nor ceremonial nor aimed at redressing private, political, or world-historical injustices. In advanced legal systems including that of Renaissance England, the public stake in detection and punishment of crime overwhelms private interests, however pressing they might be. This holds true even in capital cases, as Blackstone notes:

> In these gross and atrocious injuries the private wrong is swallowed up in the public: we seldom hear any mention made of satisfaction to the individual; the satisfaction to the community being so very great.   (4 Bl. Comm. 5–6)

Because of its interest in reaching a judgment expeditiously, the legal system can never deliver the truly balanced restitution that an offended party might legitimately expect. The dead cannot be brought back to life, nor can the survivors ever be fully repaid even if the death penalty is imposed against the offender. As far as the state is concerned, punishment is nearly always aimed at deterring delicts rather than making the aggrieved party whole.

Rights to punishment and restitution sometimes clash but remain insistent in Coke's common law theory: "Un droit ne poit pas morier . . . For of such high estimation is right in the eye of the Law, as the Law preserveth it from death and destruction, trodden down it may be, but never trodden out" (1 Institutes 279). The order in which rights are addressed is crucial to legal procedure, for civil restitution generally comes after the criminal charge has been resolved. The difficulty of achieving legal equity where private and public interests conflict is part of the play's tragic design.

This is not to imply that restitution is defective as a punishment theory because even perfectly symmetrical retribution has its failings. Coke reminds us of the place of *lex talionis* punishment in common law history: "By the ancient Law of England, he that maimed any man, whereby he lost any part of his body, the delinquent should lose the like part, as he that took away another mans life, should lose his own" (3 *Institutes* 118). Coke and other theorists understand the deficiencies of this approach, which are legion. Blackstone hypothesizes neatly that eye-for-an-eye punishment is inequitable if a victim had his only remaining good eye removed by a two-eyed aggressor. Thus, the only fair remedy under the standard of equitable retribution is the numerically inequitable one of destroying both good eyes of the offender, which was done under Solonic law. Moreover, equity under law has different standards based on cultural and historical dynamics. Punishing a beggar with capital punishment for the murder of a nobleman could never be considered equitable given the class prejudice in Renaissance England. Determining the severity of retaliation remains a difficult problem with shifting solutions, but the fundamental common law assumption holds that a victim ought to have restitution: "But the Law will, that in every case where a man is wrong and endamaged, that he shall have a remedy" (1 *Institutes* 197a).

Deciding upon remedies continues to be a thorny problem to this day, as in the case of a penniless offender being unable to repay his victim or an employee allegedly bringing down a multinational corporation through recklessness or greed.[2] Current U.S. congressional law acknowledges the limitations of restitution:

> The court, in determining whether to order restitution under section 3663 of this title and the amount of such restitution, shall consider the amount of the loss sustained by any victim as a result of the offense, the financial resources of the defendant, the financial needs and earning ability of the defendant and the defendant's dependents, and other such factors as the court deems appropriate.   (18 U.S.C. §3664a)

Full restitution is impossible in most circumstances given the inability of the offender to repay the victim for his acts. Coke argues that "treble damages" could apply in cases of forceful trespass onto private property (1 *Institutes* 257). Such a retributive imbalance would run much closer to what Blackstone calls "expiation, and not punishment" (4 *Bl. Comm.* 13). Restitution is almost always linked in complicated ways to issues surrounding retribution. Escalus's nuanced decision to banish Romeo balances his desire to maintain the peace while accommodating individual rights concerning *se defendendo* or heat of passion defenses. His decree is inadvertent as to the harm it does the marriage but it is not reckless or careless, unlike, say, Hamlet's killing of Polonius.

Civil courts offer a victim the opportunity for restitution by righting a criminal wrong through the imposition of damages. *Black's Law Dictionary* defines restitution as an equitable remedy by which a person is restored to his or her original position prior to loss or injury, but Renaissance law puts restrictions on this equation: "If in an appeal of robbery the plaintiff omit any of the goods stolen, they are forfeit to the king for the favour, which the law presumeth, the plaintiff beareth to the felon: and for that he cannot have restitution for more then is in his appeal" (3 *Institutes* 227). There can be no real restitution for a permanently disfiguring injury or death, so Romeo's banishment occupies a curious niche in the distribution of justice. There is wisdom in Friar Lawrence's perspective on banishment as "dear mercy" because the lovers are at the very least afforded the opportunity to reunite (3.3.28). Still, banishment has always been an extraordinary punishment in the English legal tradition: "For exile or transportation is a punishment unknown to the common law; and whenever inflicted, it is by the express direction of an act of parliament" (*Student's Blackstone* 18). Prohibitions against banishment are nearly absolute in English common law because that form of punishment has been reserved by the state for special circumstances.

Escalus is unaware of the marriage in part because the young lovers fear their families more than their ruler, but their status as a married couple gives them a special claim in English law. Ecclesiastical law requires restitution of conjugal rights, one indication of the state's overriding concern to defend the matrimonial bond:

> The suit . . . is also another species of matrimonial cause: which is brought whenever either the husband or wife is guilty of the injury of subtraction, or lives separate from the other without any sufficient reason; in which case the ecclesiastical jurisdiction will compel them to come together again, if either party be weak enough to desire it, contrary to the inclination of the other.
>
> (3 *Bl. Comm.* 93)

Such ecclesiastical decrees coincide with Shakespeare's effort to align the lovers with higher, supernatural laws by invoking the metaphysical imagery of star-cross'd lovers.

Further complications arise from ecclesiastical law standards, aside from affording defendants the ability to plead benefit of clergy, which Ben Jonson used to his advantage. The intent of canon law was to keep the family intact for better or worse, sometimes to the great disadvantage of women. Canonical edicts on the restitution of conjugal rights suggest the supra-legal authority behind Friar Lawrence's intercessions. The daily influence of the ecclesiastical courts would undoubtedly have been felt more overtly in the provinces, but Coke recognized their power: "For the spirituall Judges proceedings are for the correction of the spiritual inner man, and, *pro salute animæ*, to injoyne him penance; and the Judges of the common law proceed to give damages and recompense for the wrong and injury done" (2 *Institutes* 622). Common law courts had habeus corpus and other temporal powers, but Coke defended the jurisdiction of the ecclesiastical courts in tithing, marriage, heresy, adultery, and other moral matters. Civil and ecclesiastical laws were designed to bring lovers together, though the families function as a blocking force that Northrop Frye would define as the role of the senex. An ecclesiastical court would encourage their marriage bond and sanctify their love based on a putatively higher law than that which Escalus invokes. We are left to imagine what Escalus's position on banishment might be had he been made aware of their relationship.

The lovers' lack of mens rea makes them unique among Shakespeare's tragic heroes and augments the play's lyrical, Petrarchan tone. Character complications arise in the lovers' frustrations in consummating their love, regarding which Juliet's development is particularly noteworthy. Romeo's metamorphosis from worshipping Rosaline as a false idol to loving Juliet as the true one merely develops the pastoral tradition from the Spenserian eclogue regarding the difficulties of achieving one's heart's desire. Coleridge would reasonably argue, additionally, that such a change was "merely natural; it is accordant with every day's experience" (*Shakespearean* 2: 119). Romeo slays Tybalt and Paris only after both adversaries had behaved in insulting, menacing, and, in Tybalt's case, cowardly ways. Paris refers to Romeo upon his return as a "felon" (5.3.69), a pejorative which is strictly speaking true but lacking in dramatic substance. The tragedy has an emancipatory edge only insofar as the lovers cut through the Gordian knot of enduring Veronese hostility.

II. COMMON LAW EQUITY

The common law provides due process to mitigate the harsh effects of banishment, but since the play is concerned with the lovers' relationship and not mere possessions, it would be of little comfort to them to learn that the property rights of the wife hold even with the departure of the husband:

> And so it is, if by Act of Parliament the husband be attainted of Treason or Felony, and, saving his life, is banished for ever, as Belknap &c. was; this is a civil death, and the wife may sue as a *feme sole*.   (1 *Institutes* 133a)

That is, temporary exile under the law of "relegation" is in Coke's view "no civil death" (1 *Institutes* 133a). In *Richard II*, Bolingbroke, with the backing of Parliament, won back his rights of due process to prevent dispossession and waste of his hereditaments, though we may doubt his sincerity in professing to uphold the law:

> Will you permit that I shall stand condemn'd
> A wandering vagabond, my rights and royalties
> Pluck'd from my arms perforce—and given away
> To upstart unthrifts? Wherefore was I born? (2.3.119–22)

Romeo does not follow Bolingbroke's course since he has neither political nor financial aspirations nor is he interested in doctoring the scrolls of history for his own benefit. The kind of testimony and legal action that a history play might present has diminished value in tragedy even if Romeo had thought to argue for his rights with the skill of a parliamentarian.

Shakespearean tragedy thrives on inequities limiting the options that might restore a protagonist to wholeness. The actual damage here is irreparable due to the transitory purity of youthful love. This sanctified passion is seen in the law as a "reason in nature," to use Coke's phrase in the 1592 (34 Eliz.) *Case of Swans,* also called the case of *Queen v. Lady Joan Young* (*Coke's Reports* 4: 85). This case of equitable restitution concerns a dispute over ownership of swans that has as much metaphorical as legal relevance to the play if we see the young lovers as the play's swans:

> For the cock swan is an emblem or representation of an affectionate and true husband to his wife above all other fowls; for the cock swan holdeth himself to one female only, and for this cause nature hath conferred on him a gift beyond all others; that is, to die so joyfully, that he sings sweetly when he dies, . . . therefore the case of the swan doth differ from the case of . . . other brute beasts.   (*Coke's Reports* 4: 85)

At the common law, the Queen's swanherd was permitted to seize a free-swimming unmarked swan as a "royal fowl" (*Coke's Reports* 4:

84). Any marked swan raised and maintained by property owners, if seized, must be restored to the rightful owners on the grounds that property rights take precedence over the royal prerogative. The crown and landowners could as a last resort divide the swan's offspring in such disputes. Both metaphorically and in actuality, then, the prerogatives of love relationships are embedded in the common law as part of its reflection of established cultural standards.

Inequities in restitution necessarily lead to odd results. The warring families encourage slaughter but become racked with guilt over having made their children "poor sacrifices of our enmity!" (5.3.304). In the *Case of Swans*, restitution for waste of royal fowl involved punitive damages:

> And it hath been said of old time, that he who steals a swan in an open and common river, lawfully marked, the same swan (if it may be) or another swan, should be hung in a house by the beak, and he who stole it shall in recompense thereof be obliged to give the owner so much wheat that may cover all the swan, by putting the wheat on the head of the swan, until the head of the swan be covered with the wheat.   (*Coke's Reports* 4: 87–88)

Failure of restitution is evident in this case because the swans, like the lovers, ought to have a "natural liberty" even as they develop a natural sense of responsibility toward one another (*Coke's Reports* 4: 84). The conflict between natural liberty and responsibility arises when the lovers enter a marriage contract demanding that they take on personal responsibilities while being denied all due social benefits, which is the worst of all possible legal situations. They surely validate Veronese custom by attempting to finesse its strictures and blind decrees. The tactical malpractice of the intellectually and, later, physically declining Friar Lawrence leaves them all the more exposed to civil sanctions.

The basic requirement of the common law to seek equitable solutions is overriding even in a legal context favoring the rights of the aristocracy and the crown. In *Whittingham's Case* of 1602-03 (45 Eliz.), the Star Chamber upheld the right of individuals to transfer land by their own hand to their successors, including in this instance Whittingham to Prudence, his illegitimate daughter. However, when Prudence sought to transfer the same land to Stephens not in her own hand but by letter of attorney, the land reverted to the queen. This case reiterates the law's fundamental ideal of restitution, for while the crown and aristocracy have an ideological and historical claim to the land, which in Whittingham's case ultimately favored the crown due to procedural rules, the basic right of the individual to have and hold his property was one Coke was eager to defend: "Note, reader, that a condition in law by force (a) of a statute which gives a recovery, is stronger than a condition in law without a recovery" (*Coke's Reports* 3: 229). When rights and remedies are contested, the benefit of the doubt must always redound to the advantage of the aggrieved party.

Romeo is caught between the absolute liability attached to his participation in a duel and the good-faith imperatives of self-defense and defense of one's honor. His good intent leads to a gray area in the common law in instances of hot-pursuit of suspected offenders. Besides the *se defendendo* exception in a life and death struggle, *Foxley's Case* of 1601 (43 Eliz.) permits killing to defend property: "If a true man kills a thief who would (a) rob him, if the thief does not retreat, he shall forfeit nothing" (*Coke's Reports* 3: 224). This case concerns the rights of a defendant in hot pursuit of a thief and twenty apparently fleet-footed lambs. Stolen property that is abandoned reverts to the crown so that thieves might be prevented from returning later to recover their booty when the coast is clear. This regulation held if the thief waived the rights to his pelf when confronted by skeptical pursuers questioning its true ownership. Often such thieves would disclaim ownership in order to cut their losses by eluding capture. The formal waiver being spoken, care of the sheep would revert to the Queen, who had an interest in seizing stolen property when ownership was in doubt. Foxley proved that he was in continual pursuit of his sheep and that the thief had never waived the rights to them. Unwaived goods and chattel would in this case be restored immediately to the victim. A confiscatory crown interceded in disputes of property more than we would allow today, but the penalty for theft was higher as well. An essential common law principle holds that honest intent on the part of the aggrieved party in pursuit of restitution ought to be rewarded. The general good-faith condition imbues the lovers with an aura of legal as well as ethical innocence higher than that of any comparable institution in the play, this in addition to their natural common law liberty and the implicitly sacred nature of their love.

III. EQUITY AND TRAGIC THEORY

Hegel rates Shakespeare's characters as unexcelled in quality, but because Shakespearean tragedy lacks the full disclosure of ethical positions in public debate that he so esteems in *Antigone*, one senses an ambivalence in Hegel: whatever is gained in Renaissance art as to psychological and social detail involves a commensurate loss in terms of the beautifully streamlined plots and characters of Greek tragedy. Additionally, he regards as lost the Greek philosophical synthesis between art and religion which produces the concrete realization of the Ideal. *Romeo and Juliet*, painted in chiaroscuro, runs counter to Hegelian theory because the difference between the lovers and the state has nothing to do with an ethical contest. Puns on coals, colliers, choler, and collars indicate distinctions in class and punishment based on birthright, not ethics.

Romeo understands the validity of the state's prohibition against dueling, so he is on Escalus's side regarding public policy. The transcendence of state law admits contingencies leading to "misadventur'd piteous overthrows" (1.0.7), to use the Chorus's terms. A tragedy of hidden passion combined with the lovers' lack of criminal intent forwards the action and creates broad comic by-play. Somewhat like Hamlet, though, Romeo opens the play in a sour mood: "Black and portendous must this humour prove, / Unless good counsel may the cause remove" (1.1.141–42). Shakespeare will assign a fair share of blame to Hamlet, but he shields Romeo from such opprobrium. If Hamlet has a dangerous though not guilty mind, Romeo vanquishes Tybalt in a fair fight as a consequence of his failed attempt to halt the quarrel between Mercutio and his foe. While Romeo suffers from the travails of love, Hamlet worries about disease infecting the court and, by extension, the universe itself. Romeo's obstacles remain generally external, while Hamlet's are more subjective. Hegel's observation that "death is already present from the first" in Hamlet shows the aesthetic ground Shakespearean tragedy has yet to cover (*Fine Art* 4: 342), for the same cannot be said of Romeo. The deepening shadow of criminality operating in Shakespeare's tragic dramaturgy is nowhere better revealed than in the difference between these two protagonists.

Coleridge finds more tragic substance in the play from his Romantic perspective than Johnson does as a neoclassicist. Coleridge notes a pattern in Shakespeare's early tragic method as "*fondness for presentiment* and as if aware—yet reconciling with the superstition, all reconciling of opposites—of anything unusual as unlucky!" (*Shakespearean* 1: 10). Coleridge would replace the neoclassical unities of time, place, and action with terms suggesting the playwright's vision to be an organic whole: "homogeneity, proportionateness, and totality of interest" (*Shakespearean* 1: 4). Like the neoclassicists, though, Coleridge raises issues of taste by criticizing the Nurse's bawdy language and lamentations over Juliet's body as being "excellently suited to the Nurse's character, but grotesquely unsuited to the occasion" (*Shakespearean* 1: 10). His view of the play as a moral unity differs from Johnson in that, rather than invoking moral strictures, Coleridge sees Shakespeare as appealing to a supernatural religious agency.

For Coleridge, the play's dramatic action forcing ill luck and opposing desires to a tragic conclusion rises to the highest level of inspiration: "A beautiful close—*poetic* justice indeed: All are punished! The spring and winter meet, and winter assumes the character of spring, spring the sadness of winter" (*Shakespearean* 1: 11). The poetic genius Coleridge locates in the play marks a departure from Johnson, who, for example, criticizes the act two Chorus for stalling the forward action and quashing "the improvement of any moral sentiment" (*Johnson* 8: 944). The Chorus actually creates tension here by remarking on Romeo's shifting desires through an invocation of the conventions of sonnet cycles and eclogues, a delightful form of instruction of which Horace would approve. Johnson's stern moral sensibility is indicated by his desire to transcribe "lusty young men" as "lusty yeomen" (1.2.26), though to be fair he finds the play for the most part delightful and emotionally involving:

> The play is one of the most pleasing of our author's performances. The scenes are busy and various, the incidents numerous and important, the catastrophe irresistibly affecting, and the process of the action carried on with such probability, at least with such congruity to popular opinions, as tragedy requires.
> (*Johnson* 8: 956)

Assessing the intensity of the lovers' passion especially as it relates to Juliet's maturation signals the greatest divergence between Johnson and Coleridge. Coleridge reserves some of his most lavish praise for Juliet's characterization as the "imaginative strained to the highest" (*Shakespearean* 1: 8). He sees her as a worthy predecessor for Miranda, his personal favorite. By contrast, Johnson is scornful of Juliet, particularly as she prepares to drink the soporific: "Juliet plays most of her pranks under the appearance of religion; perhaps Shakespeare meant to punish her hypocrisy" (*Johnson* 8: 953). Neither critic focuses on the legal underpinnings of a tragedy in which passion brings out the best and worst of human behavior.

While literary and moral concerns have been well aired by critics, Durkheim treats political power and kinship relationships from a historical perspective and in the "external index which symbolizes it: this visible symbol is law" (*Division* 64). Criminal and ecclesiastical laws in this play are subservient to civil rule, which wields the force of the death penalty. This law is not *a priori* good but exists according to the social pressures shaping it; therefore, its presence in the play is relatively consistent with the sociological theory of Durkheim. Naturally, revenge influences the action of the play in obvious as well as subtler episodes, Lady Capulet's plan to murder Romeo in Mantua being but one example. The retributionist elements of the plot are advanced as well by tricks of fate, including Friar John's foiled attempt to deliver a letter to Romeo contradicting Balthasar's news of Juliet's demise.

A practitioner of the separation of church and state before his time, Friar Lawrence skirts the letter if not the spirit of the civil and criminal law. He implicitly follows his own ecclesiastical calling as a higher duty akin to the transcendence the lovers see in their relationship; thus, they respond to the law he represents. Romeo confides in Friar Lawrence, who consistently offers the wise if conventional advice to follow the path of moderation, counsel which the good friar fails to heed himself where legal matters are concerned. Much is made in recent literary criticism of the power inherent in the concept of the King's two bodies; that is, the crown's "naturall Capacity" and its "Royal and Politique Capacity" (1 *Institutes* 190).[3] This dualistic concept was a legal commonplace in ecclesiastical property law as to Abbots: "In respect of their several capacities . . . yet the Law (b) doth adjudge them to be severally seized. . . . So it is of any (c) body Politique or Corporate be they regular as dead persons in Law . . . or Secular" (1 *Institutes* 189a). Friar Lawrence assumes rights stemming from his religious affiliation far too expansively, with terrible consequences for the young lovers.

The motive behind ecclesiastical law is similar to the civil and criminal laws Escalus has tried to enforce, as Durkheim suggests in another context: "Religious law is always repressive: it is essentially conservative" (*Division* 78). Durkheim is quick to point out that fundamental moral laws change with the times, including the relaxing of strict ancient dietary laws or laws prohibiting the mixture of clothing fibers in our apparel. Modern lifestyles would have been greatly inconvenienced, for example, by the reimposition of the death penalty for the wearing of polyester, particularly during the 1970s. Durkheim suggests two theoretical justifications for the "social defense" of law (*Division* 108).

Punishment to preserve social cohesion is one, but the lovers experience punishment as expiation, which an offender suffers to make amends to god and society. Escalus's edict unintentionally shifts the rationale of punishment from social defense to expiation. The lovers neither constitute a threat to society nor owe expiation for committing criminal acts, though they suffer the ultimate punishment. The misapplication of laws eliminates the possibility of the "restitutive sanction," Durkheim's second justification for punishment. This sanction is "not expiatory, but consists of a simple *return in state*" (*Division* 111). The restitutive sanction would be ideal in this case, but it is precisely the road not taken. A foundational principle of common law and reason is the prevention of waste, yet two young lives are extinguished due to simple ignorance. Non-retributionist law and tragedy form the essential dialectic here that several of the other tragedies explore in divergent ways.

The lovers' position in a society that shifts its ethical and legal assumptions fits Durkheim's view of the supremacy of state power: "Human passions stop only before a moral power they respect" (*Division* 3). Verona is not unique in administering justice on the theory that force serves as a bulwark against anarchy. States generally maintain rules until their assumptions are shaken, requiring a reformulation of policy: "The moral law, then, is formed, transformed, and maintained in accordance with changing demands; these are the only conditions the science of ethics tries to determine" (*Division* 33). Shakespeare anticipates Durkheim's postulates concerning temporal laws, but in later tragedies he will concentrate more on the protagonist's inner world. Tragic heroes like Macbeth or Lear take leave of society in a vertical or metaphysical sense even if they remain in the same geographical vicinity. Not so with these lovers, whose shifting social roles and allegiances enmesh them all the more within a social embrace best described as horizontal—banishment being the ultimate horizontal punishment. The lovers' fate is a response to the essential question posed by Durkheim: "Why does the individual, while becoming more autonomous, depend more upon society?" (*Division* 37). In reacting to state power, Romeo and Juliet try to accommodate its wishes rather than oppose it like Antigone. Their marriage should make them more autonomous vis-à-vis their families and the state, but the division of labor as Durkheim and Shakespeare define it in their separate ways makes the young couple all the more dependent upon society. What is exceptional in Shakespeare's tragic exploration here is his forward-looking emphasis when others of his generation mainly adopted the retributive, backward-looking model. However enduring this tale of two lovers and their reformed city continues to be, Shakespeare produced only one tragedy scrutinizing restitutive principles akin to Durkheim's.

IV. STORYBOOK JUSTICE

Shakespeare's exploration of retribution and restitution indicates the depth of his concern for juridical issues as it relates to tragedy; for, as Durkheim says: "The task of the most advanced societies is, then, a work of justice" (*Division* 387). In this play, two patterns of social solidarity, Escalus's and the lovers', come into conflict without being contradictory. Issues of restitution dominate a play which essentially spins out a hypothetical that reveals flaws in the juridical framework. Blame is assigned in no uncertain terms to the "parents' rage" (1.0.10), the families having been reproved by Escalus on two or more prior occasions. This hostility of unknown origin is evident from the very start in the comic banter between the Capulets' underlings. The fault festers in a social arena "where civil blood makes civil hands unclean" (1.0.4). Expiation comes with the young lovers' deaths along with that of Lady Montague, who is unable to bear the strain of Romeo's banishment. The act the lovers commit by seeking to unite is neither criminal nor hypocritical, as Johnson maintains, but something the audience takes for granted in human affairs. The lovers could no more have avoided seeking a union than voluntarily cease breathing, nor would the common law require it of them: "The Law compels no man to impossible things" (1 *Institutes* 92). This play is unique in being circumscribed by obedience to aesthetic laws which can neither enforce equitable restitution nor compel a tragic playwright to bring back the dead.

Part of the play's special dramatic power lies in its choric framing device, the only tragedy to use one explicitly. Employing the strict measures of the sonnet, the Chorus seems a true and objective observer. Moreover, its poetry prepares us for the sonnet the lovers create during their initial encounter. This artistic link has further implications, for if the reconciliatory gestures the families institute seem insufficient to outweigh the loss, the restitution of art nevertheless points us toward unity as opposed to fragmentation. Restitution is held to be a valid means of rehabilitation in limited circumstances. We

are certainly given to believe that Veronese society has been emanci-
pated from hatred to an extent.[4] Such restitutions or pardons undertaken by the king were deemed by Coke a "work of grace and mercy"
(3 *Institutes* 240), particularly in restoring the blood rights of families
of felons or traitors.

Given the weight Shakespeare accords to social correctives in this
"excellent and lamentable tragedy," Hegel would not grant the play
his highest praise. His analysis of tragedy as an "*unhappy blessed-
ness* in misfortune" involves a full unveiling of the affirmative link
between external conditions and subjectivity that ultimately reveals
God and the law to man (*Fine Art* 4: 342). The means by which
Shakespeare sets off his hero from society will be the overt criminal
act, the contemplation of which ironically initiates a tragic metaphysical journey. This subjectivity flourishes in the tale of a melancholic
young prince written roughly a decade after what is by comparison an
idyllic story of unfortunate young lovers who lived together far too
brief a time in Verona.

CHAPTER 7

CORIOLANUS: PUNISHMENT OF THE CIVIL BODY

A skilled practitioner of martial law, Coriolanus ultimately favors the emancipation of peace over war. Convicted of treason in disparate jurisdictions, though, he dies for having twice outlived his usefulness as a warrior. He remains unreflective about death and never questions or alters the hypotheticals leading to his destruction, unlike Hamlet or Macbeth. His hatred of theatrical shows only makes his performance all the more arresting. Because Rome and Antium mete out excessive punishments against him for imperfectly conceived reasons of social hygiene, social cohesion is maintained in two civil arenas without its *raison d'être* of achieving permanent reform or emancipation.

The play's Roman quality appears in Coriolanus's embrace of reform through martial law as against tribunal power, not in its imitation of Roman tragedy as such. Deuteronomy provides very broad outlines for the conduct of war, but the Romans codified their own detailed regulations on tactics and discipline in the work of Ruffus, among others. Of course, given the imperatives of warfare, slash and burn tactics have been the general order of battle throughout history. As years of painful experience have shown, even unconditional surrender is no guarantee of favorable treatment. In this play, Rome remains incapable of dividing its political labor, to borrow Durkheim's terms. It refuses to accommodate the warrior's code, just as Coriolanus will stubbornly resist political socialization.

Coke refers to Roman law and its Twelve Tables in his *Institutes*, but apart from capturing deserters he treats military affairs as existing outside the purview of the common law: "There is a Law Marshal for wars" (1 *Institutes* 10a).[1] The common law mixed ancient decrees, unwritten judicial decisions, and the Norman law brought to England after the Conquest. This intermingling resulted in legal statutes being written in French and Latin, though Coke used English whenever possible so that his countrymen might better understand the law.[2] Still, Shakespeare's audiences would have been moved by the rationale guiding Coriolanus's martial conduct because of the universally understood traditions of military discipline.

In section I, I examine the conflict between martial and civil law provoking Coriolanus's defection to the Volscian side in 491 BC. Rome's transition to tribunal power commenced two years earlier, so Shakespeare chose a historical period embroiled in wide-ranging political controversy. The English were alert to the political diversity of states, including those governed by "a monarch, or . . . aristocraticall, where few be in authority, or democraticall, where the people have the chief government without any superior, saving such as they elect and choose" (3 *Institutes* 80a). Military tactics are not an issue here; indeed, the subject was ridiculed as arcane in *Henry V* through Fluellen's pedantry. Shakespeare's audience would have been aware of the harsh ad hoc regulations enforcing discipline in their own ranks as well as those of Rome. They would have had a strong sense of the patriarchal nature of Roman civil law under the *patria potestas*, the power of a father over his son. The play elevates the role of women far beyond normal Roman standards, particularly in Volumnia's characterization as a sagacious political maneuverer. Coriolanus's role in tacitly enfranchising women opens him to vicious ad hominem attacks throughout the play. The common law nevertheless deviated sharply from its Roman predecessor, the adversarial trial system being but one of the primary distinctions.

In part II, I examine slander as the tortious act enabling treason charges to be leveled so effectively against Coriolanus. Slander at common law corresponds closely to its Roman counterpart. Next, I examine Coriolanus's punishment as a tragic spectacle, his body ravaged by wars, slander, and murderous swords. The elemental display of punishment overshadows the psychological and political issues in the play, however appealing they might be. The play reduces the outward show of tragedy to its essentials: the banishment, supplication, and slaughter of a hero too psychologically shallow in a modern sense to have an Oedipus conflict and too much the peacemaker to be played as a stage Nazi.

The criminal and tort law tradition is grounded in the concept that reason and justice lead us toward emancipation. Coke confirms this when he states that "every man desireth to be at naturall liberty" (2 *Institutes* 589). Coke's understanding of liberty differs from ours today, especially in the U.S., where individual rights are respected far more than the law would have allowed in Renaissance England. For Coke, it was natural that the subject should serve his king and the common good, while in return the law would prevent the king from annoying his industrious subjects with unjust levies and punishment. Aside from the new rights granted the plebes through their tribunes, the play's vision of reform or emancipation appears only through the lens of tragic waste in the form of the denunciation and murder of the hero.

I. CIVIL VS. MARTIAL LAW

A complicated division of civil and military codes gives their respective adherents—Coriolanus, the tribunes, the plebes—absolute confidence in the validity of their positions. The intensity of rage expressed derives from each party's belief in its political rectitude. In typical Shakespearean fashion, the plebes buffoonishly alter their opinions as the winds blow. The tribunes press for expansive, self-serving civil powers, which does not inherently invalidate them or their political ideas. Coriolanus aligns himself with the patricians to the extent that they share his sense of military discipline.

Martial law is a blanket set of regulations applicable to the civilian and military population in zones of active conflict. By contrast, military law is a code of conduct limited to military personnel. Coriolanus thrives in arenas of active warfare when pitted against a worthy opponent. He relishes the imposition of martial law in Corioles:

> Condemning some to death, and some to exile;
> Ransoming him, or pitying, threat'ning th' other;
> Holding Corioles in the name of Rome,
> Even like a fawning greyhound in the leash,
> To let him slip at will.   (1.6.35–39)

He creates a military order outside the city that the Romans have themselves repudiated in favor of a republican state, yet whose existence serves their imperial aspirations.

Under martial law, Coriolanus can exercise autocratic power to enlarge the empire. He invokes the quintessential rule of battlefield discipline during the assault on Corioles: "He that retires, I'll take him for a Volsce, / And he shall feel mine edge" (1.4.28–29). Roman troops reject his orders, allowing him to be trapped alone within the besieged city. Under the Roman military law of Ruffus, their conduct would be actionable: "If any person, in war . . . fails to execute a command, he shall be punished with death" (Brand 159). Roman military law uses legal overkill to ensure that orders from above are obeyed and that individual soldiers are made responsible for the actions of their legion. Units that retreated unlawfully were "decimated," meaning that one-tenth of a legion would be randomly "run through with spears by the other legions for breaking the line of battle and causing the flight of others" (Brand 157).[3] The *Corpus Juris Civilis* echoes this command: "All disobedience of a general or the Governor of a province should be punished with death" (*Corpus* 11: 193). With a few minor variations, this theme of military discipline remained in force during the Renaissance and beyond, as for example in the British navy's 1661 Articles of War: "Every Person . . . who through Cowardice, Negligence, or Disaffection, shall in Time of Action withdraw, or keep back, or not come into the fight or engagement . . . shall suffer death" (Rodger 24). Partly because the heroic gesture is his *métier*, Coriolanus does not exact due punishment against his men, but their conduct explains his fury over corruption in Rome paralleling the breakdown of military discipline before Corioles. The play's first capital crime under military and civil law is committed by the plebes, not by Coriolanus.

The tribunes are newly privileged, mid-level politicians apt at manipulating public opinion to increase their influence. They represent plebeian rights in public trials and enforce their juridical power with ædiles. Sicinius seeks to thwart Coriolanus to the extent of denying that a valid consulship election ever occurred. Coriolanus's patrician backers are willing to "surety him," (3.1.177), or make his bail, as the banishment proceedings unfold. Older, consensus-seeking patricians like Cominius and Menenius appease the tribunes to retain their own authority. Thus, class relationships go far beyond the simple issue of plebeian versus patrician rights, as Kenneth Burke puts it in his elegant analysis of the play. True, Sicinius urges the crowd to cast Coriolanus from the Tarpeian rock, but Aufidius plots Coriolanus's death in Antium without the assistance of plebes. Burke thereby overstates the importance of plebeian class hatred in his formula whereby Coriolanus becomes a fit sacrifice for the tragedy. Burke's critique is influenced by cold war politics, evident when he remarks that pseudo-socialist dictators loot their impoverished nations' coffers while planning lavish retirements on the Riviera. Had he written the piece today, he might have added pseudo-democratic dictators to the list of rulers seeking golden parachutes. Burke's wit leads him to round off some legal and political edges that deserve closer scrutiny. Cominius's reference to Rome as a "falling fabric" legitimates martial law as one means to preserve the state from ruin through the misdeeds of various citizens (3.1.246).

Coriolanus conflates martial and civil law when he ponders the flight of his soldiers at Corioles: "This kind of service / Did not deserve corn gratis" (3.1.124–25). Linking acts of war with politics is inappropriate. Furthermore, having just been informed of a Volscian attack and the nullification of his election, he urges his colleagues to consider abrogating the rights of "the multitudinous tongue" (3.1.156). This request goes further than merely suggesting that free dispensation of corn nurtures sedition in Rome as it had in Greece. Such opinions align him with those whose intentions are dishonorable, including the nameless patricians who, in all probability, have been hoarding grain. Because Coriolanus refuses the spoils at Corioles, we can fairly assume he is not involved in monopolistic practices in Rome. Coriolanus's contempt for the plebes is mitigated by his attempt to reward a commoner who came to his aid at Corioles. He seems to adopt informally what IMT prosecutor Charles Dubost calls the "three precepts of the classical Roman jurists: 'Honeste vivere, alterum non lædere, suum ciuque tribuere.' (Live honorably, inflict no harm on another, give each his due)" (*IMT* 6: 425). The audience can of course weigh his failure to remember the almsman's name as it wishes.

Tribunes ratchet up the charge of usury as a way of poisoning the jury in advance of the time that they can arraign Coriolanus for treason. No evidence exists that Coriolanus sought tyrannical power, however rude his behavior may be toward those he considers deserters under martial law. The second charge leveled against him concerning the failure to distribute corn is a bootstrapping technique to make the treason accusation more palatable, a clever bit of lawyering designed to blind the populace to the real issues at stake. The tribunes seek to channel plebeian rage toward Coriolanus in order to make a conviction inevitable. Up to now, he has merely violated custom by refusing to display his scars; indeed, he remains thus far more innocent of felony than the cherubic Romeo. Coriolanus skirts the margins of political criminality with his expressions of ill-will toward the new order though he has always regarded Roman rule as immoral, not illegal. His emotional response to the verdict: "I banish you!" (3.3.123), constitutes a tactical failure; however, such invective is mild compared to the accusations made against him. One indication of the weakness of the tribunes' case is that they settle for the lesser punishment of banishment. Our faith in *Corpus Juris Civilis* is not strengthened when Cominius tries to convince Coriolanus that a repeal might be expected at some future date.

The 1607 Midlands corn uprisings are taken for granted in many circles as having directly influenced the play, but even if true they are not essential to its legal complexities. Andrew Gurr argues that Coke would have taken the commons' side in these disputes:

> 'Commons' here need mean no more than the plebeian faction, of course, but when the tribunes describe the citizens' statutory rights as
>
> > Your liberties and the charters that you bear
> > I'th'body of the weal (2.3.179–80)
>
> they are unequivocally echoing Coke, Chief Justice of the Common Pleas, who upheld Magna Charta as the great unwritten record of common rights.
> ("Body Politic" 68)

Gurr is right to find profound legal tensions in the play revolving around an expansive interpretation of the term, "commons." Coke certainly upheld the rule of common law based on Magna Carta, but he also argued on behalf of a powerful monarch. He defended the common law as the guarantor of a state order balancing the powers of the king, aristocracy, and commons.

Coriolanus seeks no such balance when he reiterates his allegiance to martial law upon entering Antium as an exile. He expects no quarter from Aufidius given their past enmity: "If he slay me, / He does fair justice" (4.4.24-25). His position in Roman military law is tricky because the regulations against desertion demand the death penalty, though he joins Aufidius only as a result of being unjustly banished himself. Shakespeare's work is filled with banished leaders returning home with foreign assistance to vie for power, but the Roman martial law to which Coriolanus adheres is categorical: "Those who flee from the Roman side to the enemy may be killed with impunity, as enemies" (Brand 167). Since the purpose of banishment is to neutralize rivals threatening the state from within, for Coriolanus to do the same from without would suffice to incriminate him in Rome. Such treason in Roman or common law makes intent a moot point.

During the *drôle de guerre*, the tribunes who engineered his banishment express delight that peace has apparently been restored. The populace cooperates by remaining silent about his fate, but upon hearing of his renewed assault, the plebes and tribunes who consented to his banishment forgive him with comical celerity. Class warfare, then, seems an almost entirely inessential component of the play's rising action. Burke finds Coriolanus to have been "appropriately punished" due to "excesses" which "lead necessarily to his downfall" ("Delights" 202, 195, 187). Burke's tactic of prophesying "after the event" in this instance falls short of explaining why Coriolanus dies (185). He sees equity, balance, and order in the tragic equation producing Coriolanus as the perfect victim bringing catastrophe down upon himself. From a legal perspective, though, we might find disorder, waste, and inequality marking the path of the hero's descent.

In preparing to leave Rome, Coriolanus consoles himself by noting: "There is a world elsewhere" (3.3.135), but unfortunately the political dynamics of Antium differ little from those of Rome. While the Roman charge of treason is plainly unfounded, Aufidius's accusation has legal merit because Coriolanus plans to give up present and future Volscian gains. Seen from the perspective of treason statutes in Renaissance England, Aufidius's charge lies midway in terms of seriousness between a direct threat to the safety of the king and his family and counterfeiting or altering English coins or importing base ones. Punishing evil figures prominently in the rationale of the death penalty, but Coke also argues that deterrence is a necessary component:

> By intendment of the law the execution of the offender is for example, . . . but so it is not when a mad man is executed, but should be a miserable spectacle, both against law, and of extreame inhumanity and cruelty, and can be no example to others.   (3 *Institutes* 6)

Shakespeare aligns himself with Coke's theory by proving the converse of this rule in having Coriolanus punished via Aufidius's rage. If Aufidius's evidence is more compelling than that of the tribunes, it is equally self-serving: "He sold the blood and labour / Of our great action; therefore shall he die, / And I'll renew me in his fall" (5.6.46-48). The Volscians cannot help but see merit in Aufidius's position, though a few urge that legal procedure be observed to stay the execution, if only for the sake of appearances. The Volscian conspiracy works its deadly effect because Coriolanus has become a political liability. Aufidius's passion and political maneuvering ironically confirm the link between Antium and Rome.

Retribution by conspiracy robs us of the wager of battle we might have expected between the principals. Coriolanus does not recognize Aufidius as his inferior until too late, though we have known it all along. Aufidius is a better administrator than warrior, having cleverly used Coriolanus as a stalking horse for his political ambitions: "When, Caius, Rome is thine, / Thou art poor'st of all; then shortly art thou mine" (4.7.56–57). Shakespeare regards Aufidius's subsequent demise as unworthy of report. The disaster befalling the Volscian camp and its leader the following year as reported by Plutarch might have appeared in the denouement of a Shakespearean history play. Here, we end by witnessing a cowardly act of stunning ferocity.

II. Slander Law

Punishment for slander has softened considerably over time, while the definition of the act itself has broadened in scope. Blackstone refers to the tyrant Dionysus ordering a subject executed for slander merely because he recounted a dream in which the ruler was slain. The *Corpus Juris Civilis* is almost as harsh: "When any one publicly abuses another in a loud voice, or writes a poem for the purpose of insulting him, or rendering him infamous, he shall be beaten with a rod until he dies" (1: 70). We define slander today as a personal tort based on false and defamatory declarations which may or may not have caused demonstrable harm. Slander is the oral version of libel, which is actionable language appearing in print. In some cases, words are prima facie slanderous; that is, action lies when the charge imputes criminality, horrible illness, or great immorality to another, notably when it results in loss of trade. Common law cases contain some key elements of the tort as it exists today, though certain concepts were defined in ways we would deem irrational.

Slander cases flourished in Coke's time, but to succeed they required that criminality be overtly alleged. As a matter of moral and public policy, Coke wished to prevent feuds of honor from erupting on the street:

> He who kills a man with his sword in fight is a great offender, but he is a greater offender who poisons another; for in the one case he, who is openly assaulted, may defend himself, and knows his adversary, and may endeavor to prevent it: but poisoning may be done so secretly that none can defend himself against it, for which cause the offence is the more dangerous, because the offender cannot easily be known; and of such nature is libelling, it is secret, and robs a man of his good name, which ought to be more precious to him than his life.   (*Coke's Reports* 3: 255)

Blackstone refined Renaissance case law as to libel theory:

> The words scoundrel, rascal, villain, knave, miscreant, liar, fool, and such like general terms of scurrility, may be used with impunity, and are part of the rights and privileges of the vulgar. To constitute legal slander, the words must impute a precise crime; hence it is actionable to say a man is a highwayman, but it is not so, to say he is worse than a highwayman. (3 *Bl. Comm.* 125n)

Given how Renaissance law distinguished slanderous speech from other forms of invective, a reasonable Jacobean spectator would likely have viewed the tribunes' libelous remarks as both reprehensible and patently illegal.

Generalized references to mens rea absent a criminal act do not rise to the level of slander even though such speech might cause the hearer to fly into a rage. Two cases recounted by Sir George Croke, a renowned jurist under Charles I, illustrate the distinction in Renaissance law. In *Edward's Case* of 1582 (24 Eliz.), the slanderer describes an intent by the plaintiff, Edwards, to commit a crime: "Jo. Edwards did wrap Gunpowder in a piece of Tow, and laid it under my Window, and put fire to it, minding to burn my house" (1 *Croke* 6). The case for the slandered Edwards was upheld because his accuser links mens rea with the arson allegation. The 1599 (41 Eliz.) case of *Davies v. Taylor* demonstrates how slander would be actionable when inferences of mens rea or moral turpitude might reasonably be drawn. Suit was brought for these words: "*Thou art rotted with the pox*, And . . . adjudged, that the Words were actionable: For it is to be intended of the *French Pox*" (1 *Croke* 648). The slander found here does not suggest the commission of any crime, but it leaves the accused open to the public perception that he is a moral or physiological outcast.

Slander cases against women were forced to meet an unreasonably high test by today's standards. In the 1596–97 (38–39 Eliz.) case of *Pollard and his Wife v. Armshaw*, suit was brought for these words: "*Thou art a Whore, and J.S. hath the use of thy Body: The Cart is too good for thee*" (1 *Croke* 582). Surprisingly, the court held that no slander lay in the accusation. This apparent double standard given the outcome of *Davies v. Taylor* was nevertheless viewed as reasonable at the time. English common law privileged attacks on property over those against a woman's honor: "But, if one saith to a Woman, which keepeth an Inn, or a Tabling-House, *Thou keepest a house of bawdry*. It is Actionable; For thereby her house is slandered" (1 *Croke* 582–83). Such were the social lines drawn in English Renaissance common law on the use of hurtful speech.

Remedies for slander against women were held to a similarly high standard of proof in Coke's age. In the *Holwood v. Hopkins* case of 1600–01 (42–43 Eliz.), Holwood claimed that allegations of her being an "arrant whore" put an end to her marriage plans (1 *Croke* 787). Words like whore and heretic, being "spiritual Slander and Defamation" (1 *Croke* 787), generally remained safe from common law action; however, they could be punishable in the ecclesiastical courts, which had a vital interest in sustaining the institution of marriage. Legally speaking, loose talk about character is one thing, but if such charges were "purposely intended to hinder the marriage, the Action had been maintainable for the loss, which she sustained" (1 *Croke* 787). Holwood was unable to convince the court that Hopkins's vile remarks directly resulted in such a termination. A 1606 (4 Jac.) case, *Dame Morison v. Cade*, succeeded when innuendoes of moral turpitude were leveled against a widow. Cade reported to Morison's suitor that Askot "*had the use of her body*" (2 *Croke* 162). Upon hearing this, the suitor broke off his pursuit of Morison. Cade had argued successfully in a lower court that his accusation caused no direct harm on the rationale that a physician could literally be said to have use of a woman's body without imputing immorality. This lower court decision was reversed on appeal because the "usual and common sense" inference of the charge was found by the higher courts to be damaging (2 *Croke* 163). The initial lower court ruling against Dame Morison is less outrageous than it might appear to us because common law courts were scrupulous about circumscribing their decisions to the letter of the law. The lower court ruling confirms, however, that women held a lower status in the common law.

Coriolanus is vulnerable to slanders employed by his foes to validate their treason charges. Both Coke and Blackstone permit loopholes in speech acts of precisely the sort Shakespeare uses to advance his dramatic action. Any actor would understand Blackstone's remarks on oral interpretation:

> But now it seems clearly to be agreed that, by the common law and the statute of Edward III, words spoken amount only to a high misdemeanor, and no treason. For they may be spoken in head, without any intention, or be mistaken, perverted, or mis-remembered by the hearers; their meaning depends always on the connexion with other words, and things; they may signify differently even according to the tone of the voice, with which they are delivered; and sometimes silence itself is more expressive than any discourse. As therefore there can be nothing more equivocal and ambiguous than words, it would indeed be unreasonable to make them amount to high treason.
>
> (4 *Bl. Comm.* 79–80)

Words generally had to be linked with deeds to constitute treason, as with other felonies, though as we have seen there were important exceptions to the rule: "An overt act must be alleged and proved" (4 *Bl. Comm.* 79). Because Coriolanus's initial remarks decrying the tribunes' power constitute mere political opinion, not subversive intent, his foes set verbal snares to inflame the hero's passion.

The main slanders against the protagonist relate to usury, Volumnia's influence, and his political bias. Despite being warned about using slanderous speech, a citizen openly accuses Coriolanus of fixing corn prices in Rome.[4] Because the emotional charge is legally insubstantial, the mob soon shifts its focus to the question of Volumnia's influence on her son. During this extraordinarily well-ventilated debate on the character of one of Rome's leading figures, the citizen who made the usury charge now attacks Coriolanus as being motivated "to please his mother, and to be partly proud, which he is, even to the altitude of his virtue" (1.1.38–40). Besides foreshadowing the eventual success of Volumnia's supplication, this accusation permits Menenius to raise the issue of legally actionable words in the context of the *patria potestas*: "You slander / The helms o' th' state, who care for you like fathers" (1.1.76–77). Volumnia complicates psychological questions surrounding Coriolanus through her use of such innocent phrases as "if my son were my husband" (1.3.2–3). Psychological elements recur when Volumnia suggests that bleeding wounds are fairer than Hecuba's breasts and that Romans will "put our tongues into those wounds" (2.3.6–7). If Coriolanus has an Oedipal complex, so apparently does all of Rome.

Critics have turned to Freud to evaluate the effect of Volumnia's influence on her son. A. C. Bradley sees the final reconciliation as being good for Coriolanus's soul, but many psychological critics find neurotic implications in the relationship. Earlier Freudians assert that Volumnia dominates her son much as Gertrude haunts Hamlet. Critic Rufus Pitney calls the play a "tragedy ensuing from an oedipal mother-son relationship" and finds Volumnia to have structured her son's superego so that "his conscience compels him to choose his own death rather than his mother's" (380, 381). Psychiatrist Charles Hofling finds "morbid" elements in the mother-son relationship that affect Coriolanus's healthy marriage by causing a "phallic-narcissist" condition (427, 428). Critic Janet Adelman sees a "phallic aggressive pose" making Coriolanus a "rigid and cold" tragic hero (133, 141). The hero seems to me to be anything but frosty, nor does the play provide proof that a homoerotic "alliance" exists between Coriolanus and

Aufidius, as Lisa Lowe suggests (87). Lowe uses psychological criticism while distancing herself from other Freudian feminist critics, including Coppélia Kahn, Janet Adelman, and Madelon Gohlke. Lowe suggests that Coriolanus has a "castration" complex brought about by patriarchal, not matriarchal, pressures (93). This observation might be more salient given a clearer historical context, for Lowe refers to "Elizabethan England" as the play's backdrop (89), when it is of the Jacobean period.

Shakespeare diminishes Volumnia's role in the supplication scene by having Coriolanus greet Virgilia first, contrary to Plutarch. Virgilia's humility is hardly a novelty in military marriages, but the presence of Valeria as a disinterested and unimpeachable presence along with Virgilia further reduces the mother's influence. Volumnia is a strict disciplinarian, though in light of the authoritarian standards of Rome she is not overly harsh. Roman wives had no more standing in the family than their children, but this patriarchal order did not mean that male offspring were necessarily well positioned. Many were cruelly mistreated by their fathers, and only after three extraordinarily harsh cases of abuse and disowning could a son wrest himself free of his father's grasp. Still, one of Coke's forerunners, Bracton, confirms an essential bias in the common law: "Women differ from men in many respects, for their position is inferior to men" (2: 31).[5] The Roman citizens, whose amateur psychological opinions count because they decide Coriolanus's fate, resign themselves to having ambivalent feelings about Volumnia's influence: "What he cannot help in his nature, you account a vice in him" (1.1.41–42). Aufidius makes the same psychological evaluation of his old nemesis after they have joined forces. The play consistently links psychological readings of the hero with the tactics of slander to divert our attention from issues of substantial public interest.

The slander that decisively shifts the play relates to Coriolanus's political leanings. Sicinius is a master at stage-managing baseless accusations of intentional criminal wrongdoing to strengthen his position:

> We charge you, that you have contriv'd to take
> From Rome all season'd office, and to wind
> Yourself into a power tyrannical,
> For which you are a traitor to the people. (3.3.63–66)

Sicinius leads the populace up to this accusation very carefully, perhaps more so than necessary given the discontent over poverty and starvation. Coriolanus, he says, demonstrates the requisite intention by words alone to be deemed a traitor, an argument so weak and overreaching that he pronounces the death sentence before the trial begins. Knowing that Coriolanus will be unable to restrain his fury upon hearing the illogical charges, Sicinius feels confident of his victory in the court of public opinion. Political speech operates here and elsewhere in a middle ground between slander and flattery, implying one whenever possible while engaging in the other. Coriolanus has already been blamed by one of his own soldiers for unnecessary vituperation: "Now, to seem to affect the malice and displeasure of the people is as bad as that which he dislikes, to flatter them for their love" (2.2.21–23). Without the tribunes' intervention, the reaction of the mob would have remained bifurcated, for when he is not being slandered, Coriolanus is hailed for his martial skill.

Coriolanus's opponents work themselves into a slanderous frenzy to blunt perceived threats to their personal and political well-being. Sicinius reveals the personal animosity he feels toward Coriolanus by insisting that the citizenry abuse the hero as he is led beyond the city walls. Further undercutting the tribunes' position is the vital Nicanor spy scene, in which a countryman is shown in fact to be working actively on behalf of the enemy: "I am a Roman, and my services are, as you are, against 'em" (4.3.4–5). Ruffus on military law is most explicit on this sort of demonstrable treachery: "Deserters to the enemy, and those who reveal our plans to the enemy shall be burned alive or hanged upon the gibbet" (Brand 60). This concept of law is identical to Coke's:

> If a subject joine with a foraine enemy, and come into England with him, he shall not be taken prisoner here and ransomed, or proceeded with as enemy shall, but he shall be taken as a traytor to the king.   (3 *Institutes* 11)

For such overt disloyalty to go unsuspected or unreported while Coriolanus's bad manners are treated as treason is the kind of legal imbalance that a reasonable audience would regard as outrageous, ginning up the tragic effect through an inequitable distribution of justice.

By siding with the Volscians, Coriolanus becomes the traitor he was falsely alleged to be in Rome. He describes his motivation for revenge during the supplication scene, yet his rage is laced with a desire to reform Rome rather than seek its destruction. He is no stock revenger because he does not target old adversaries like Sicinius or Brutus. Perhaps this is the source of Aufidius's jealous awe of

Coriolanus, a feeling shared by many of the play's characters. The virulence of the Volscian leader's final response is shocking: "*Draw the Conspirators, and kills Martius, who falls; Aufidius stands on him*" (5.6.130). This gross exhibition is pure desecration. We move beyond the legal realm of punishment to a tragic theatricality whereby a hero is insulted beyond all recognized bounds of decency. Shakespeare herein casts any legal impulse for reform into confusion.

III. THE SPECTACLE OF TRAGIC PUNISHMENT

Coriolanus's body is used as a metaphor for political life and its diseases, with his immune system breaking down entirely at the end in a violent spectacle of capital punishment. He demonstrates a special reluctance for political acting, which is theatrical acting writ small. Politics requires displays that strike Coriolanus as unbearable flattery. If Hamlet delays, Coriolanus refuses to act at all, which creates a tension endangering the forward action of the tragedy. Coriolanus despises ham acting much as Hamlet does dishonest shows, but he thinks his way through his dilemma as a military tactician. He leavens his flattery with contempt of those who desire it: "I will counterfeit the bewitchment of some popular man, and give it bountiful to the desirers" (2.3.101–02). Armed with a new ironic distance from his role, Coriolanus injects the bluster learned in his capacity as a military commander to hector his fellow Romans as he would his foes: "Your voices? For your voices I have fought!" (2.3.126). Receiving the approval of the crowd despite refusing to display his wounds, he overleaps the obstacle occasioned by his refusal to act by making a pretense of it, while Hamlet pretends in order to arrive at true action itself.

Coriolanus rejects ham acting on personal grounds, but the premise that honor and policy might join harmoniously—Durkheim's aim—is impossible given the political tensions. Norman Rabkin is thus correct to assert that "rational and humane order cannot really be restored because it cannot exist in society" to the extent that he means Roman or Volscian society (21). The contradiction is evident in Menenius, who praises the hero's nobility while chastising him for failing to soothe the populace. Coriolanus believes in cognitive behaviorism, fearing that unworthy practices will "teach my mind / A most inherent baseness" (3.2.122–23). The distanciation involved in the classical acting style he adopts enables him to stand for consulship once he realizes that he need not take his own political gestures seriously. When

Cominius promises to stage-manage the action: "Come, come, we'll prompt you" (3.2.106), theatrical and legal issues begin to overtake the psychological and political aspects of the play.

For all his seeming superficiality or inflexibility, Coriolanus remains an irresistible figure in part because of his ironic attitude toward acting. Cominius is forced to admit that there is something admirable about Coriolanus even after the defection. The plebes' sense the loss of Coriolanus, though they express their remorse illogically: "And though we willingly consented to his banishment, yet it was against our will" (4.6.144–45). The Senators respond in kind when news of Coriolanus's peace offer reaches them, so Kenneth Burke is right to detect a catalytic quality in the hero's nature that affects Rome and Antium equally. But rather than revealing any fault or criminality within the hero, as Burke maintains, Coriolanus's non-performances constitute great acting that incites others to perform legal or illegal acts, as they will. His authoritarian streak accords with his military rank, though his contempt for the plebes as better suited for the gibbet than the battlefield is far too harsh. It is, nonetheless, a distinct curiosity in critical reaction to the play that a military man who proposes peace for the general good should be castigated so strongly as an unfit or emotionally crippled leader.

Coriolanus is not so much an absolutist as fully formed from the start, which cannot be said of Romeo, Hamlet, or Othello. His foes catalogue his defects in moral terms of "pride," "[defect] of judgment," or "nature" (4.7.37, 39, 41). Menenius refers to any alliance between Rome and Antium as unthinkable, a "violent'st contrariety" (4.6.73). Because she understands her son's martial disposition, Volumnia wins him back by arguing that reconciliation would constitute not a retreat but a double victory. The supplication scene creates theatrical metaphysics equal to the power of Greek tragedy, though without its supernatural dimensions. In this respect, too, the play differs from *Macbeth*, *Hamlet*, or *King Lear*. Coriolanus can no longer pretend to act as a public figure might. Reminded that the role of a conqueror is merely assumed, he responds with a theatrical analogy: "Like a dull actor now / I have forgot my part, and I am out, / Even to a full disgrace" (5.3.40–42). Silence reigns as Volumnia takes his hand in a restoration of the hero's private identity. In the theatre the silence is deafening, with many actors exploiting it for a minute or longer. The suppliants kneel before a theatrical hero, but he responds in a way that rejects the premise of the *patria potestas*. He finds their submission to be "unnatural" (5.3.184), which contradicts the patriarchal foundations of the *Corpus Juris Civilis.*

Coriolanus seeks an emancipation that is unknown in Roman law and scarcely visible in Renaissance law and tragedy. Shakespearean tragedy rejects the possibility of full emancipation here as it had in *Romeo and Juliet.* That Coriolanus should be asked for mercy by Rome is terribly ironic because he is in no position to dispense it. As one who has been exiled, it is he who should by rights be seeking pardon from those who banished him. Mercy of this sort must come from the leader, a point Coke emphasizes as essential to the common law: "Mercy and truth preserve the King, and by clemency is his throne strengthened. And hereupon is the law of England founded" (3 *Institutes* 233). Coriolanus appeals for peace, but he cannot overcome the legal and theatrical traps awaiting him.

The validity of the martial code guiding Coriolanus's civil behavior is established once and for all in contradistinction to the political discourse of Menenius, which can be pierced immediately by the military mind. When Menenius attempts to bluff his way past the Volscian guards, they quickly take him to be a "liar" and a "decay'd dotant" because he is incapable of distinguishing between the ranks of captain and general (5.2.31, 44). Coriolanus regards war and peace simply as the initiation and cessation of hostilities. For him, action constitutes eloquence in war, while eloquence is the less honorable action of civil peace. His peace proposal is rebuffed by Aufidius, who can speak both languages simultaneously and fluently. When Coriolanus weeps before him, he slanders this image of Mars with a devastating rejoinder: "Name not the god, thou boy of tears!" (5.6.100). By pleading for mercy, Coriolanus has threatened to breach his contract to serve Aufidius, but the Volscian leader violates a theatrical contract of his own in mixing the language of the politician and warrior. We, like Aufidius's giddy servingmen, rightly sense that Coriolanus could "thwack our general" (4.5.178–79). In view of Coriolanus's martial and theatrical superiority, the Volscian lords must search hard to find mitigating factors for the assassination: "His own impatience / Takes from Aufidius a great part of blame. / Let's make the best of it" (5.6.144–46). Aufidius's murderous premeditation is apparent to all, yet the Volscian lords seek to calm the political waters in precisely the same manner as their Roman counterparts.

The desecration of Coriolanus's body is a shameful and self-defeating act that is at once high theatre and an imitation of a primitive act of domination equivalent to Clytemnestra's treatment of Agamemnon. Aufidius senses his own disgrace: "My rage is gone, / And I am struck with sorrow" (5.6.146–47), but the solemnity that ensues cannot erase the horror of the act. Death is the only emancipation for the tragic hero, which is in reality a non-emancipation. At Stratford in 1959, the conspirators heaved Olivier over the balcony to hang by his heels. This *coup de théâtre* links the Roman punishment of throwing offenders off the Tarpeian Rock with the savage conspiracy engineered by Aufidius. That the prime conspirator receives no punishment is thoroughly unfair, but if the historians are correct, Aufidius has only one more year to live before he dies in a botched attempt to conquer Rome. In the play, though, Coriolanus's death never brings with it a believable promise of general peace, as Burke suggests it does.

IV. THE ENDS OF CIVILITY

The body is killed by slander in civil law and by death in criminal law, both punishments being combined to form the basis of this tragedy. Coriolanus's demeanor ranges from tender to severe, like Othello's, but his actual theatrical role is put to the test far more than that of the Venetian general. Othello commits murder out of simple jealousy under English Renaissance law.[6] The slander suffered by Coriolanus under the body of Roman and Renaissance law is as plain as the criminality involved in his banishment and murder.

For a Shakespearean tragic protagonist to propose peace in his final moments is quite unusual. Generally, such heroes succumb after a prolonged state of excitement. Romeo, Hamlet, Macbeth, and Othello all reach heights of physical and emotional animation before they expire. Apart from a last minute argument with Aufidius, which merely marks a return to his old form, Coriolanus dies in a mood as forgiving as that of the Roman citizens and leaders who now desperately wish for his return. More successfully focused than *Julius Caesar* as to the fate of a singular hero, this play gives Coriolanus a theatrical bewitchment, some touch of the gods, that elevates him.[7] Hence the furtiveness of a slaughter that completes the destruction of his body begun over a multitude of military campaigns. The final vicious insult is inflicted by his inferiors, including vicariously the audience, which can contemplate its emancipation only in the most ironic fashion.

CHAPTER 8

TIMON OF ATHENS AS UTILITARIAN TRAGEDY

Timon of Athens reverses key elements of the legal formula by which guilt is established, particularly as to the protagonist's actus reus and mens rea. Timon's self-enforced banishment and death, probably an extended *felo de se* suicide, are abetted by Athenian corruption and his own misplaced generosity. A non-political figure who eschews bloodshed, Timon violates laws of the most mundane variety—matters of contract and debt, mainly. His bankruptcy falls far short of the metaphysically charged inciting actions of the other tragedies. His death portends no general calamity. The disproportionate punishment our ascetic hero receives for his failure to repay debts is a model of deterrence gone awry. Restitution is not an option for Timon; consequently, the concepts of guilt and corresponding punishment become disjoined. The play anticipates Jeremy Bentham's utilitarian analysis of punishment as deterrence because Timon's misery ensures the temporary continuity, or pleasure, of the state.

Timon dies for an act disproportionate to the crime if we examine the formula for establishing guilt: the act plus mens rea leading to an illegal result absent a valid legal defense equals the guilty verdict:[1]

$$A + MR \gg R \text{ w/o } DEF = G$$

Being harried into death or banishment for debts is an inequitable outcome by any standard, though Timon never qualifies as the victim he believes himself to be. Except for a brief interval he is continuously wealthy, even if what he intends to accomplish with his gold changes drastically. So while Antony and Cleopatra soar beyond the reach of the common law, Timon's acts scarcely rise to the level of serious juridical concern. Instead, public policy disputes relating to social contracts and indebtedness surround the central conflict. Timon's non-contractual goodwill is repaid by legal parchment from his creditors. Having sought to better the lot of his city-state, he is, in fact, undone by Benthamite principles when he seeks to undermine its corruption. While Timon sees the social contract as binding, his peers hold him absolutely liable to the strictures of contract law.

Timon of Athens raises the spectre of talionic law while holding it at arm's length. Alcibiades objects to the death sentence imposed on a quick-tempered but otherwise worthy Athenian soldier, a plea which is rejected by the First Senator: "We are for law, he dies, urge it no more / On height of our displeasure" (3.5.85–86). Later, Alcibiades rather surprisingly emphasizes Timon's plight as a rationale for assaulting his city: "Those enemies of Timon's and mine own / Whom you yourselves shall set out for reproof / Fall, and no more" (5.4.56– 58). His volubility seems excessive given that he has Athens on the brink of unconditional surrender while neither redeeming nor relieving Timon's suffering. Shakespeare widens the gap between retributive theory and tragedy in favor of addressing more nuanced, if esoteric, utilitarian law.

In part I, I address Renaissance case law on debt, which holds out little succor for our hero. Part II explores the nature of utilitarian punishment, the enforcement of which is more prevalent than audiences might generally believe. Part III treats Timon as a study in Benthamite punishment. Because of its seemingly unpolished concluding acts, the underdeveloped relationship between Alcibiades and Timon, and the curious dual epitaph scene, the play has rarely been regarded as one of Shakespeare's finest efforts. The utilitarian theory of justice presented as part of the tragic action constitutes an added layer of perplexity for an audience steeped in retribution theory.

I. DEBT AND CASE LAW

Few sparks of controversy fly in Renaissance juridical circles about the procedures for repaying debts of the kind Timon incurs. Settled opinion based on the reasonable person standard guided tort resolutions. Cases that tested this rule on technical irregularities were subject to rather hasty dismissal.

The 1596 (38–39 Eliz.) Exchequer case of *Woodward v. Parry* was an action of debt for an outstanding sum of £14. Parry admitted to owing the money but asked the court to quash the complaint because the contract presented in court indicated that he owed exactly £20.

Parry argued for dismissal on the grounds that the plaintiff "ought to have Counted upon the Bill, as it is" (1 *Croke* 537). The court rejected this maneuver because the receipt "was good enough: For there is but £14 due upon this bill" (1 *Croke* 537). Woodward was granted relief. Similarly, in a 1597 (37 Eliz.) Common Pleas case of debt, *Capp v. Lancaster*, the plaintiff sought return of £70, with the defendant arguing that no repayment was required since no formal demand had been proffered. The judges ignored this technicality, finding that the case was made "well enough: For It is a Duty *maytenant*, and therefore there needs not any Demand" (1 *Croke* 548). Renaissance courts held that bringing an action in itself fell into the category of making a demand. In a suit postdating the staging of the play, the 1611 (9 Jac.) King's Bench case of *Els v. Clark* saw a defendant try to elude repayment through a different sort of technicality. The defendant objected "that the words in the bond have a construction that he obligeth himself in fiftieth pounds, and not fifty pounds" (2 *Croke* 290). The court rejected this fine distinction by determining that the bond "shall be construed to be all one sense, and the intent of the parties" (2 *Croke* 290), which was to repay the £50.

The court had long experience regulating public transactions efficiently. It had an interest in deciding cases by objective standards of reason rather than by subjective issues, including voluntarism and the like, which might arise in a criminal action. In its view, a contract was a contract as long as it conformed to normal standards. Closer scrutiny of the letter of the law entered into the prosecution of criminal treason trials. In the 1606 Gunpowder Plot trial of *Rex v. Fawkes et al*, Coke invokes the Psalms to support death sentences for crimes "beyond all example, whether in fact or fiction, even of the tragick poets who did beat their wits to represent the most fearful and horrible murders" (*St.Tr.* 2: 167).[2] Since Papal intrigue was constantly raised as an issue in treason trials, Coke expanded the conspiracy to include Henry Garnet, Superior of the Jesuits, because he gave the Eucharist to the defendants. Admitting only to a "general knowledge" of the plot (*St.Tr.* 2: 356), Garnet was nevertheless targeted because of his high status in a religious order deemed threatening to Jacobean society. The reasonableness standard was not strictly invoked in criminal cases, which in this instance hurt Garnet. A famous saying by Common Pleas Chief Justice Brian in 1477 indicates the degree of objective liability inherent particularly in tort law: "The thought of man is not triable; the devil alone knoweth the thought of man" (Hart

1968, 188). Justice Brian is voicing a minority juridical opinion as to criminal liability in the Renaissance, but his maxim held much more securely in tort cases.

II. BENTHAMITE PUNISHMENT

Timon's feelings of persecution are obvious, but objectively speaking Athens must regard his indebtedness as a crime threatening to unbalance her political and commercial security. Timon has no rejoinder in law to fend off action by his creditors. Elsewhere in Shakespeare, such as in *The Merchant of Venice*, a civil proceeding of a utilitarian nature would soften the impact of an unforeseen bankruptcy. Renaissance England had a special court, the "Court for the Commissioners upon the Statute of Bankrupts," which considered bankruptcy to be very nearly criminal and certainly immoral. The offender was seen to be "consuming of his estate in riotous and delicate living" (4 *Institutes* 277). Statutes were enacted in the reign of Henry VIII against English merchants who "had rioted in three kinds of costlinesses, viz. costly building, costly diet, and costly apparel, accompanied with neglect of his trade and servants, and thereby consumed his wealth" (4 *Institutes* 277). These descriptions apply neatly to Timon apart from his humanitarian streak, which gives him psychic pleasure while providing a windfall for his erstwhile friends.

Even the harshest legal systems apply utilitarian theories in practice, theory, and distribution if only by deciding which cases ought to come to trial. The Benthamite response based on objective social criteria would reject Kant's moralistic solution, though it is true that reasonable arguments can be made that Kant was not a moral extremist. Ralph C. S. Walker theorizes that despite language that is "vague," "old-fashioned," and "unfortunate," Kant believes that people should always be treated as ends in themselves:

> But he does *not* differ from the utilitarians over the requirement to promote happiness. Where he differs is that for him that requirement derives its value from the moral law, as every ethical requirement must. For utilitarians things are the other way round: if the moral law (or anything else) has a value, it is because of its tendency to promote happiness.   (Walker 11)

Given certain extreme statements and hypotheticals, it is probably fair to suggest that Kant is at best inconsistent at times in his juridical theory. Kant's decree that a society must, even at the hour of its disbanding, execute the last remaining murderer to repay evil deeds and to relieve its members of blood-guilt contrasts sharply with the utilitarian perspective. Bentham holds that society ought to restrain itself from enforcing talionic punishments because it has a counter-interest in dispensing pain:

1. The general object which all laws have, or ought to have, in common, is to augment the total happiness of the community; and therefore, in the first place, to exclude, as far as may be, every thing that tends to subtract from that happiness: in other words, to exclude mischief.
2. But all punishment is mischief: all punishment in itself is evil. Upon the principle of utility, if it ought at all to be admitted, it ought only to be admitted in as far as it promises to exclude some greater evil.

                                                                    (*Principles* 158)

Kant's social cathartic is Bentham's necessary evil. Kant's last murderer would be spared by Bentham, for such punishment would be deemed "*unprofitable*" and legally "*groundless*" because a society in dissolution has no need to prevent mischief as a matter of public policy (*Principles* 159).

Deterrence directs punishment not so much against the offender as against others who might commit the same offense in the future, though harsh sanctions may very well exist under a utilitarian regime. Coke saw deterrent effects flowing from retributive punishment and the symbolism inherent in its enforcement:

For to deterre and to detain men from committing of Treason or felony, the Law hath inflicted . . . punishments upon him that is attainted of Treason or Felony. 1. He shall lose his life, and that by an infamous death of hanging between heaven and earth, as unworthy in respect of his offence in either.

                                                                    (1 *Institutes* 41)

Punishment resulting from bad laws or an unjust verdict remains a problem for retribution theory. So too is punishment of a crime which, as Hart puts it, "does not entail moral guilt" (*Punishment* 18). Such a case might include prosecution of a corporate executive whose workers manufactured fatally flawed automobile parts without his knowledge. Hart's sense that "no individual is to be punished who lacks the capacity to obey" indicates how deeply ingrained the mental element is in Anglo-American defenses (*Jurisprudence* 284).

Known for imposing uniformity on criminal procedure and punishment throughout England, thereby curbing the whims of individual judges, Bentham would apply only the minimum force necessary to advance the goals of a peaceful society. Moral responsibility is downplayed while the concept of placing a tariff on bad behavior is elevated. As Hart suggests, the law cannot in practice impose eye-for-an-eye punishment because court officials would have to slander slanderers, rape rapists, and so on. Freed by the imaginative space of the theatre, Shakespeare can see the logic of retribution through to its final consequences. The plays implicitly criticize invoking the death penalty for relatively minor offenses, including, for example, the delict of fornication in *Measure for Measure*. Similarly, *The Merchant of Venice* discourages the kind of disproportionate sentence Shylock would carve out of his debtor's hide. Bentham's principle of proportionality suggests that punishment should exceed the crime only to the extent that bad acts can be prevented. Proportionality is a particularly difficult concept for Timon, who is incapable of making reasonable choices between what Bentham calls the "governance of two sovereign masters, *pain* and *pleasure*" (*Principles* 11). Timon's pain is apparently also his pleasure. The hard labor Bentham recommends as deterrence for most offenses, notably white collar crimes, would have little effect on individuals like Timon placed in unfamiliar, threatening circumstances, as indeed it would fail to deter most Shakespearean tragic heroes. Capital punishment has no educative effect, for instance, on one who sees himself as a martyr. On the other hand, Bentham would favor preventive detention, a policy many today view as utterly abhorrent.

Punishment theory in *Timon of Athens* becomes a hypothetical which pushes Bentham's social-corrective doctrine to an extreme. While Bentham makes a strong case for ignoring victimless crimes, he argues that illicit acts against society cannot go unchecked: "There are few cases in which it *would* be expedient to punish a man for hurting *himself*: but there are few cases, if any, in which it would *not* be expedient to punish a man for injuring his neighbor" (*Principles* 292). Bentham stretches the notion of what ought to be criminalized in his own philosophy far beyond what would be deemed acceptable in America. Current European law follows Bentham's theory in criminalizing the failure to intervene on behalf of a helpless victim. For example, bystanders must in ordinary circumstances lift an unconscious victim's face out of a puddle of water: "Why should it not be made the duty of every man to save another from mischief, when it can be done without prejudicing himself" (*Principles* 293). This position has ethical merit because Bentham wishes to save lives, but it also implicitly recognizes Timon's dilemma of having his peers know-ingly drain off his resources. Timon's assumption that his false friends are motivated by mutually held feelings of benevolence provides him a strong moral but not legal claim to their allegiance when he suffers a financial reversal. His misguided generosity becomes as upsetting to good social order as parsimony or outright theft.

Bentham stands apart from Kant mainly in his vision of the perfect-ibility of man and society. His reference to the corpus of the law as a sophisticated timepiece would be utterly foreign to Kant:

> A body of laws is a vast and complicated piece of mechanism, of which no part can be fully explained without the rest. To understand the functions of a balance-wheel you must take to pieces the whole watch: to understand the nature of a law you must take to pieces the whole code.   (*Principles* 299n)

Bentham would regulate crime through transactions rewarding those who conform to the interests of society at the expense of those who do not, much like Athenian law does in the play. Timon becomes the hypothetical model of an individual punished to deter the kind of be-havior that leads to bankruptcy. Today, white-collar criminals charge that such selective targeting is an abuse of the law. However mis-guided these individuals might be, the charge has some validity. The IRS investigates and convicts tax evaders selectively in order to deter more widespread fraud.

While incorporating elements of deterrence, the common law has always supremely valued the rights of the individual. Thus, neither Benthamite deterrence nor Kantian retribution has ever been accepted in the common law in its pure form. Even today's popular "three strikes and you're out" laws contain elements of deterrence and retribution. The play exploits the tension between the two theories in common law because Timon comes to share the core belief of the most vehe-ment retributionist as Bentham distastefully conceives it: "If you hate much, punish much; punish as you hate" (*Principles* 25). The pro-tagonist comes to hate men greatly after loving them too much; never-theless, his passion seems less harmful than the Athenian laws which, when misused, drive him to despair.

III. Timon's Punishment

Though no Athenian is directly culpable, Timon dies without having committed a capital offense. The play complicates each element of the equation by which guilt is determined under traditional common law principles. Bentham understands this formula, though he employs his own terminology concerning the "act," "circumstances," "intentionality," and "consciousness" (*Principles* 75):

A *(act)* + MR *(intentionality)* » R *(circumstances)* w/o DEF *(consciousness)* = G

Regarding the *act* (A), neither Timon nor his creditors commits an illegal deed justifying a fatal resolution. What Bentham calls *intentionality* corresponds to mens rea (MR). No one in the play intends to commit murder, though many are negligent as to the evil that might result from bad or rigid applications of the law. Malignant attitudes, as we have seen, cannot be prosecuted except as they pertain to the life of the king. The result (R)—what Bentham calls *circumstances* and the law *res gestae*—refers to the chain of causality and events surrounding the act. Finally, *consciousness* (DEF) for Bentham includes various positive defenses, including automatism, false consciousness, and the like. Far from wishing Timon's ruin, his creditors probably hope that he could somehow be restored to financial health so that they might continue to exploit him. Regarding Timon's fate, then, the play presents a non-act, corresponding non-intentions, excessive results, and at best indirect guilt requiring no proffer of an affirmative defense. The punishment formula never coalesces except in the wounded imagination of the principal character.

Timon's valuing of pain over pleasure constitutes the main reason he stands at odds with an acquisitive society. His creditors meet the common law threshold for contractual validity, but only barely: "In every contract there must be *quid pro quo*" (1 *Institutes* 47a). Parasitic behavior constitutes an unjustified risk to Timon's well-being; however, it would reach only the lowest level of mens rea guilt. The proof would still by no means be certain. The legal definition of a defense obviating guilt requires evidence of some self-defense, such as shooting at someone who is about to fire at you. Timon has no positive self-defense in tort law. The fact that he does not understand his financial plight is no defense, though we sympathize with his better nature. He might escape his debts in a modern court under some plea of "imperfect," or mistaken, judgment or by declaring bankruptcy, but at the common law he has no standing.

Bentham's discussion of the difference between intentions and motives is useful for assessing character: "The causes of intentions are motives" (*Principles* 134). What an actor would call an intention is roughly equivalent to mens rea, while motives would mean roughly the same thing in the law and theatre. Intentions correspond directly with the act. If on a sunny day a foe accelerates and swerves across three lanes to aim his car at a victim as he walks through a pedestrian crossing, the intention, or mens rea, is to hit and kill. Mens rea or intention thus refers to the immediate purpose involved in accomplishing the act itself. Motive refers to deeper-lying attitudes, ranging from hatred, anger, delusions of grandeur, a sense of martyrdom, and so forth. Timon's intention in dispensing cash varies greatly during the play. Initially, he does so to strengthen the bonds of interpersonal and societal relationships through what he sees to be benevolent acts. Later, he hurls gold coins with the intention of destroying those he now considers to be his implacable foes. His motive remains singular in that he wishes to save society even if he means to destroy it by the play's end. Bentham regards all people, even ascetics, as directing their efforts toward pleasure; thus, were he to critique the play, he would note that Timon's malice involves a pursuit of his pleasure: *"There is no such thing as any sort of motive that is in itself a bad one"* (*Principles* 100). Retributionists would disagree that evil motives do not exist. It is likely that Shakespeare would disagree with Bentham on this point too given his portraits of Macbeth and Iago, but this play is generally utilitarian in its determination of guilt and punishment considering the retributivist legal traditions of his age.

The play outlines various levels of culpability relating to intention but not motive, since the motives of the central characters remain remarkably stable. Intention refers to positive acts or refusals to act in cases of willful blindness. Timon retains the motives of an apocalyptic reformer whatever his tactics. Alcibiades is a thoroughly crass opportunist, but all Athenians act out of varying degrees of self-interest, including outright greed. Even Timon's servants are self-interested if only because human survival depends upon it to a certain degree.

Current law recognizes four main levels of criminal culpability as to mens rea: purpose, knowledge, recklessness, and negligence. In distinctions based on the reasonable man standard discussed in *Macbeth*, purpose involves a conscious, harmful, and direct objective, such as uncoupling the brakes in a foe's automobile. Knowledge is marginally less direct, connoting an awareness that a disastrous result could not help but occur from an act. A car accident resulting from an otherwise competent driver speeding and passing through a series of blind curves

on a busy highway raises mens rea to the level of knowledge. Recklessness invokes a still lower level of culpability indicating malicious
disregard for human safety. Late-night drag racing on quiet public streets
is a form of reckless behavior. Negligence stands at the lowest level of
criminal intent. A luxury ocean liner taking to sea despite unfinished
repairs might reasonably raise questions of negligence on the part of
the ship's owners or managers. The play presents Athenian society
operating on all levels of intent where Timon is concerned, but in
Renaissance common law, Timon would not be seen as a victim because he mismanages his financial affairs: "Lord Timon will be left a
naked gull, / Which flashes now a phoenix" (2.1.31–32). Shakespeare
largely severs criminal intent from the criminal act here, giving us mens
rea without the actus reus.

Timon's servants are enlightened, committed workers who suffer
privation to an admirable degree before being forced to desert their
self-flagellating master. The long-suffering Steward, who fought vainly
to balance Timon's unbalanced books, is left to mitigate the effects of
the collapse: "Good fellows all, / The latest of my wealth I'll share
amongst you. / Where ever we shall meet, for Timon's sake / Let's
yet be fellows" (4.2.22–25). A Senator employs the reasonableness
standard in critiquing Timon's passion for charitable deeds: "It cannot
hold, no reason / Can sound his state in safety" (2.1.12–13). In the
face of the threat posed by Alcibiades, however, the Senators quickly
try to intercede on Timon's behalf. Bentham takes it for granted that
societies like that of Athens will act in a self-interested manner:

> The principle of asceticism never was, nor ever can be, consistently pursued
> by any living creature. Let but one tenth part of the inhabitants of this earth
> pursue it consistently, and in a day's time they will have turned it into a hell.
>
> (*Principles* 21)

Timon's fate serves as a deterrent to other would-be reformers, including Alcibiades, who is finally too self-serving to risk sharing his
friend's pain and privation.

Bentham's calculation for deterrence requires that the state exact
more prospective psychic and corporal punishment than Timon can
accumulate in wealth. To put it another way, Timon's punishment must
be greater than his cost of doing business, if he can be said to behave
in a business-like way:

> The value of punishment must not be less in any case than what is sufficient
> to outweigh that of the profit of the offence. . . . It is a well-known adage,

> though it is to be hoped not a true one, that every man has his price. It is commonly meant of a man's virtue. (*Principles* 166, 166n)

Bentham's dry remark means precisely that society assumes each individual to have his price. Regrettably, Timon did not have occasion to read Bentham, for it might have had a salutary effect on him. By contrast, Alcibiades understands the calculus of deterrence by arriving at Athens' city gates with overpowering military strength. His bargaining strategy is more effective than Timon's since he negotiates with real force behind him. The ineffectiveness of Timon's moral suasion is unusual in Shakespeare because the tragic hero generally manages to win the emotional or intellectual debate even if his antagonists cannot comprehend his vision in its entirety. Timon mainly exudes unlimited gall in attacking society, though he also has the uncanny ability to generate unending supplies of gold. Unlike the Athenians, he is never forced to choose between financial pain and pleasure for long. Death is the only punishment that can outweigh his almost magical ability to generate destructive wealth.

Though the facts surrounding Timon's demise remain unclear, Bentham, like Shakespeare before him, knew that it is mainly the perception or threat of punishment that deters potential offenders: "It is the idea only of punishment (or, in other words, the *apparent* punishment) that really acts upon the mind" (*Principles* 178). Timon's death reverses the formula by which guilt is assigned, for it relieves the state of direct responsibility for having to carry out a lesser, though still serious, punishment. The play's formula for punishment concludes in the following manner:

$$(\text{-})A \; + \; (\text{-})MR» \; R \; \text{with DEF} \; = \; (\text{-})G \; \text{with Punishment}$$

That is, we end with a non-act, no mens rea, and with imperfect self-defenses all leading to an absence of guilt in Timon's death. Underlying this formula is the unstated assumption that the Athenian social contract is inviolable. Timon accepts his misery and humiliation with the consolation that Athens will fall, an awareness shared by Shakespeare's audience many centuries after the fact.

The procedure for evaluating Timon's culpability involves three steps: first, determining the precise description of the illegal act; second, defining the precise mens rea attached to the act; and third, establishing whether or not the defendant has that mens rea. As to point one, Timon is factually guilty of failing to repay his debts, which in the common law opens him to an action of debt, as Blackstone remarks:

> The legal acceptation of *debt* is, a sum of money due by certain and express
> agreement: as, by a bond for a determinate sum; a bill or note; a special
> bargain, or a rent reserved on a lease; where the quantity is fixed and spe-
> cific, and does not depend upon any subsequent valuation to settle it. The
> non-payment of these is an injury, for which the proper remedy is by action of
> *debt*, to compel the performance of the contract and recover the special sum
> due.   (3 *Bl. Comm.* 154)

Timon's nude contracts have no standing beside his creditors' legal
ones, but the play complicates points two and three. Timon refuses to
accept the significance of his financial negligence. Mens rea attaches
because, though Timon does not at first intend to cause harm, he
blocks restoration by wastefully flinging at his creditors the very gold
that might satisfy their demands—with interest in the form of his insults.

As a utilitarian, Bentham would say that Timon's nude contracts
are bad for society per se, while legal contracts, though not always
charitable, promote the progress of society. Coke would have none of
Timon's foolishness and would regard any resistance to due restoration of debt to be a continuation of the original unlawful act. Coke
makes this point in the case of seizure of another's property:

> If the Lord is going to the Land holden of him for to distrein for the Rent
> behind, and the Tenant hearing this, encountreth with him, and forestalleth
> him the way with force and arms, or menaceth him in such form, that he dare
> not come to his Land to distrain for his Rent behind, for doubt of death or
> bodily hurt, this is disseisin, for that the Lord is disturbed of the means whereby
> he ought to come to his rent.   (1 *Institutes* 161a–162)

The Athenians' desire to collect their debts is valid even if their motives remain absolutely cynical.

Timon's mens rea puts into question what critics assume to be his
misanthropy, a perspective based logically enough on Timon's own
self-description as *"Misanthropos"* (4.3.54).[3] He gives freely but ex-
presses no intent to repay his loans. This refusal arises not from greed
but from a lack of interest in the city's economic welfare. Instead of
making restitution, he prefers to abscond to the woods in pursuit of
his ascetic pleasure. He rebuffs the somewhat basened coin of Athenian goodwill by trading in the currency of rage, but he cannot be
called a pure misanthrope because he merely refuses repayment in a
legal sense. Timon lavishly dispenses gold to whomever requests it at
his cave. Willingness to repay debts negates some of the ground of
action against him, though his method of repayment is quite improper.
The Senators, fearing Alcibiades's approach, implore Timon to return

as their leader with full "recompense" or immunity from old debts (5.1.150). If accepted, this offer would terminate all legal action against him. By refusing their plea, he reinstitutes the retributive conditions on which their action was founded.

The play's cautious ideological stance is developed in the relationship between the Poet and Painter. Both pay lip service to the virtues outlined by Sidney in *The Defence of Poetry* on behalf of the golden world of art. They make a pretense of having acquired the requisite *sprezzatura* in their labors. The Poet's offering is "a thing slipp'd idly from me," while the Painter terms his work "a pretty mocking of the life" (1.1.20, 35). Despite the Poet's claim of effortless ingenuity, his art being the "[gum], which [oozes] / From whence 'tis nourish'd" (1.1.21–22), his tale of fortune's blows is the oldest of conceits, as the Painter remarks sarcastically. Later, when word of the miraculous financial rebirth spreads, they return to Timon bearing an unfinished satire emphasizing the evils of flattery. Before driving them off with his curses, Timon reveals their corruption when he extracts their consent to plot his foes' death. In a famous essay, Marx interprets this scene as reflecting the degrading effects of capitalism upon the human spirit, but the play indicts moralistic art and retributive justice of all sorts by attacking their advocates as pseudo-artists and self-serving politicians. The play's modified utilitarian perspective, unlike Bentham's, suggests a deep skepticism concerning the perfectibility of man's social relationships.

Timon's malevolence toward Athenian society becomes pronounced at the end: "If Alcibiades kill my countrymen, / Let Alcibiades know this of Timon, / That Timon cares not" (5.1.169–71). To the extent that Timon cannot fathom the split between his motives and intention, he remains un-selfconscious as a tragic hero. This lack of consciousness creates difficulties for the exaction of punishment in Shakespearean tragedy. *King Lear* dispenses justice inequitably but is satisfying as a tragedy because of the relatively full awareness demonstrated by its main characters. This play punishes Timon without suggesting that he reasonably comprehends why he is blamed. By extension, there remains a gap between Timon and the audience as ersatz judges of his case:

> *Equity* is a construction made by the Judges, that cases out of the letter of a Statute, yet being within the same mischief, or cause of making the same, shall within the same remedy that that Statute provideth: And the reason hereof is, for that the Law-Maker could not possibly set down all cases in express terms.   (1 *Institutes* 24a)

Timon leans toward modernity as a tragic hero because of his lack of consciousness, breaking the retributivist legal conventions of his age and the playwright's general practice of creating tragic heroes who disclose, implicitly or explicitly, the ethos of their existence.

Timon remains a fascinating, exploratory character in an innovative play which accepts neither retribution nor deterrence wholeheartedly. He is a symbol of Renaissance nobility shattered on the reefs of a social order that will eventually refuse to sustain the aristocracy with largesse out of deference to a privileged hierarchical structure. At Coke's common law, contracts have already acted as great levelers: "For, the value of money being the measure of all contracts, &c, is in effect the value of every man" (2 *Institutes* 577). The play verges on being a "problem" tragedy, but it is far too complicated and troubling to be taken as a polemic. Timon's solitary death is an innovation that elevates the action by virtue of the tenacity of the hero, which taken alone would meet with Hegel's approval. A better understanding of the utilitarian influences in common law might force a reevaluation of the play, though this seems a remote prospect.

CHAPTER 9

JULIUS CAESAR AND THE PUNISHMENT OF WAR CRIMES

"Defend Norway. Enlist in the German Navy."
—Nazi Propaganda in Norway (*IMT* 7: 19)

The brutal assassination of Caesar anticipates only in miniature the criminal acts committed by the Axis powers during World War II. The allies eschewed the rough style of justice avenging Caesar's murder in favor of a novel legal forum designed to punish Nazi war criminals. Chief American prosecutor Justice Robert Jackson explicitly justified the legality of the International Military Tribunal [IMT] based on the development of English common law. He consulted ancient legal procedures, modern international statutes, and juridical opinions from the U.S., England, France, and the USSR in presenting his case. He invoked relevant international peace conventions and treaties, including those of the Hague, Locarno, Geneva, the Kellogg-Briand Pact of Paris, and the Treaty of Versailles.[1] He drew most heavily of all upon English common law theory regarding conspiracy, mens rea, and the actus reus. I am less interested in finding parallels between Rome and the Third Reich than suggesting that the play can be said to envisage the unique horrors of World War II if only because all murderous *coups d'états* are in many ways alike. Shakespeare's world had seen no calculating monster of Hitler's proportions, but the play's conspiracies, murders, and war make the comparison apt in terms of tragic punishment.

I will first review Renaissance war crime theory, then examine the elements of Nazi war crimes as they bear upon the play. These two sections might seem hopelessly condensed given the gravity of the subject, but I doubt that any single book could adequately treat IMT

transcripts and evidence covering 40 volumes, countless other trea-
tises on war crime theory, and still more volumes documenting the
history of wartime atrocities from Rome to the present day. I can
categorically state my opinion that the Axis powers bear absolute responsibility for the war and its miseries. In part III, I discuss
Shakespeare's distribution of responsibility for war crimes to the opposing sides. To conclude, I address the play's central orations as
metaphors for the representation and resolution of the greater criminal conspiracy that divides Rome.

Shakespeare makes political murder and its justification a tragic
issue of world-historical importance. Factional strife infects clan relationships in *Romeo and Juliet,* where death occurs in the heat of
passion or by misadventure. *Julius Caesar* takes the decisive step of
treating assassination as public policy while remaining indifferent as
to the fate of its central characters. Shakespeare's interest lies in the
artistry with which he shapes the debate. The play thus creates sufficient aesthetic distance between plot and character to afford a glimpse
of the full tragic potential realized a few years later in *Hamlet.*

I. THE LAWS OF WAR

Renaissance political theory required the showing of good cause to
begin wars (*jus ad bellum*) but dealt little with the need to adjudicate
their prosecution (*jus in bello*). This crucial distinction derives from
biblical sources and the politically sagacious Church fathers who followed their teachings. Deuteronomy prescribes how war is to be con-
ducted if a city fails to submit to God's anointed army:

> . . . then thou shalt besiege it: and when the LORD thy God hath delivered it
> into thine hands, thou shalt smite *every* male thereof with the edge of the
> sword: but the women, and the little ones, and the cattle, and all that is in the
> city, *even* all the spoil thereof, shalt thou take unto thyself; and thou shalt eat
> the spoil of thine enemies.   (Deut. 20: 12–14)

Church fathers like St. Augustine saw war as prudent and necessary
retribution for the imperial aspirations of renegade states despite the
moral and physical damage caused by such conflict, which "would still
be a matter of grief to man because it is man's wrong-doing" (*Works*
2: 311). The need to correct the political failures that result in the
carnage of war outweighs the deep ethical problems surrounding the
conduct of military campaigns.

St. Thomas Aquinas struggles with the distinction between just cause and just acts in terming the slaughter of innocents to be "against natural law" (*Summa* 28: 93). Still, he regards the preservation of the state by war as just: "*Wars are waged to achieve peace*" (*Summa* 42: 17). Aquinas spends most of his intellectual capital focusing on the moral issue of maintaining one's courage in battle and stressing the need for generals to conduct themselves professionally. The Church might determine the justness of the cause, but the acts of those engaged in war remained largely a matter of individual conscience and discretion. Given persistent attacks by neighboring nations against its allies, the medieval European Church granted states the right to defend themselves by any effective means.

It was not until 1625 that Hugo Grotius outlined humane protocols for war, but of course his treatise postdates Shakespeare's death. Still, the playwright seems cognizant of the two central issues surrounding the Renaissance debate over the conduct of warfare. Henry V struggles—vainly, many believe—to find just cause for his invasion of France in a comic scene with the Archbishop of Canterbury involving the intricacies of Salic law. To his credit, the young monarch comports himself reasonably well during the invasion, though it could be said he is acting out of self-interest in treating innocent bystanders humanely since it was his intent to retain the French territory he conquered.

Coke viewed war as an impediment to the domestic growth and industry that the common law sought to promote: "Time of peace is the time of law and right, and that of War is the time of violent oppression, which cannot be resisted by the equal course of law" (1 *Institutes* 249a). He ascribes the suffering of war to contests between peoples over increasingly limited space and resources. Nevertheless, he saw slow but discernible human rights progress in the development of warfare. Captives formerly executed or turned into villeins were now granted some legal protection. Attributing these and other social advances to the rule of law, he sought to limit the jurisdiction of courts martial strictly to matters extrinsic to the internal affairs of England. Disputes concerning native soil, treason, or crimes committed within eyeshot of England were to be dealt with by the common law courts. He permitted martial courts to retain their important symbolic functions domestically only insofar as they organized state ceremonies and categorized martial orders and emblems.

English courts martial fell under the authority of "The Honorable Court of Chivalry before the Constable and Marshall" (4 *Institutes*

123). The Lord Constable, well versed in the common law, decided whether cases ought better to appear before the common law courts. If cases were to be decided by courts martial, he was to be joined by the Earl Marshall, also a learned judge, whose role it was to enforce the court's decision by arranging combat or other punishments. The Chivalric Court remained a lower court to the extent that appeals from it could be heard by the King's Bench. A minor jurisdictional case arose before the Queen's Bench in 1582 (24 Eliz.), *Vast versus Gaudy*, in which the defendant was charged with allowing the escape of a Marshalsea prisoner, one T.B. The plaintiff was nonsuited because Gaudy proved that he had been shown a Queen's Bench order of "Attaint to Reverse the Judgment" (1 *Croke* 5). Coke moved increasingly to constrain the overweening Admiralty, or Marshalsea, courts. Given the ability of the English navy to seize valuable prizes in international waters, the power and wealth accruing to the martial courts made them ever more likely to encroach upon the jurisdiction of the common law.

International treaties and conventions were observed during Shakespeare's age mainly out of convenience: "A league may be broken by leavying of war, or by Ambassador or Herald" (4 *Institutes* 152). Ambassadors from foreign nations could reasonably be assured of enjoying the usual immunities and safe passage during the conduct of their business. Ensuring their safety was considered good policy by all sides, though exceptions were made for diplomats committing high crimes during their tenure. International laws were maintained on a bilateral basis rather than by any higher jurisdiction. Thus, international disputes could quickly surface as to the distinction, for example, between piracy and lawful taking of valuable prizes on the high seas.

One such complicated jurisdictional case arose in June 1614 involving Samuel Palache, ambassador for Morocco to Holland. England came into possession of several Spanish ships hijacked by the opportunistic Palache, who had intended to steer his prizes to Holland but instead found himself driven to England by bad weather. A joint hearing by the Chief Justice, Master of the Rolls, and the Admiralty convened under the ægis of the King's Bench to consider the disposition of the vessels. England had good relations with both Spain and Holland, though the latter two were in a state of war. Through her English attorney, Spain asked for the return of her ships, fully expecting a positive outcome. The decision reached by the English panel indicates the precision with which common law jurisdiction had been established: "It was resolved by the whole Court of the King's Bench upon conference and deliberation, that the Spaniard had lost the property of the goods for ever, and had no remedy for them in England" (4 *Institutes* 154). Palache, a bona fide ambassador, was released from the prison wherein he had languished pending the ruling.

Because the seizures took place on the high seas in a state of war, the King's Bench determined that it had no jurisdiction to order the return of the ships. The Bench resolved that since the cargo contained within those ships had found its way to England's shores by extra-legal means, Spain could sue for its recovery in the common law courts, though not in the Admiralty courts. No outcome of the common law case is recorded, but the English lawyer representing Spain was deeply distressed by the decision, apparently feeling that the Admiralty court had constituted his best hope for a win. He should not have been too surprised, however, because the King's Bench in the 1610 (8 Jac.) *Case of Piracy* had ruled that the king could seize the personal possessions of felon pirates and hold in protective custody all other goods until suit was made for recovery by merchants armed with valid bills of lading. Foreign merchants and the Admiralty court were losers in this case because "goods robbed from others . . . did not pass" to the Marshalsea courts but only to the jurisdiction of the king and the common law courts (*Coke's Reports* 12: 7). Even when a friendly foreign power was involved, then, English courts would follow strict jurisdictional procedures concerning the facts surrounding such seizures and the venues that should hear the matter.

Jurisdictional disputes were managed intelligently by the IMT, which dealt inclusively with the juridical concerns of the signatory nations pursuing their cases against the Nazi war criminals. It could do so freely because Germany had become occupied territory, with all Reich laws having been placed in a permanent state of suspension. Thus, the allies could impose English common law and other statutes upon contemporary German defendants. The IMT borrowed what it wished from various domestic and international legal systems while refusing to bar interested nations from pursuing their own cases against war criminals as they saw fit at some future date.

II. War Crimes

Coke viewed war, particularly civil war, with distaste because it undermined the power and institutions of the common law. War remained governed by loosely applied maxims and traditions until the late nine-teenth century. The just-cause rule was perhaps the most powerful moral restriction on aggression, but any consideration given to the treatment of innocents or soldiers was granted ad hoc. By the time the IMT convened, though, there existed a series of European and international treaties to which the major Axis and Allied nations were party. As a result, the Nazi defendants could be charged under one or more of the following counts:[2]

Count One—The Common Plan or Conspiracy
Count Two—Crimes Against Peace
Count Three—War Crimes
Count Four—Crimes Against Humanity   (IMT 1: 29–65)

Where Coke built a wall between the common law courts and courts martial, the IMT made the conceptual leap of combining domestic law with international law in a military tribunal setting. This innovative mixture led the defendants to argue that they could not be tried for violating laws which were abrogated for obvious reasons before the commencement of their aggression. As British prosecutor Sir Hartley Shawcross put it in common law terms, the defendants claimed that they were being charged under what amounted to bills of attainder; that is, they were being tried either *post hoc* or *in absentia*. The defendants pressed this common law procedural issue as forcefully as they could through their attorney:

"No punishment without a penal law in force at the time of the commission of the act." This maxim [*Nulla Poena Sin Lege*] is precisely not a rule of expe-diency but it derives from the recognition of the fact that any defendant must needs consider himself unjustly treated if he is punished under an ex post facto law.   (IMT 1: 169)

The *post hoc* argument required a response because of its standing in the common law, however ill it suited the defendants in question. Had Justice Robert Jackson only international statutes upon which to rely, the argument might have had greater merit. He was able to thwart this gambit by referring to even more basic concepts and statutes in the common law:

The Fourth Count of the Indictment is based on Crimes Against Humanity. Chief among these are mass killings of countless human beings in cold blood. Does it take these men by surprise that murder is treated as a crime?
                                                    (IMT 2: 145)

With regard to the first two counts of conspiracy and waging of aggressive war, international treaties signed by the Axis powers were used to refute the defendants' suggestion that they had crossed international boundaries in self-defense or out of altruistic motives. The defendants employed other transparent ruses designed to evade responsibility, including claims that they had invaded countries like Poland to prevent allied nations from invading them first. Such arguments were seen as irrational, akin to the notion that one ought to murder A first to prevent B from doing the same. Their excuses were as flimsy as Brutus's consent to assassination on the grounds that Caesar would be relieved of the mental strain of pondering his eventual death from natural causes. So as far as the IMT was concerned, international law began where domestic common law ended, providing a relatively seamless case with which to prosecute the defendants.

English common law was particularly helpful for Jackson on other fronts. It was no accident that he quoted Coke directly on at least one occasion:

> The Charter of this Tribunal evidences a faith that the law is not only to govern the conduct of little men, but that even rulers are, as Lord Chief Justice Coke put it to King James, "under God and the law." (*IMT* 2: 143)

This reference helped to overcome the argument that the defendants were mere conduits transmitting illegal orders from a higher authority to their inferiors. They could not be insulated from prosecution by claiming that they were merely following orders since all men are, as Jackson and Shawcross remarked, equally responsible to defend human rights under the law. It was shown in many instances that the defendants conceived the means by which the Führer's general policy goals would be enacted. In other words, they were not intermediaries but agents of crime. Armed with this basic common law precedent, the prosecution could blunt what they knew to be the last line of defense; namely, that European political tradition prior to the mid-nineteenth century held leaders blameless for initiating aggressive wars under the just cause doctrine.[3] Because the Reich's brand of total war, involving genocide, false imprisonment, torture, economic spoliation, and military devastation, had previously been outlawed by international convention, the defendants could not arbitrarily ignore the German signatures on those treaties.

Jackson found inspiration in the common law to surmount the procedural obstacle the defense would raise concerning the legitimacy of the Tribunal itself. He readily admits that there existed "no judicial precedent for the Charter" (*IMT* 2: 147), which was formulated in London on 8 Aug. 1945. No system of laws, he maintained, was ever expected to anticipate every possible misdeed, including crimes of the magnitude perpetrated by the Nazis. The fact that the court was guided by military regulations did not go unnoticed by the defendants' counsel, who argued that the Tribunal could not remain neutral without including a German representative. This argument was very poorly received, treated as a rough equivalent to the old joke about the parricide who throws himself on the mercy of the court on the grounds that he had become an orphan.

The Tribunal's implicit response to all defense objections was that the defendants were lucky to have been granted any legal protection at all given the Nazis' summary execution of partisans and POWs as well as their disproportionate reprisal executions. The USSR would have been more than willing to execute the defendants on the spot along with thousands of their cohorts, most of whom maintained a united front against the charges. The Tribunal allowed the inclusion of documents favoring the defendants when the evidence warranted it. It would also direct the prosecution to read material into the record detrimental to the defendants' case, to interrogate witnesses in the Continental style, to dispense with the technical rules of evidence familiar to common law courts, and to speed the proceedings along by evaluating evidence as to its relevance and probity. Whether the Bosnian war crimes trials at the Hague will fare as well with less assistance from military law regulations to help produce evidence, arraign major defendants, and thwart dilatory tactics by the defense remains to be seen. Defense counsel before the IMT were able to stall the proceedings to a minor extent even in the face of a total German surrender. On the other hand, the demilitarization of war crimes tribunals might represent the natural evolution of this form of international common law. Jackson himself saw the court's mixed jurisdiction as developing according to "the Common Law, through decisions reached from time to time in adapting settled principles to new situations" (*IMT* 2: 147). The Tribunal readily adopted Jackson's arguments on the dynamic nature of international law as it pertains to prosecuting modern aggressors, with their new technologies of mass destruction.

Coke approved of the outlawing of defective statutes by remarking that "three things (it is said) overthrew the flourishing state of the Roman empire: *Latens odium, Juvenile consilium, & Privatum lu-*

crum."[4] *Julius Caesar* theatricalizes not only these faults but implicitly contains the first two IMT counts of conspiracy and crimes against peace as charges worthy of convicting Caesar's foes before a metaphysical court of law. Coke saw martial law as corrosive to the common law intent of guaranteeing individual rights. These rights of individual freedom were, with important exceptions, secure by the time the IMT was gaveled into session from 14 Nov. 1945 to 1 Oct. 1946.

The military component of the tribunal helped to create order and dispense punishment in the rubble of post-war Germany. Revisionists charge that the trial was merely victor's justice. Some of them point to the atomic bombings of Japan as military outrages that went unpunished. Given the anger of the USSR over the release of several of the defendants, it could equally well be said that the verdicts were too compassionate. Despite the criticism, the IMT established itself as a model for international law in the arena of war crimes prosecution. Constructive innovations in law must at times appeal mainly to our imaginative or even aesthetic understanding, which Coke understood could raise as many questions as it answered:

> There is an old legall word called [Guidaguin] which signifieth an office of guiding travellers through dangerous and unknown ways; here it is appeareth, that the Lawes of the Realm hath this office to guide the Judges in all causes that come before them in the ways of right Justice, who never yet misguided any man, that certainly knew them, and truly followeth them.
>
> (2 *Institutes* 526)

Shakespeare's tragedies guide us through similarly dangerous territory but leave no conclusive or over-arching formal answers as to how to punish, which would be the objective of a lesser dramatist. Debate over the propriety of the IMT verdicts continues, but the fact that prosecution of Nazi war crimes is pursued in civil and criminal courts to this day, some 50 years after the war, is a vindication of the work of the Tribunal. The statute of limitations on the victor's justice theory would from any reasonable perspective seem to have long since expired.

III. JULIUS CAESAR AND WAR CRIMES

Shakespeare's Roman civil war presents no slaughters comparable to those of World War II, but the violent *putsch* instigating them includes similar criminal elements of conspiracy, subterfuge, premeditation, propaganda, murder, aggression, and retribution. To these the Nazis added genocide and torture on an unprecedented scale. The absence of an international body to which Shakespeare could appeal led him to employ theatrical devices soliciting the metaphysical realm. Caesar's Ghost reminds Brutus of past crimes and future punishment, a symbol of the spirit world Shakespeare had exploited in *Richard III* and would do in *Macbeth*. Critics have long debated Brutus's merits, but by killing Caesar, he tumbles headlong into a logical error worthy of *Alice in Wonderland* by arriving at a "sentence first—verdict afterwards," a process sanctioned by only the most brutal tyrants throughout time. Brutus's claim to be a supporter of republican values fails certain legal tests; however, the play defends him on other grounds to bring the antagonists more nearly into dramatic balance.

Favoring the causes of Antony, Brutus, or Caesar becomes problematic because each succumbs to the ambition so reviled by the Roman polity. Antony's self-promoting tactics are obvious, while Caesar appears all too willing to flirt with the prospect of absolute rule. A recent production by the Moving Theatre with Corin and Vanessa Redgrave at Houston's Alley Theatre led Corin to pronounce Caesar a "bastard,"[5] but this is an epithet one could assign to many characters in the play. Brutus's suggestion that the conspirators steep their arms in Caesar's blood is a particularly gruesome addition to the historical record that visually undercuts the professed nobility of his cause. Heavy blame falls upon Brutus for the conspiracy and slaughter that leads Rome into an unpopular civil war. Left with no defense in law, he sets out to defend himself in the court of public opinion, a task for which he is shown to be inadequately prepared.

For its part, the Roman populace affords the audience little hope for legal enlightenment. It is sullen and devious enough to make jokes about mending soles but irrational enough to kill the wrong Cinna for his verses. Skittish as they are, the plebes nevertheless alter the calculations of Rome's political leaders at every turn. The play exploits the theatrical nature of Roman political decorum. Brutus sheathes his dagger at the request of the mob for the same reason that Caesar rebuffs Antony's public offering of the crown. Most important of all, the crowd provides Antony the means by which he can revenge himself against the conspirators by delivering an oration far superior to Brutus's plodding circumlocutions.

Brutus commits a capital crime to redress wrongs Caesar had not yet committed, but such false steps mark most such criminal conspiracies. Hitler's decision to invade the USSR preemptively was one of several foolhardy, illegal acts that doomed him. The conspirators' plea for Publius Cimber's repeal is as clear a pretext as the provocations sown by Nazi organizations along several national borders to "justify" their invasions. Upon the murder of Caesar, Cinna cries: "Liberty! Freedom! Tyranny is dead!" (3.1.78), when no unusual state of despotism can reasonably be said to exist. Thus, Caesar's Ghost returns as a symbol of Brutus's mens rea, not merely of his impending misfortunes.

The first of the major charges against the Nazi defendants concerned their conspiracy to wage aggressive war. The secret association led by Brutus and Cassius took as its primary aim the removal of a perceived political impediment. Cassius admits subterfuge in planning the *coup d'état*:

> Now know you, Casca, I have mov'd already
> Some certain of the noblest-minded Romans
> To undergo with me an enterprise
> Of honourable-dangerous consequence. (1.3.121–24)

Cassius describes his plot in euphemistic terms by employing code words like "enterprise," a term, incidentally, used by Nazis in their pre-war correspondence. Cassius's personal animosity toward Caesar diminishes the conspirators' expressed republican ideals, though it should be noted that Brutus was previously inclined toward murder: "It must be by his death; and for my part, / I know no personal cause to spurn at him, / But for the general. He would be crown'd" (2.1.10–12). Brutus can neither claim that he was duped nor deny that his role in the act was essential to its completion. Furthermore, rumors surrounding the conspiracy were relatively well-aired compared to the furtive criminality of other Shakespearean overreachers like Richard III or Macbeth, who limited their associations strictly to the needs at hand. Discontented back-benchers could thereby lend their moral support to the principal conspirators as they made their way to the Capitol. Still, secrecy reigned among those within the loose conspiratorial circle, while obfuscation prevented those outside it from divining the nature of the crime about to unfold. On a personal level, Brutus's refusal to discuss his conspiracy with Portia reveals a guilty mind. By contrast, Caesar's openness is highlighted by his relationship with Calphurnia, who agrees to disagree with him about his public appearances during the ides of March.

Count Two of the charges before the IMT dealt with the violation of peace and its attendant international treaties, what Justice Jackson succinctly terms the Nazi leaders' orders to "goose-step the Herrenvolk across international frontiers" (*IMT* 19: 399). It is a logical successor to Count One because brazen assassinations inevitably foster opposition groups at home or abroad. Brutus tacitly admits this eventuality in demanding that the conspirators appear as "purgers, not murderers" (2.1.180). Yet their act succeeds only in marring a successful and legitimate reign; indeed, the ease with which they kill Caesar owes to the fact that no compelling cause exists for such violence. The quashing of Pompey's legacy creates minor discord but the empire exhibits no extraordinary signs of festering discontent from mass starvation or repression of the nobility. Brutus wishes the populace to see the boldness of the slaughter as a symbol of forthrightness. He hopes his feigned regret will be taken as a sign that the act was unavoidable. Good theatrical use could be made of Plutarch's record that Brutus's death stroke went to Caesar's groin, hardly a noble thrust. Brutus's first thought after the murder is to disperse the conspirators amidst the populace to allay its fears. His professed republicanism becomes a cover for a guilty mind aimed at averting a just response.

Shakespeare uses highly theatrical means to suggest that the conspirators disturb the civil peace. Characters interpret these quasi-supernatural events with varying degrees of sincerity. Cassius finds the tempests buffeting Rome so exhilarating that he would brave fortune with his bare chest. Casca is more circumspect, allowing that the tempests might signify "civil strive in heaven, / Or else the world" (1.3.11–12). Caesar refuses to entertain the notion that supernatural signs portend doom, which can be taken as an indication of pride, political sagacity, or common sense. There is little doubt of his pride, but his refusal to heed the Soothsayer is based partly on the political urgency of maintaining his preeminence in the Senate. Seemingly idle warnings from street peddlers cannot reasonably be taken as grounds to suspend normal political procedures. Like Hamlet, Caesar accepts the inevitability of death, but while the Prince contemplates a providential pattern, Caesar rejects related fears out of pride of position:

> Cowards die many times before their deaths,
> The valiant never taste of death but once.
> Of all the wonders that I yet have heard,
> It seems to me most strange that men should fear,
> Seeing that death, a necessary end,
> Will come when it will come.   (2.2.32–37)

Caesar views his assassination stoically after realizing that the conspiracy has been engineered by his friend: *"Et tu, Brute?—*Then fall Caesar!"* (3.1.77). The premonitions of death have come to pass by human agency, but a metaphysical sign of justice not anticipated by the conspirators arrives in the form of Caesar's perturbed spirit. The peace shattered by the conspirators throws nature and society into disorder, the two thematic strands becoming interwoven in a monistic plot structure.

Because no just cause exists for continued military action, just execution of warfare is rendered impossible. The twin pillars upon which the rationale for warfare rests collapse in illegality even by Renaissance standards. Brutus and Cassius end as mere personalities gambling their fortunes at the expense of the citizenry they pretend to serve. They argue over unpaid bills in an irrational manner given the high stakes at Philippi. Thus, we are as surprised as Cassius at the news Brutus has held back concerning Portia's dreadful suicide. She becomes, in effect, the first to have judged him. Antony calls Brutus the best of the conspirators, but it is left to the audience to decide whether heading a conspiracy to assassinate a rightful ruler and leading his troops into aggressive, unpopular wars render him deserving of praise. Legally, he is not, nor does the play attempt to make him so apart from the pro forma panegyric at the close.

IV. Tragic Orations

Besides being forced to vacate his place in the empire, Brutus loses the decisive theatrical debate at the play's center in rather short order. Antony's three opening words: "Friends, Romans, countrymen" (3.2.73), expand outward in geographical and social definition just as each word does in syllabic length, giving his salutation a sense of dynamic forward movement. By contrast, Brutus's "Romans, countrymen, and lovers" meanders both directionally and syllabically (3.2.13). He fares no better with the remainder of his speech, which has a modicum of rhetorical structure but no particular logic. To paraphrase, since to quote him would be uninspiring, he entreats the mob to hear him that they might hear, believe him that they might believe, and judge him so that they might judge. Antony's speech has formal unity and logical development. Suggesting by innuendo his immediate purpose: "I come to bury Caesar, not to praise him," Antony aims a series of unforgettably ironic barbs at his foes: "But Brutus says he was ambitious, / And Brutus is an honorable man" (3.1.74, 86–87).

He convinces the mob with factual proof contained in the will that Caesar was not ambitious, ergo Brutus must be dishonorable. His speech has already established the groundwork for a factual demonstration by suggesting that Brutus's act was in itself dishonorable, therefore Brutus must be wrong as to his calumnies against Caesar's character. Antony regains sympathy for Caesar, plants the seeds of mutiny against the conspirators, and with rhetorical legerdemain forces the mob to demand that he read the will confirming Caesar's benevolence. Every other line is a show-stopper, whipping the audience into a frenzy of anger that sweeps the conspirators out the gates of Rome. Having brought the house down, Antony pauses briefly to admire the mischief he has sown by his "blunt" speech.

The power of Antony's debunking oration can hardly be overstated in terms of its influence on successive generations of audiences. English prosecutor G. D. Roberts must have had it in mind when in cross-examination he too employs "honour" ironically and repeatedly to contrast the Axis leaders' early promises of peace with their hostile actions: "Was any protest made by any of these honourable men at the breach of Germany's pledged word?" (*IMT* 9: 117). With such ironies the forensic qualities of the courtroom and stage merge perfectly. The theatricality of this scene runs right down to the plebes, who clap and hiss at their political leaders as if on cue at a stage play. Antony not only reduces Brutus's sophistical arguments to rubble, he reveals him to be the murderer that he is. Where Brutus obfuscates the truth, misrepresents his intentions, and hides facts about the conspiracy, Antony unearths the truth through irony and deduction, transforming what was said to be an honorable sacrifice into dishonorable murder.

Others may differ in this harsh assessment of Brutus, of course. A. C. Bradley believes he acts out of a "full conviction of right" (*Shakespearean* 22). Against those who claim Brutus's centrality as a tragic hero to be overstated, a group in which I include myself, Ernest Schanzer locates the unity of the play in Brutus's moral struggle between republican ends and Machiavellian means. He finds a stoic depth in Brutus's speech, which purports to have the best intentions of the empire at heart:

> For he has to defend the murder of the 'foremost man of the world' on a charge which he cannot substantiate. And all Antony has to do is discredit Brutus' allegation of Caesar's ambition in order to nullify his entire argument.
>
> (3–4)

Antony must not only demolish Brutus's argument but check the military force behind it. Entering the stage the weaker of the two men, Antony is forced to create a political counter-movement out of mere words while Brutus, fresh from an act of terrorism, merely attempts to suppress any response from a timorous public.

Julius Caesar marks the final tack in course before the great tragedies to follow. Shakespeare has distanced himself in this play and hereafter from his tragic figures and their fate. By contrast, Juliet, Romeo, and the Andronici enlist our strong support. The RSC's inspired Barbican staging of *Titus Andronicus*, with Brian Cox in the lead, struck me at first as being occasionally sentimental, though upon further consideration I believe that such emotions are written into the play as we witness the characters' Job-like suffering. Agony per se, however, does not necessarily constitute tragic punishment. *Julius Caesar* is relatively unsentimental and lean while providing the surplus of punishment that marks the great tragedies.

Brutus aims to hide conspiracy and murder in plain sight. Antony cannot prove conspiracy on short notice but he can deduce it. He cannot prove murder, but he can infer it by acting as a kind of Renaissance coroner, or murder investigator, and in so doing taint his foes. It is Shakespeare who links the inevitability of war and war crimes with such an act. Brutus and Cassius refer to Caesar as their revenger as they die *felo de se*, their guilty consciences confirming the same kind of criminality as was leveled in the indictments against the Nazi defendants.

Coke refers to Rome in evaluating James's political power: "The King which is Supream and Imperial is equivalent within this land to the power and authority that Caesar can challenge within his own Dominions" (4 *Institutes* 343). Caesar, like James, was limited by law and tradition in a way that did not constrain Hitler. Our World Wars have altered tragedy because we have responded in two divergent ways to their evils. First is the sort of legal action so bravely taken up by the IMT and which is being adopted along different procedural lines in the Hague as to Bosnian war crimes. In this vein, too, Catharine MacKinnon is currently helping to gain civil remedies on behalf of victimized Bosnian women. Second and more immediate to drama is the hollow, sardonic laugh that we hear responsively in Beckett's tragedies, for example. Today, neither the law nor tragedy can contain the horror of recent human barbarity; indeed, our civilizing institutions are often regarded as impotent or irrelevant. We have yet to assimilate the disasters of our century in a way that can be represented on stage without diminishing either drama or reality. Modern drama generally wrestles with moral and aesthetic issues without seeking assistance from the law, while Shakespeare found a way to do so by integrating foundational legal concepts into his tragic vision.

CHAPTER 10

TITUS ANDRONICUS AND 'INCORPORATE' ROME

The limited franchise granted by incorporation creates and dissolves the tragic subject in Shakespeare's Rome. The play theatricalizes the contradiction between the rights of citizens in a "realm of ends," to borrow Kant's terms (*Fundamental* 52), and the terrible punishment visited upon its victims. Unchecked revenge breaks down all distinctions between the order of imperial Rome and the world outside, where anarchy is presumed to reign. Intruders like Tamora carve out a legal niche in the body politic: "Titus, I am incorporate in Rome, / A Roman now adopted happily" (1.1.462–63). Fluid identities shape tragic figures in new and often terrible ways via the "Corporation, or a body incorporate, because the persons are made into a body" (1 *Institutes* 250a). Corporate laws of a more benevolent nature govern Shakespeare, the players, and his Renaissance audience by virtue of their presence at the theatrical event.

I will first treat the corporation in Renaissance case law as well as in the context of Kant's theory of retribution. Lucius slaughters Saturninus while uttering curses decidedly retributionist in nature: "There's meed for meed, death for a deadly deed!" (5.3.66). In Part II, I focus on Kant's punishment theory in relationship to the subject, using Hegel's ideas as a counterpoint. I will attempt to mitigate the fact that Kant's views are presented at something of a disadvantage here because the play carries the logic of retribution to extremes. If cannibalism is the zenith—or nadir—of corporeal revenge, then no better image of retribution exists than that of Titus and Lavinia collecting the ingredients for their ghoulish banquet. Part III evaluates the unique dialectic created in Shakespearean theatre between the corporation and the subject, with the edicts of the former becoming inscribed on the latter, for better or worse.

I. THE VIOLENT CORPORATION AND KANTIAN JUSTICE

Political institutions lacking what Kant calls "distributive justice" are unworthy of legal respect (*Metaphysics* 121), like Rome in this play. U.S. Chief Justice Marshall tells us that the corporation is "an artificial being, invisible, intangible, and existing only in contemplation of law."[1] Though conceptually elusive, it is a definition dating back to the Romans, steeped in the tradition of Coke and Blackstone, and rehearsed in countless trials, including the 1816 case of *Trustees of Dartmouth College v. Woodward* in which Marshall's remarks appear. This landmark decision allowed Dartmouth's trustees to act as an independent corporate body to manage the growth of the institution free of state control.[2] Similarly, the rationale in the 1591 (33 Eliz.) case of *The Warden of All-Souls Colledge in Oxon v. Tanworth* makes it a requirement that the corporation retain its original distinct identity, or "capacity" (1 *Croke* 232), to use the term favored by Renaissance jurists. Failing to do so puts its privileges and very existence at risk. So it is with Shakespeare's Rome, whose charter is too permeable for the good of its members.

Rome's defects predate Tamora's arrival because the political infighting at the outset shows the commonwealth to lack regular procedures for settling questions of succession. Given the *Black's Law Dictionary* definition of the corporation as a body with "a personality and existence distinct from that of its several members," corporations are to be treated apart from the misdeeds of their initiates, which is to forgive a great deal in this play. Aaron's acts parallel the difficult hypothetical situation described by Peter Arenella of a killer who seeks immunity from punishment by claiming to have been socialized apart from civil standards of moral accountability: "There are many forms of human evil but some do not issue from moral agents" (1622). Evil actions both originate from and endanger the Roman corporation because they are foundational and systemic. Titus, for example, never regrets sacrificing Alarbus, while Tamora, who spoke so movingly of the need for compassion where her son was concerned, shows none for Lavinia. Instead, pure revenge becomes the norm in Rome.

How the corporation deals with massive illegality is a perceived problem in both Renaissance society and the play. The 1623 (21 Jac.) case of *Dalton v. Episcopum Eliens* demands that corporations endure despite the actions of individual members. In this case, a bishop granted use of church land to Dalton, but the court restricted Dalton from extending his ownership by favoring the rights of the corporation: "Usurpations shall bind the Bishops who suffer them, but shall not bind their successors" (2 *Croke* 673). This opinion confirms prior common law rulings. The decision in *The Aldermen of Chesterfeilds Case* of 1584 (26–27 Eliz.) required that the corporation behave in such a way as to sustain rather than dissolve its charter. In this case, land granted by the Queen to the town of Chesterfeild [sic] was ordered to remain in trust rather than be sold because the corporation has the "capacity to take, but not to grant the Land to another" (1 *Croke* 35). The legal point is that by permitting evil to thrive, Rome fails to control bad behavior and distribute punishment in a manner that would otherwise keep its charter whole.

Kant's theory grants the lawgiver categorical immunity from prosecution on the grounds that he who dispenses punishment must logically be immune from punishment himself:

> But it cannot *punish* him (and the saying common in England, that the king, that is, the supreme executive authority, can do no wrong, means no more than this); for punishment is, again, an act of executive authority, which has the supreme capacity to *exercise coercion* in conformity with the law, and it would be self-contradictory for him to be subject to coercion.
> (*Metaphysics* 128)

Kant misconstrues the English maxim, however, for when Coke states that "the King being Gods Lieutenant cannot doe wrong" (2 *Institutes* 681), he means that the king's power of adjudication and punishment has been dispersed to the courts. Implicit in Coke's remark is the notion that the courts cannot do wrong because the aim of the laws by which they exist requires them to issue only good rulings. Kant does not understand that the English king already occupies a power-sharing role in Coke's theory. Kant's edict that the ruler must be obeyed even if he issues illegal or immoral orders would be only slightly less illogical to Coke than it would be to us today. Equally pertinent in Kant's theory is the passion with which he conveys his views on retribution:

> Accordingly, whatever undeserved evil you inflict upon another within the people, that you inflict upon yourself. If you insult him, you insult yourself; if you steal from him, you steal from yourself; if you strike him, you strike yourself; if you kill him, you kill yourself.   (*Metaphysics* 141)

The rhetorical elements of parallelism and repetition are designed for maximum emotional impact on the reader. Derrida points out the irony of this sort of emotionalism given Kant's attack on the passion he attributes to other contemporary philosophers.[3]

Though Kant assigns absolute priority to reason, it is nevertheless possible to give passion a legitimate place in retribution theory. Samuel Pillsbury concurs with Kant's essential moral vision but finds the emotion of righteous satisfaction to be a valid element in the rational dispensation of justice. Pillsbury's position is the Augustinian one of embracing biblical *agape,* wherein we hate the criminal deed while respecting the individual worth of the offender:

> This need not contradict the first principle of caring for all persons because we can still care for them as persons while hating their bad choices. . . . In retributive punishment, therefore, it should be appropriate—and sufficient— for the sentencer to hate the criminal deed.   (688)

Pillsbury separates the crime from the criminal out of a fundamental respect for the individual and would search for mitigating circumstances before imposing a sentence. In this, Pillsbury is more compassionate than Kant, who rates punishment against the criminal "in proportion to his *inner wickedness*" (*Metaphysics* 142). For Kant, punishment is a social and moral sanction that puts an end to the delict. Pillsbury's empathetic position is actually closer to Hegel, for whom the effects of punishment do not end with sentencing because the accused remains free to change in a positive or negative way as a matter of choice given the dialectical development of human thought. In the nineteenth century, Justice James Fitzjames Stephen promoted virulent hatred of criminals as good public policy with a somewhat caricatured version of Kant's position: "The sentence of the law is to the moral sentiment of the public . . . what a seal is to hot wax" (*History* 2: 81). Shakespeare critiques the effects of emotionalism in his Roman world perhaps more carefully than Kant does in his realm of ends.

Shakespeare approaches the issue of despotic rule in a more practical vein than Kant and therefore sees defects as inevitable under such systems, one possible outcome being the reign of terror.[4] In the perception of those who rule, like Richard III, Wolsey, or Tamora, personal power rises to the level of what Kant calls universal desire. No Shakespearean despot could find fault with Kant's categorical imperative: "I am never to act otherwise than so *that I could at the same time will that my maxim should become a universal law*" (*Fundamental* 17). If Kant does not endorse tyranny, he offers no serious checks to the abuse of power: "The head of state has only rights against his subjects and no duties (that he can be coerced to fulfill)" (*Metaphysics* 130). Kant's exemption fails conceptually as an apodictic principle of the categorical imperative, due more, no doubt, to ambiguous wording than poor judgment.

The 1884 case of *Regina v. Dudley and Stephens* tests the validity of Kantian juridical extremism, besides coincidentally invoking the theme of cannibalism. In this case, three seamen and a ship's boy were forced to abandon ship in a storm 1,600 miles off the Cape of Good Hope. After eighteen days at sea in a life boat with virtually no water or food and with no foreseeable hope of rescue, Dudley and Stephens initiated private discussions about killing the dying ship's boy for sustenance. A third sailor, Brooks, refused to give his assent. Dudley and Stephens nevertheless killed the boy with a knife wound to the throat. All three sailors lived off the boy's remains for four days until they were rescued by a passing vessel. That the ship's boy would have died before the rescue seems a virtual certainty because the three surviving sailors barely escaped their ordeal. The question before the bench concerned whether the act was one of murder or self-preservation.

Speaking for the court, Lord Coleridge found the two conspirators guilty on the grounds that the youth could neither resist nor consent to the act. The opinion was laced with lofty phrases concerning "the moral necessity, not of the preservation, but of the sacrifice of their lives for others, from which in no country, least of all, it is hoped, in England, will men ever shrink, as indeed, they have not shrunk" (Kadish 1983, 185). The link between morality and law to which Kant refers reappears in Lord Coleridge's ruling:

> Though law and morality are not the same, and many things may be immoral which are not necessarily illegal, yet the absolute divorce of law from morality would be of fatal consequence; and such divorce would follow if the temptation to murder in this case were to be held by law an absolute defence of it.
>
> (Kadish 1983, 185)

Though Kant would probably side with Lord Coleridge's verdict, his requirement that humans be treated as ends in themselves rather than as means to ends remains a valuable contribution to punishment theory in whatever form it might be adopted by the state. Still, taking his punishment theory literally tends to vitiate nuances that might point to a defendant's innocence.

Renaissance society granted relatively greater rights under the law to those fortunately placed in terms of class and economic standing. The 1606 (3 Jac.) case of *Predyman v. Wodry* illustrates the crown's unique ability to turn land transactions to its advantage. In this case, leased land seized by the king under attainder of treason was determined to be "vendable for his best profit" (2 *Croke's* 109). Ordinary citizens would have to jump through legal hoops to dispose of such land as a commodity. Similarly, Roman justice for those in authority is so partial as to make prey of its own citizens. Rome, like Tamora, will cannibalize her own children, an enlargement manifested symbolically on stage.

II. 'Incorporate' Retribution

If the weak king is said to create instability in Shakespeare's history plays, the danger in the tragedies springs from the strong king—he who makes his own will the law for himself and others. This is Sidney's point as well when he argues that tragedy "maketh kings fear to be tyrants" (*Defence* 96). For Kant, the risk of political instability outweighs some considerable loss of personal freedom. Faith instead of reason binds Kant's state. He admits that full justification for his authoritarian vision lies "wholly beyond the capability of all human reason" (*Fundamental* 82). Even Kant's "court of pure reason," the highest conceptual court in the land, "cannot explain the absolute necessity of an unconditional practical law (such as the categorical imperative must be)"; instead, we can merely "comprehend its *incomprehensibility*" (*Fundamental* 62, 84). While Kant allows that understanding, judgment, and reason interact in imaginative "free play" (*Judgement* 117), this union operates in a subjective realm that cannot finally decipher the real world beyond the finite limitations of human cognition. Kant demands that the subject link his free will to the state, not strictly to moral norms. As we have seen, however, the corporate state is not necessarily constrained by moral laws.

Treating retribution as a moral imperative, Kant shows relatively little interest in the process by which a despot might come to power: "The command 'Obey the authority that has power over you' does not inquire how it came to have this power (in order perhaps to undermine it)" (*Metaphysics* 177). Such inquiry is precisely what drives Shakespearean tragedy in its apodictic phases. Some of what the play lacks in overt metaphysical reflection it gains in its critical assessment of the self-destructive civil corporation. To show the corporate body destroying itself through imperial adventures or despotic rule is to reveal a logical lapse that Kant seems to overlook:

> To permit any resistance to this absolute power [*Machtvollkommenheit*] (resistance that would limit that supreme power) would be self-contradictory; for then this supreme power (which may be resisted), would not be the lawful supreme power which first determines what is to be publicly right or not.
>
> (*Metaphysics* 177)

Kant's logic is circular here; supreme power may not be questioned because it would not ipso facto be supreme.

The static nature of Kant's politico-moral philosophy is its main weakness from a dramatic standpoint, though the cognitive faculties of artistic appreciation to which he refers are in themselves formidable powers. His refrain that everyone has his own taste, which cannot be legislated, is a concession to this bifurcation of concepts and aesthetics: "The aesthetical Judgement is therefore a special faculty for judging of things according to a rule, but not according to concepts" (*Judgement* 38). While the political dynamic in Shakespearean tragedy shifts constantly, Kant's very imagery of a court of reason aligns his moral and metaphysical inquiry with preexistent authoritarian models, whether biblical or civic. His court downplays procedural questions and mitigating circumstances involving mens rea, evidence, and proof—all of which make a legal system legitimate. Even his prescribed punishment of symmetrical retribution is surprisingly unyielding and derivative, while, as Coke and Shakespeare know, details and exceptions necessarily alter the unfolding of legal decisions as well as tragedy.

To be incorporate in Rome is the sole aim of Romans and barbarians alike, but this status neither brings the state its requisite security nor endows its leaders with good judgment. No family is more essentially Roman than the Andronici, yet no family is more severely punished. Given Tamora's incorporation, Marcus speaks contradictorily when he asserts: "Thou art a Roman, be not barbarous" (1.1.378). Such incorporation nonetheless would be valid in Renaissance law:

> If a man be created by Letters Patents Duke, Marquesse, Earle, Viscount, or Baron, the dignity is so incorporated to him, according to the State given unto him by those Letters Patents, as the Duke, &c. by the common Law might be named by his Christian name, and by the name of his dignity, which standeth in lieu of his surname: as *Præcipe Johanni Duci Lancastreæ*. And

> the reason thereof is, for that the King by those Letters Patents creates him
> to the state, honour, and degree of Duke, &c. . . . and albeit a creation by writ
> hath not the same words, yet it has the same effect.   (2 *Institutes* 666)

Kant would agree that the identity of the commonwealth evolves politically: "The civil union *is* not so much a society but rather *makes*
one" (*Metaphysics* 121). At the same time, Kantian justice remains
rigid, creating friction between law and politics in the state. Tamora
finds that the quickest way to enfranchisement is through a liaison
accomplished by bodily as well as spiritual incorporation.

Shakespeare's tragic conception of Rome is not so much of a hierarchical structure which the ambitious seek to climb as they would a
ladder, however much this might be assumed by his characters; rather,
it is of a corporation with a permeable, horizontal, and dynamic structure in which various factions rise and fall over time. There is, finally,
very little support in the play for Aaron's assessment of his queen's
new position: "Now climbeth Tamora Olympus' top, / Safe out of
fortune's shot, and sits aloft" (2.1.1–2). Aaron's perspective is utterly
confounded by the leveling action of incorporation upon which
Shakespeare's play relies.

Shakespeare's corporate model here is very broadly pre-Hobbe-
sian, though without Hobbes's royalist assumptions. The play's images of the body politic as a grotesquely self-destructive machine strike
me as anticipating Hobbes's vision of a leviathan or behemoth:

> But as men, for the atteyning of peace, and conservation of themselves thereby,
> have made an Artificial Man, which we call a Commonwealth; so also have
> they made Artificial Chains, called *Civill Lawes*, which they themselves, by
> mutuall covenants, have fastned at one end, to the lips of that Man, or As-
> sembly, to whom they have given the Sovereign Power; and at the other end
> to their owne Ears.   (149)

For Kant, though, reason dictates that humanity see its "final purpose
of creation" as moral (*Judgement* 371), even if we cannot apprehend
the categories circumscribing our thought processes. Through reason, we can firmly "assume the being of a *moral* author of the real
world, that is, a God" (*Judgement* 384). Curiously, Hobbes admits a
broader range of extenuating circumstances than Kant, though his
treatise is on its surface more deterministic.

Hegel would agree with Kant that the subjective element can be
taken too far in legal decisions. Hegel regards the fascination with
subjectivity as a primary defining principle of modernity: "It is one of

the commonest blunders of abstract thinking to make private rights and private welfare count as *absolute* in opposition to the universality of the state" (*Right* 85). The assumption behind each philosopher's definition of subjectivity leads to divergent results. For Kant, reason preexists and organizes subjective and objective realms without contradiction. Subjectivity cannot be so neatly bifurcated for Hegel, who objects to the notion of an uncontradictable categorical imperative as being "productive of nothing, since where there is nothing, there can be no contradiction either" (*Right* 254). For Hegel, art can reveal any content, which is defined as the concept given a fully self-determined reality and consciousness. The work of art as well as the human soul can thus be the "medium for the existence and manifestation of the Absolute" (*Fine Art* 3: 17). Hegel finds Shakespeare's characters to have the "subjective freedom" of modernity while retaining the heroic proportions he admires in the characters of classical antiquity (*Right* 84), though he understands Kant's point implicitly when he derides the *Sturm und Drang* productions of his own age as irrational celebrations of absolute subjectivity.

Hegel remains ambivalent about the relationship between law and philosophy because idealistic visions of state order "always come on the scene too late" to dispense accurate social prescriptions (*Right* 12). Both Hegel and Kant favor a strong central authority, in Hegel's case a constitutional hereditary monarchy, but Hegel's flexible approach suggests that he would adopt positions closer to Coke, notably regarding mens rea. Coke's practicality would lead him to regard crime as being immoral, disruptive of public order, and therefore deserving of punishment under the proper rules of adjudication. Hegel treats crime more philosophically as a defect in subjectivity: "Crime, as the will which is implicitly null, *eo ipso* contains its negation in itself and this negation is manifested as punishment" (*Right* 72). He is relatively unconcerned with punishment as the satisfaction of the public's retributionist urges; nevertheless, he regards crime as an evil: "Crime is contingency as subjective willing of evil, and this is what the universal authority must prevent or bring to justice" (*Right* 146). More crucial to Hegel's essential dialectic, though, are the synthesis and reconciliation transpiring via the subject's cognitive faculties. He would thus consider any extreme pursuit of retribution to be an irrational or, at minimum, a wasteful act.

The subjective life of the individual, despite its vagaries, remains Hegel's starting point for the concrete realization of a full ethical existence. He criticizes Kant's public policy view that the law operates necessarily as a "restriction" of personal desires (*Right* 33). Though in some cases such impositions must arise, Hegel prefers that the individual grow into an understanding of his complete familial, social, and civic relationships. He presents his own hypothetical that complicates Kant's more absolutist stance:

> When St. Crispin stole leather to make shoes for the poor, his action was moral but wrong and so inadmissible. . . . Hence it is only the necessity of the immediate present which can justify a wrong action.   (*Right* 252)

To think in terms of such concrete exceptions puts the issue of mens rea into play, which Kant generally seeks to avoid. Hegel believes that the individual can ultimately know the thing-in-itself. Art can give external shape to the internal content of spirit; therefore, education for Hegel as for Coke becomes a more integral element in the subject's legal status than for Kant, where fear or avoidance of punishment predominates. The dialectic between particulars and universals that engrosses Hegel depends upon the continuing education of the subject.

For Hegel, advances in philosophy as such create the need for his dialectic since it alone can best address modernity. He refers to classical characters as proof that the mental element was far less compelling formerly because, as in the case of Antigone, punishment would have been accepted without question in its entirety. Antigone's metaphysical and social contract requires her to submit to both the just and unjust aspects of her fate: "It is a striking modern innovation to inquire continually about the motives of men's actions. Formerly the question was simply: 'Is he an honest man? Does he do his duty?'" (*Right* 251). Modern philosophy and art make these distinctions by definition; thus, Hegel addresses himself to the development in philosophy that splits the act and the intent. What is real and simultaneously ideal in Hegel's world is not a heavenly command or a structure embedded unalterably in consciousness but rather the idea that arises through reflection. The mind "gives itself actuality in world-history and is the absolute judge of the state" (*Right* 279). Hegel, in fairness, acknowledges that his unified view of reality builds upon Kant's position.

The belief in the efficacy of reason links both philosophers just as it associates them inevitably with legal issues. Hegel's dialectical definition of reason goes beyond what Anglo-American law can make of it, which owes perhaps to the fact that his points invariably respond to philosophical issues:

> Form in its most concrete significance is reason as speculative knowing, and content is reason as the substantive essence of actuality, whether ethical or natural. The known identity of these two is the philosophical Idea. (*Right* 12)

Hegel locates human emancipation in the unity of form and content in law, art, philosophy, and indeed all human affairs, which are all directed properly toward what he would call "the March of God in the world" (*Right* 279). This expansive view of the relationship between various humanistic activities contrasts with Kant's restrictive approach to the law, though both seek to define how the demands of the ethical state can be fulfilled.

It is only fair to lay out in brief Hegel's deficiencies relating to the legal positions he adopts, as has been done with Kant. Hegel's sense that the four great world-historical realms are those of the Orient, Greece, Rome, and the Germanic nations reveals a trace of chauvinism. Unlike Kant, he sees no need for international laws, which he regards as unworkable given the diversity of national interests. Strange, too, is his notion that war has a curative effect between peoples: "Just as the blowing of the winds preserves the sea from the foulness that would be the result of a prolonged calm, so also corruption in nature would be the result of prolonged, let alone 'perpetual' peace" (*Right* 210). He takes a swipe at Kant's call for world peace while on the other hand strongly opposing tyranny as an obnoxious system. Finally, though this cannot be considered a deficiency given that the English legal system is not immune from criticism, he regards the common law as overburdened with customs, traditions, and "eccentricities" (*Right* 266). Coke would no doubt reply that these eccentricities, exceptions, and delays help to ensure that individual rights are maintained under the common law. Between the generally forward-looking Hegel and the backward-looking Kant lies Renaissance common law, which is idiosyncratic and relatively unformalistic as compared to the Continental models that were inspired in part by these two great philosophers. Coke's instinct to distribute authority among various parties reveals itself perhaps most clearly in his historical evaluation of one of the great documents in English legal history: "The

Statute of Magna Charta is but a confirmation or restitution of the Common Law" (1 *Institutes* 81).[5]

III. THE INCORPORATE THEATRE AND THE REALM OF ENDS

Peter Brook calls the violence in *Titus Andronicus* a "ritual of bloodshed" (*Space* 47), and reasonably so. Still, Olivier's 1954–55 starring role in Brook's production was noted for its gritty, realistic presentation of an old warrior speaking to the audience through an "ocean-bed of fatigue" (Tynan 104). Olivier's performance gave credibility to the stage-worthiness of what had been a neglected tragedy. *King Lear* contains roughly as much violence as *Titus Andronicus,* but critics like Dr. Johnson view it as exceeding all bounds of propriety and poetic justice: "The barbarity of the spectacles and the general massacre which are here exhibited, can scarcely be conceived tolerable to any audience" (8: 750). In Deborah Warner's 1987–88 production, which I was fortunate to see at the Barbican, physical violence was not ritualized but played realistically to evoke compassion.[6] The play puts violence under a microscope rather than asking us to view it as though from afar.

While Marlowe introduces metaphysical division into his world view, and Kyd pathos, Shakespeare takes a new slant on metaphysics by focusing on the civic pathology of the Roman corporation. Aaron, we discover, pursues revenge out of mere inclination. This diminishes him as an overreacher relative to Tamburlaine, Faustus, or Gaveston because he, like the slightly ridiculous Edmund in *King Lear*, is merely an accessory to the tragic action. Saturninus's unorthodox succession parallels the legal doctrine of *suum cuique* enunciated by Marcus in justifying Bassianus's elopement: "This prince in justice seizeth but his own" (1.1.281). This doctrine rapidly splinters the factions constituting Rome's power base. Against this backdrop of political dissent and Tamora's ascent, Aaron's bombastic speeches merely parody Marlovian visions of an Ovidian paradise. By the logical extension of disproving the negative, Shakespeare would appear to endorse the concept of a corporation of sharers rather than of rulers or stars as the best alternative for the development of the Renaissance corporation, theatrical or otherwise.

Titus Andronicus is not merely sensational, though it has less apparent philosophical depth than the best contemporaneous tragedies or Shakespeare's later works. *Doctor Faustus,* the most amusing and least violent of Renaissance tragedies, uses devils, angels, and the Seven Deadly Sins as comic types to construct a profound psychological and intellectual world view based on the retributive model. The same juridical pattern is, however, present in *The Massacre at Paris* and *Tamburlaine*, which litter the stage with bodies. Shakespeare's representation of torture here goes beyond the metaphysical tradition from which Marlowe and other Elizabethan playwrights drew their inspiration.

In reacting passionately to his torments, Titus echoes not so much Marlowe but Thomas Kyd, notably in Hieronimo's grief over the loss of his son, Horatio. Unlike Titus, Hieronimo is an actor, lawyer, and impresario by profession, trained for orations including the ones he performs *non compos mentis*. From the start, then, Shakespeare forges a middle road between Kyd's rhetorical flourishes and Marlowe's poetical conceits. John Webster will come closest to understanding the complicated link Shakespeare establishes between human dignity and punishment, but even he takes an easier path by treating the law as a tool for satire and ridicule. Webster possesses more pure legal knowledge than Shakespeare, though he uses it to create tricks of plot and revenge, as in *The Devil's Law Case*, which concludes rather sententiously: "Bad suits, and not the law, breed the law's shame" (4.1.72). The legal rationale in Shakespeare's tragedies transcends its usefulness as fodder for plot devices.

Employing various stock characterizations in this play, including that of the revenger, Shakespeare uses them for dramatic ends wholly his own. In the otherwise unscintillating dialogue between Quintius and Martius, the stage trap is referred to as a "detested, dark, blood-drinking pit" with "ragged entrails" (2.3.224, 230). Enveloped in darkness, it is somehow illuminated artificially by a ring lying deep within it. This magical aura makes the pit comparable to "[Cocytus'] misty mouth" or a "swallowing womb" (2.3.236, 239). It mysteriously saps the strength of brothers flush with victory over the barbarians. The trap becomes a body laced with blood, a slaughtered and slaughtering force, a womb that swallows but does not expel, a hell-mouth bringing forth theatrically vibrant demons, devils, and attendant vices which serve Marlowe so well as symbols of depth psychology in *Doctor Faustus*. This fearsome earthen pit is also cast as a body subjected to outrageous pain and punishment, like a wounded predator that is to be both feared and pitied. Shakespeare's theatrical and philosophical aim is new to the extent that he refuses to employ the usual stage devils, props, and other such devices for traditional retributivist purposes.

Subtle new dramatic challenges emerge even in this violent play. The eulogy for Bassianus is surpassed in its effect by Marcus's elegy to the battered Lavinia. Marcus describes her pain for her as he sees the tortured, bewildered creature standing before him:

> Alas, a crimson river of warm blood,
> Like to a bubbling fountain stirr'd with wind,
> Doth rise and fall between thy rosed lips,
> Coming and going with thy honey breath.   (2.4.22–25)

The green world imagery that opened the hunt is transformed by physical torture as Marcus catalogues her injuries. Deborah Warner's production theatricalized the physical shock that would accompany the atrocities inflicted upon her. In dramatic terms, then, Shakespeare trumps a scene of lamentable carnage surrounding Bassianus's death with the spectacle occasioned by Lavinia's pathetic entrance. So dreadful is her situation that Titus momentarily forgets his despair over his sons' imminent execution. There exists a dramatic action of overreaching expressed not so much through the Faustian character as a social or metaphysical climber but by the play's very structure. It is a patterning that reflects the ongoing self-destruction of Rome, of sorrow heaped on sorrow, and of the self-mutilation that will soon visit Titus himself.

The battered body reveals signs of imposed corporate punishment. Self-mutilation as a visible symbol of fidelity to civic justice seems a reasonable policy to Titus if it can spare his sons. Parallel with such horrible displays is the silence with which Romans observe the damage that they inflict upon one another. Silences connote compassion, as when a messenger enters with "*two heads and a hand*" (3.1.233). It is a tricky matter to prevent such scenes from being taken for black humor because the silences are effective only for a short while, as Shakespeare seems to know. Marcus, who had just urged Titus to control his emotions, now overflows with anger: "Now let hot Aetna cool in Sicily, / And be my heart an ever-burning hell!" (3.1.241–42). Titus and Lavinia say nothing during this outburst; instead, she kisses him, adding a layer of theatrical sophistication to a play deemed overburdened with gore and injecting a tender note at a moment of ghoulish cruelty. These moments of silence are admittedly more subtly handled than Titus' outrage in the fly-killing scene, which often provokes nervous laughter in the theatre. The scene makes sense, though, because the fly is to Titus yet another being not merely killed but mutilated in an atmosphere of savage revenge. Shakespeare's lines come near enough to being as powerful as Marlowe's even early on, but he distributes his theatrical effects across a broader palette. Young Lucius's horror and confusion at the sight of Lavinia's shattered visage is but one indication of tragic greatness to come.

The revenge tradition Shakespeare inherited piled misery upon misery. Mutilation and justice are linked by Kyd when the distracted Hieronimo shocks his poor petitioners by tearing their parchments with his teeth. Such disfigurement intensifies when Hieronimo bites off his tongue rather than reveal his secrets. In the *First Part of Hieronimo*, Andrea equates tragedy with distress: "This misery / Aims at some fatal pointed tragedy" (vii. 95–96). The goal of Revenge in *The Spanish Tragedy* is similarly to turn the characters' "joys to pain, their bliss to misery" (1.5.10). Shakespeare remolds the genre with Titus's laughter in the depth of his despair:

Marcus:	Why dost thou laugh? It fits not with this hour.
Titus:	Why, I have not another tear to shed.
	Besides, this sorrow is an enemy,
	And would usurp upon my wat'ry eyes,
	And make them blind with tributary tears;
	Then which way shall I find Revenge's cave? (3.1.265–70)

Where Kyd and his script doctor, Ben Jonson, heighten scenes of woe, Shakespeare treats them with a new, more complicated coloration by mixing emotions which if not handled properly can produce an unwanted reaction from the audience. Titus's request that Lavinia exit bearing his hand between her teeth is grotesque, though with effective staging the tragic action can be realized.

If Shakespeare elicits sympathy for his battered characters, he also heightens suspense during Lavinia's disclosure of the identity of her assailants. It is perhaps unrealistic to assume that so much time would pass before she would carve her tormentors' names in the sand, but it is a plot contrivance we accept if the performers have registered the full agony of these assaults, thereby sparing us facile stage recoveries from the violence. Hereafter, Titus's rituals and vows mark him as a revenger. A second ritualistic swearing scene with Titus confirms the exact course the revenge will take. By asking that Lucius employ the Goths to overwhelm Rome, Titus would have his city be engorged by the chaos that lies beyond her walls. Retribution is redefined as personal justice writ large, making Titus' private will the will of all, to borrow Kant's phrasing.

Displays of physical pain predominate over psychological disorders because the play makes only an initial foray into the mental element of tragedy relative to the more mature works. Titus is generally perceived to have become mentally incompetent, but it is a condition logically borne of despair and physical torment. In other words, when Aaron refers to Titus as being mad, he sees his foe as another Hieronimo. Titus is fooled by appearances for a time, a common enough malady, but his distraction is motivated by outrage over wrongdoing of the kind represented in *The Spanish Tragedy*. *Titus Andronicus* cannot be said to have too much gratuitous violence; instead, there is as yet perhaps insufficient concomitant reflection upon the full legal and psychological implications of the slaughters to match the physical horrors of revenge punishment.

The self-devouring corporation theatricalizes itself when Tamora enlists stage types to attempt to dupe Titus: Tamora taking the part of Revenge, Chiron of Rape, and Demetrius of Murder. Titus plays along with his foes' theatrical game: "How like the Empress and her sons you are!" (5.2.84). Titus's feigned inability to penetrate their disguises suffices to convince Tamora that his madness is real. She and her associates laugh at him as an ineffectual ranter who can discern only their superficial identities as symbolic demons and criminals. Retaining the mask of a madman, Titus asks them to punish themselves in a formulation much like Kant's retribution theory: "And when thou find'st a man that's like thyself, / Good Murther, stab him, he's a murtherer" (5.2.99–100). The play presents a wryly comical aspect of suspense when Titus confirms his own plot in an aside: "I knew them all though they suppos'd me mad, / And will o'erreach them in their own devices" (5.2.142–43). He uses a spectrum of emotional tones to enact his vengeance, but this is not madness, for in Rome, to be mad is to be unable to revenge oneself upon one's foes.

A vision of revenge in the form of Banquo's ghost interrupts the banquet in *Macbeth* because the action is more psychologically centered and metaphysically complex. Here, revenge leads Titus to prepare a banquet in which newly enfranchised Roman citizens are literally to eat their young:

> Hark, villains, I will grind your bones to dust,
> And with your blood and it I'll make a paste,
> And of the paste a coffin I will rear,

And make two pasties of your shameful heads,
And bid that strumpet, your unhallowed dam,
Like to the earth swallow her own increase. (5.2.186–91)

As Titus's communion of human self-consumption is fulfilled, he shocks everyone by slaughtering Lavinia. The delicacies have scarcely had a chance to cool before Rome has made a complete banquet of the banqueters. With the aid of the invading Goths, Lucius absorbs Rome, Aaron faces torture, and Tamora's remains will be devoured by birds of prey.

In near-benedictory tones unusual in a Shakespearean denouement, Marcus asks that Rome forgive these punishments for the sake of unity: "O, let me teach you how to knit again / This scattered corn into one mutual sheaf, / These broken limbs again into one body" (5.3.70–72). Marcus's fear is Rome's perpetual reality, but the play may be said to suggest that it is a present theatrical condition as well. Titus orders arrows to be shot into the heavens, to whose inhabitants he had prayed for divine justice. Marcus asks that the arrows be directed "into the court" (4.3.62), though whether the shots are mimed or actually loosed to the sky, possibly into the Thames, remains unclear. The court to which Marcus refers lies beyond the theatrical walls. Like fictional Rome, London stands just outside the walls of the South Bank playhouses. Aaron, the unrepentant, culpable anti-corporation at the heart of the corporation, will be "fast'ned in the earth" before our eyes (5.3.183). Perhaps in a comic gesture, this character will remain on stage, watchful, as the actors and audience depart to their respective civic corporations.

Shakespeare's corporate model mirrors the predicament of the Elizabethan theatrical company. Shakespeare lived in an age of contracts, mutual sharers, and players who sought to form corporations, purchase property, and construct playhouses legally under the auspices of highly placed political figures. The theatre itself could, of course, obliquely present juridical and other verbal forms of contestation. It could refer to punishment in London, which was harsh and visible. Alarbus's sacrifice is not unlike the hanging, drawing, and quartering so voluminously documented by contemporary sources and recent theoreticians, as for example by Foucault.[7] Shakespeare's London theatre also had its rules of reward and retribution, its joint-stock mergers and acquisitions. Actors were hired and fired; plays toured outside of London and even outside the country. Will Kempe, then of Strange's Men, is thought to have played Elsinore circa 1586. The Strange's,

Worcester's, and Admiral's Men became the 1590–91 Admiral's Strange's Men, which in turn evolved into Pembroke's Men and Burbage's company. After fits and starts, by 1594 members of Pembroke's Men in large measure formed the Lord Chamberlain's Men. In 1603, this company became the King's Men, in which Shakespeare had a one-fifth to one-twelfth share depending upon the number of sharers that were allowed to incorporate themselves into the group. This amorphous structure of actors and playwrights in a few instances developed a slightly unstable but enlightened new corporate arrangement to benefit England's most skilled performers.

The basic outline of Shakespearean tragedy as the representation of excessive punishment in exceptional circumstances appears in this early play. *Titus Andronicus* can therefore be favorably compared to such Renaissance works as *Arden of Feversham* and *A Yorkshire Tragedy*, which, despite their other virtues, present criminal characters whose motivations are unexceptional and who receive at best perfunctory punishment.[8] Though England produced an era of theatrical richness unparalleled since the age of classical Greece, the transitory alliances and personnel shifts in companies during the period when *Titus Andronicus* was staged must have seemed wrenching even to relatively secure theatre professionals. The tone of many of these early tragedies, including this play, treads the borderline between tragedy and comedy and thus corresponds to what must have been felt in the theatre when performers, widely perceived to be rogues and vagabonds, could aspire to mold themselves into legitimate companies with permanent standing. John Heminge and Henry Condell provide further evidence of such security by having produced a folio of Shakespeare's works, memorializing their finest playwright and valued colleague. The dislocation caused by the corporate administration of theatrical justice is reflected conceptually in this play by the audience's departure from the performance itself, when the Londoners returned to their version of Rome.

NOTES

INTRODUCTION

1   It was high treason merely to "compasse or imagine the death of our lord the king, of my lady his queene" (3 *Institutes* 2). A preemptive blow against such a perceived intruder would be uncontroversial in the law.

2   Shakespeare undoubtedly took an interest in the actions to which he was party, but a modicum of research and observation went far enough in his chosen profession toward grasping a few broad legal concepts and procedures. A full account Shakespeare's personal legal activity can be found in the work of E. K. Chambers or S. Schoenbaum, among others. The execution of his will was a matter for the ecclesiastical "Prerogative Court" (4 *Institutes* 335). Shakespeare successfully used various lower courts to sue for recovery of small debts as well as to establish himself as a gentleman by reconstructing the accomplishments of his father, John Shakespeare: "A Knight is by creation, and not by descent: a Gentleman is by descent" (2 *Institutes* 595).

Witnesses had cause for concern when appearing before Renaissance courts. The playwright's demeanor as recorded in his Belott-Mountjoy deposition of 11 May 1612 is subdued, understandable given the consequences of providing inaccurate testimony. This deposition in a matter of dowry and inheritance was taken in the Court of Requests, a lower court that often served as a traffic junction for determining whether cases ought to proceed to higher common law or Chancery courts:

> To the ffourth interrogatory this deponent sayth that the defendant promised to geue the said complainant a porcion ~~of monie and goodes~~ in marriadg<e> with Marye his daughter, but what certayne ~~some~~ **porcion** he rememberethe not, nor when to be payed ~~yf any some weare promissed~~, nor knoweth that the defendant promissed the ~~defendant~~ **plaintiff** twoe hundered poundes with this daughter Marye at the tyme of his decease.   (Chambers 2: 92)

The deponent avoids areas of ambiguity out of an abundance of caution. The courts were probably viewed ambivalently even by industrious citizens like Shakespeare, who may not themselves have been the focus of legal action.

CHAPTER 1
OTHELLO: COMPLICITY AND TRAGIC RETRIBUTION

1   5.2.294. All citations from Shakespeare's plays refer to *The Riverside
     Shakespeare*, 2nd ed., 1997. Legal citations observe the MLA guidelines.
     For clarity, U.S. legal references follow the Harvard *Bluebook* (16th ed.).

2   The occasional stridency of the law and literature debate in the 1980s has
     given way to a more conciliatory tone for three major reasons. First, Posner,
     West, Weisberg, and others have fine-tuned their earlier opinions. Second, a
     tacit understanding has taken hold that no useful purpose is served by fighting
     old ideological wars in this new field. Robin West sensed this problem as early
     as 1986: "The use of literature may have merely shifted the battleground"
     ("Submission" 1456). Third, these leading figures have felt the need to reject
     inappropriate labels that became assigned to them.
         Judge Posner has responded to the charge that he is a knee-jerk, right-
     wing capitalist: "I do not believe that economics holds all the keys to legal
     theory. Rather, I believe that economics is one of three keys," along with
     pragmatism and classical liberalism (*Overcoming* viii). Posner has always con-
     tributed greatly to the debate with his approach to law and economics and his
     juridical expertise. Similarly, for Richard Weisberg to be termed Nietzschean
     is to invite misinterpretation. Weisberg is no nihilist (and whether Nietzsche is
     one remains a complicated question): "The Law and Literature task here is to
     revivify the lawyer's grasp of rhetoric, but then to undertake the highly diffi-
     cult task of associating an esthetic or technical tool like rhetoric with a moral
     and abstract realm, which is ethics" ("Family" 73). Robin West is more con-
     cerned with improving society than scoring rhetorical points on behalf of a
     narrowly defined political agenda. Her studies of Kafka show that conscious-
     ness and human actions are extraordinarily complicated; therefore, she main-
     tains that "without understanding of this sort, we cannot attain true commu-
     nity, we cannot attain any meaningful justice" ("Economic" 877). A consensus
     has emerged that literature ought to be an elevating force in legal studies, a
     point first espoused by Justice Cardozo and later by James Boyd White, though
     with different assumptions.
         Judith Schenk Koffler critiques literature intelligently while arguing on be-
     half of political action: "I propose two defining attributes: one, an alliance
     that aims at generating political friction; . . . and two, an effective agitation of
     the organs of power" ("Forged" 1375). Another reformer is Stanley Fish, who
     has spent his recent theoretical energy questioning the validity of original
     intent, or objective, construction:

     . . . I'll put my faith in the convictions that grip me, and put my efforts into
     trying to get those convictions enacted into law. If this means the imposi-
     tion of my values on others, I prefer it to the imposition on me of the
     values thrown up by a process that is either guided by nothing or guided by
     forces and agents hiding behind it even as they preach the false (because
     impossible) gospel of neutrality.   ("Dueling" 19)

3 A robust law and literature debate raged one century ago over Shakespeare's education in light of the plays' many legal allusions. Those discounting the likelihood that Shakespeare had legal training include J. M. Robertson, who believes: "Shakespeare had no more law than half a dozen other Elizabethan dramatists . . . who were not lawyers" (*Baconian* ix). William C. Devecmon argues that Portia "makes five distinct rulings which are bad in law, logic, and in morals" (*In Re* 43). Another disbeliever is F. Lyman Windolf, who finds the gravediggers' chop-logic in *Hamlet* to be nothing more than "parodies" of legal thinking (*Reflections* 46).

    In the opposing camp, W. L. Rushton argues that the playwright must have been at least a student-at-law because "*recognizances, fines, double vouchers*, and recoveries are somewhat . . . technical and abstruse" (Rushton 7). A contemporary fellow-traveler is Sir Dunbar Plunket Barton, who finds the plays' legal citations compelling, though he wrongly asserts that Coke "derided poets as 'fools' and actors as 'vagrants'" (*Links* 59). Coke had tremendous respect for the great English poets, including Chaucer.

4 Cultural criticism centered on race and sex has dominated recent *Othello* criticism, counterbalancing older, less sensitive interpretations such as those of Thomas Rymer in his 1693 remarks on the playwright's use of an African protagonist: "He bestows a name on his *Moor*; and styles him the *Moor of Venice*: a Note of pre-eminence which History nor Heraldry can allow him" (*Tragedy* 87). Eamon Grennan finds "the theme of female abuse at the heart of the play" particularly in the violence surrounding the marriage bed ("Women's" 282). A. L. Little, Jr., argues that the play aggravates racial and sexual phobias surrounding interracial marriage by "associating it with other culturally horrifying scenes of sexuality, especially bestiality and homosexuality" ("Primal" 306).

5 7 *St. Tr.* 157. Sir James Fitzjames Stephen finds Iago guilty as accessory "for one single remark—'Do it not with poison, strangle her in bed',", but he notes that given Othello's suicide: "Iago, in the then state of the law, could not even have been brought to trial in England" (*History* 8). Presumably Sir James considers only Desdemona's murder relevant here. Sanford Kadish resolves "the problem of whether Iago can be convicted of a crime greater than Othello" by finding Iago guilty on the grounds of causation (*Blame* 182). John Kaplan and Robert Weisberg agree that Iago's mens rea makes him "more culpable" than Othello and allow that modern statutes separate the accessory's culpability from that of the perpetrator (*Criminal* 633).

6 Marvin Rosenberg believes that Iago suffers from a "familiar, severe functional disorder," or neurosis, which he calls "the ulcer 'type'" ("In Defense" 155), but he does not object to Iago's punishment. Coke describes pain *fort & dure* inflicted on those refusing to testify at criminal proceedings:

> The judgement is, that the man or woman shall be remanded to the Prison, and laid there in some low and dark house, where they shall lie naked on the bare earth . . . and one arme shall be drawne to one quarter of the

house, and the other arme to another quarter, and in the same manner shall be done with their legges, and there shall be laid upon their bodies iron and stone, so much as they may beare, and more. (2 *Institutes* 178)

7   Renaissance law required the coroner, or murder investigator, to establish seven facts before bringing a charge: "The fact [i.e., cause of death], 2. the year, 3. the day, 4. the hour, 5. the time of the King, 6. the Town where the fact was done, and lastly, with what weapon" (2 *Institutes* 317).

8   "Apocalyptic" 95. Deconstruction is an affirmative if skeptical literary theory, though the term has become twisted in everyday parlance to mean "destruction" or some other unrelated notion. I retain my interest in recent theorists including Jacques Derrida, Michel Foucault, and Paul Ricoeur, but for a more detailed study the reader can turn to my *Critical Hermeneutics and Shakespeare's History Plays*, New York, Peter Lang, 1992.

CHAPTER 2
MACBETH AND THE REASONABLENESS STANDARD IN LAW

1   For *Calvin's Case*, see 77 Eng. Rep. 377-411 (K.B. 1608). For *Reniger v. Fogossa*, see 1 *Plowden's Rep.* 1-20a.

2   Coke gave full control of juridical policy to Parliament:

The jurisdiction of this Court is so transcendent, that it maketh, inlargeth, diminisheth, abrogateth, repealeth, and reviveth, Laws, Statutes, Acts, and Ordinances, concerning matters Ecclesiastical, Capital, Criminal, Common, Civill, Martiall, Maritime, and the rest.   (1 *Institutes* 110)

According to Coke, the king had "distributed all his whole power of judicature to several Courts of Justice" (4 *Institutes* 70).

3   Psychoanalytical criticism follows Freud's basic paradigms and his focus on gender and morals: "It would be a perfect example of poetic justice in the manner of the talion if the childlessness of Macbeth and the barrenness of his Lady were the punishment for their crimes against the sanctity of generation" (*SE* 14: 321). Arthur Kirsch implicitly assigns blame to Macbeth by regarding parricide to be "like the denial of God, a negation of one's source of being" (280). In a similar vein, Robert Watson observes: "Macbeth is everyman; except that his ambitious impulses are cursed with the efficacy of action" (12). In Harry Berger's modified scapegoat theory, Duncan androgynously provides his subjects with "blood and milk" (25). Following Adelman, David Willbern discusses the pathology of gender roles: "*Macbeth* manifests a fatal con-fusion between 'feminine' otherness and 'masculine' ambition" (540-41). Norman Holland draws a flattering psychological image of the playwright: "A man who, like Shakespeare, can accept such imaginings and not only come to grips with them, but transmute them into moral, even bourgeois, drama, such a man has extraordinary strength and beauty of mind" (133).

4   Jury nullification throws the entire concept of a division of labor into up-
    heaval. IMT prosecutor Sidney S. Alderman defines the economy of knowl-
    edge and responsibility in American law courts:

> If I may be allowed to interpolate, an old law professor of mine
> used to present the curiosity of the law: that a judge is held to responsibil-
> ity for no knowledge of the law whatsoever, that a lawyer is held to a
> reasonable knowledge of the law, and a layman is held to an absolute knowl-
> edge of all the laws. It works inversely as to facts, or facts of common
> knowledge.   (*IMT* 2: 246–47)

CHAPTER 3
HAMLET AND THE WAGER OF LAW

1   Hamlet's moot court trial staged at the Supreme Court focuses not on com-
    mon law matters but on the prince's psychological status as a defense for
    killing Polonius. Expert defense witness Dr. Thomas Guttheil argued that
    Hamlet suffers from "bipolar manic depression" involving "rapid cycling"
    ("Trial"). His opinion was roundly rejected by a jury composed of legal
    noteworthies. The guilty verdict pronounced against Hamlet conveyed tones
    of a backlash against current "abuse excuse" theories. The jury suggested
    (through Justice Ruth Bader Ginsburg, if memory serves) that Hamlet be pros-
    ecuted for facilitating Ophelia's suicide.
        Hegel sees Hamlet's vengeance against a ruler lacking ethical stature as
    illustrative of the ethical imbalance to be found in Renaissance modernity:

> The real collision, therefore, does not turn on the fact that the son, in
> giving effect to a rightful sense of vengeance, is himself forced to violate
> morality, but rather on the particular personality, the inner life of Hamlet,
> whose noble soul is not steeled to this kind of energetic activity, but, while
> full of contempt of the world and life, what between making up his mind
> and attempting to carry into effect or preparing to carry into effect its
> resolves, is bandied from pillar to post, and finally through his own pro-
> crastination and the external course of events meets his own doom.
>   (*Fine Art* 4: 334–35)

This is a romantically leaning interpretation of Hamlet, but Antigone might
have responded differently and sooner in the same circumstances.

2   *Wigmore on Evidence* cites the relevant passage from 1 Ed. VI. c.12: "No
    person [shall be indicted or convicted of treason unless he] be accused by two
    lawful and sufficient witnesses, or shall willingly and without violence confess
    the same" (3: 293). Coke recognizes the need for multiple witnesses:

> Two lawfull accusers . . . are taken for two lawfull witnesses, for by two
> lawfull accusers, and accused by two lawfull witnesses . . . is all but one:
> which word (accusers) was used, because two witnesses ought directly to
> accuse, that is, charge the prisoner, for other accusers have we none in the

common law, and therefore lawful accusers must be such accusers as the law allow. (3 *Institutes* 25)

3 Wigmore defines the general hearsay rule: "When the statement of a person not in court is offered as evidence of the fact stated, the real ground of objection is that it has not been subjected to the test of trustworthiness which the law regards as desirable before listening to any testimonial evidence, namely, the test of cross-examination" (*Wigmore* 3A: 651).

4 Lee Ann Rappold's dissertation on *Hamlet* and the common law focuses on Fortinbras's rights and the burial of Ophelia: "Elizabethan common law was essentially land law; legal elements in *Hamlet* manifest the cultural obsession with land ownership, the chief sources of wealth, social prestige, and political power" (Rappold). Coke's remarks on criminal law and administration are equally extensive, of course. Benefits can be derived from the principle of organizing property ownership along clear lines even if one does not condone the manner in which it was distributed in Coke's age.

CHAPTER 4
KING LEAR AND THE LEGALITY OF MADNESS

1 For more on the *Prærogativa regis*, see W. S. Holdsworth, 1: 473 ff.

2 In his magisterial study, *Madness and Civilization*, Michel Foucault links insanity with apocalyptic images of death in the Renaissance: "In Shakespeare, madness is allied to death and murder. . . ." (31).

3 An "irresistible impulse" defense overcame traditional mens rea standards in *Daniel M'Naghten's Case* of 26 May 1843 (8 Eng. Rep., Lords, 718–24). This ruling was debated for nearly a century until statutes in the U.S. and England clarified the issue. Under current U.S. guidelines, insanity cannot hold if at the time of the offense the defendant understood the "nature of his act, and knew it was criminal and that if he committed it he would be doing wrong and would be punished" (18 USCS §1111, n 24 at 44). Convincing psychiatric testimony must support insanity defenses in court today.

4 Edmund does to himself what *Holwood v. Hopkins* of 1599–1600 (42 Eliz.) would consider libelous: "And for the calling one Bastard an Action lies, for Bastardy is triable by our Law" (1 *Croke* 787).

CHAPTER 5
VISIBLE GODS: *ANTONY AND CLEOPATRA*

1 H. A. Mason is rankled by comparisons of Antony to the deities since he regards the protagonist as not having adequately contemplated Heaven and Shakespeare as not having adequately essayed tragedy. Of Antony's Elysian fields speech, Mason declares: "This was a never-never land, even for a Roman" ("Telling" 343). Leonard Tennenhouse regards Antony's bond with

Cleopatra to be a deplorable, apolitical fantasy: "His sexual bond to Cleopatra strips Antony of his military judgment, deprives him of prowess in battle, and deceives him into committing suicide" (*Power* 144–45).

2   Critics question Antony's fidelity to patriarchal values. Maurice Charney suggests that the lovers' bedroom play, with its light-hearted cross-dressing, suggests his loss of mastery: "Cleopatra's dominance involves control of her lover's sword, the symbol of his manliness and soldiership" (*Roman* 130).

3   Antony's sensuality has drawn the most critical fire. Dr. Johnson and Coleridge seem to visualize the Antony created by Dryden, who, interestingly, gives Enobarbus's burnish'd throne speech to the protagonist. L. C. Knights finds Antony's revelries to be "self-consuming" stimulants nourishing an otherwise empty lifestyle: "Antony, in short, is galvanized into feeling; there is no true access of life and energy" (*Shakespearean* 147). For Kay Stockholder, Antony is unclear as to the influence women have on him, which in her Freudian analysis consists of him seeing women as whores and mothers: "Antony can afford to indulge erotic love only when he feels his identity protected by martial honour" (*Dream* 160). While Coleridge regards the play as perhaps the "most wonderful" of all Shakespeare's works, he still finds a "sense of criminality" in Cleopatra's sensuality, which by extension diminishes Antony (*Shakespearean* 1: 77).

4   Lawyer Wendy Kaminer describes the genesis of the Indianapolis law as involving an unusual alliance: "In 1984 anti-porn legislation devised by Andrea Dworkin and Catharine MacKinnon, defining pornography as a violation of women's civil rights, was introduced in the Indianapolis city council by an anti-ERA activist, passed with the support of the right, and signed into law by the Republican mayor, William H. Hudnut" (Kaminer 112). According to Dworkin, she and MacKinnon drafted a controversial Minneapolis statute on which the Indianapolis statute was modeled: "With Catharine MacKinnon, I drafted the first civil law against pornography" (Letter 15). MacKinnon's drive for censorship is based on a deep political conviction: "Sexuality is to feminism what work is to Marxism: that which is most one's own, yet most taken away" ("Feminism" 515). Judge Posner covers aspects of this topic with a different rationale (*Overcoming* 357–67).

CHAPTER 6
ROMEO AND JULIET: THE FAILURE OF RESTITUTION

1   Athenian law is emphatic in enforcing capital punishment for sacrilegious crimes, according to Durkheim:

> Yet these faults, so easily redeemable, were the ones that Athenian law punished with the greatest severity. They were:
>
> 1. Profanation of any *locus sacer*;
> 2. Profanation of any *locus religiosus*;
> 3. Divorce in case of marriage *per confarreationem*;

4. The coming of a male issue from such a marriage;

5. Exposure of a dead person to the rays of the sun;

6. The accomplishment without bad intention of some one of the scelera inexiabilia.   (*Division* 162)

2   Problems of restitution arise in the recent collapse of Barings Investment Bank's Singapore branch. The alleged misdoer, Nicholas Leeson, lost $1.4 billion for the company by engaging in untimely futures trades. Leeson could never begin to repay the sum, of course, so the moderate prison term he received was based on a calculus of decisions relating to modern German law that lie outside the provenance of this study. His case has inspired "A City Opera" for the Spitalfields Market Opera of London, whose artistic director, Philip Parr, suggests without naming Leeson that "it is quite obvious where the origin of the piece is" ("Barings" A10).

3   I treat Ernst Kantorowicz's application of this concept in *Critical Hermeneutics and Shakespeare's History Plays*.

4   David B. Stires reports that "perhaps the most striking element of juvenile restitution, however, is its rehabilitative effect on offenders" ("Beyond" A17). He cites several studies to support this remedy, aimed mainly at youthful offenders.

CHAPTER 7
CORIOLANUS: PUNISHMENT OF THE CIVIL BODY

1   Coke distinguishes common law from military court procedure:

And all matters done out of the Realm of England concerning warre, combate, or deeds of armes, shall be tryed and termined before the Constable and Marshall of England, before whom the trial is by witnesses, or by combate; and their proceeding is according to the civil law, and not by the oath of twelve men.   (1 *Institutes* 261)

2   Coke describes the mixture of Roman, Norman, and other laws in English common law:

For so many ancient Terms and words drawn from that legal French, are grown to be *Vocabula artis*, Vocables of Art, so apt and significant to express the true sense of the Laws, and are so woven in the Laws themselves, as it is in a manner impossible to change them, then if they were expressed in pure Latine.   (1 *Institutes* 9a, pref.)

Coke always favored strong parliamentary rule for reasons of national security: "The Romans vanquished our Ancestors the ancient Britains, for that they assembled not, they consulted not in common with them, nor Common Councels" (4 *Institutes* 9).

3   Desertion is a felony in the common law: "All idle and wandring souldiers or mariners, or idle persons wandring as souldiers or mariners, shall be reputed felons, and suffer as in case of felony" (3 *Institutes* 84).

4   Coke detests usury because it stifles normal human industry: "Usury is a contract upon the lone of money . . . directly against the Law of God . . . as a means either to exterminate, or to depauperate" (3 *Institutes* 151). He regards the practice as being "against the law of nature" (3 *Institutes* 152). The doubling of rent, for example, would qualify as a usurious practice (2 *Institutes* 89). He is by our standards entirely too sanguine about the mistreatment of Jews in English history, though to be fair it is he who records that English kings were the beneficiaries of supposed Jewish business practices between the reigns of Henry III and Edward I to the tune of £420,000. Coke admits gross hypocrisy in the annals of English legal history, which singled out Jews for deportation on charges of usury. The "Courts of the Justices assigned for the government of the Jewes" ended in 18 Ed. I when, by statute, the Jews were "utterly banished" from the realm (4 *Institutes* 254). A Chancery bureau continued through Coke's time: "The house annexed to his office, is called *domus Conversorum*, so called because H.3. founded this house to be a house of Jews as should be converted to the true religion of Jesus Christ, and there should have maintenance and allowance, which continueth to this day" (4 *Institutes* 95).

5   The second class status of women is obvious in Renaissance inheritance and property laws:

> If a man give Lands to a man, To have and to hold, to him and the heirs Males of his body, and to him and to the heires Females of his body, the estate of the heirs Females is in remainder, and the daughters shall not inherit any part, so long as there is issue Male, for the estate to the heirs males is first limited, and shall be first served; and it is as much to say, and after to the heirs females, Males in construction of Law are to be preferred.
>
> (1 *Institutes* 377)

6   Coke's definition of murder requires the element of malice aforethought, wording which today has been eliminated because it does not apply, for example, to a professional "hit":

> Murder is when a man of sound memory, and of the age of discretion, unlawfully killeth within any county of the realm any reasonable creature *in rerum natura* under the king's peace, with malice fore-thought, either expressed by the party, or implied by law, so as the party wounded, or hurt, &c. die of the wound, or hurt, &c. within a year and a day after the same.   (3 *Institutes* 47)

7   Shakespeare's innocent intimation of the capital crime of witchcraft is an anachronism that would have interested James. Coke defines a witch as "a person that hath conference with the devill, to consult with him or to do some

act" (3 *Institutes* 43). Also, minor Renaissance courts could prosecute scold-
ing; thus, Coriolanus's incorrect assertion to Aufidius: "'tis the first time that
ever / I was forc'd to scold" (5.6.104–05), had tangential legal implications.

Chapter 8
Timon of Athens as Utilitarian Tragedy

1   My introduction to this formula in criminal law theory came in a course taught
     by Professor Samuel Pillsbury at Loyola Law School, Los Angeles, where I
     studied briefly in 1993. My development of this topic reflects my own re-
     search; therefore, any faults herein are strictly my own.

2   Coke cites biblical authority for the death sentence in cases of treason:

> But this treason doth want an apt name, as tending not only to the hurt,
> but to the death of the king, and not the death of the king only, but of his
> whole kingdom, *Non Regis sed Regni*, that is, to the destruction and dis-
> solution of the frame and fabrick of this antient, famous, and ever-flourish-
> ing monarchy; even the deletion of our whole name and nation: 'And there-
> fore hold not thy tongue, O God; for so lo thine enemies make a murmuring,
> and they that hate thee have lift up their heads: They have said, Come, and
> let us root them out, that they be no more a people, and that the name of
> Israel may be no more in remembrance Psal. lxxxiii, 1–5. (*St.Tr.* 2: 167)

3   In Susan Handelman's Freudian analysis, Timon is a primitive, narcissistic
     ego engaging in a "demonstration of the rage which refuses to accept loss"
     (47). For Handelman, Timon becomes "Misanthropos, monster, and beast"
     (49), though she views Alcibiades as a responsible figure. G. K. Hunter speaks
     of Alcibiades favorably, too, terming Timon's emotionalism "so monomaniacally
     fixed in hatred of society that it is obviously as dependent on Athens now as it
     was in the old days of acceptance" (14). Una Ellis-Fermor assesses the play as
     an unfinished work. She regards the central character as "negative" and thus
     entirely lacking the stature of the great tragic heroes (280). For her, Timon is
     "inadequate to the theme," while the action fails to "knit together his fate
     with that of the other people in the play" (282). Harry Levin views the play as
     an increasingly dark "monodrama" that forced the playwright to reject his
     protagonist: "Shakespeare himself was so far from being Misanthropos, so
     very far from hating all mankind, that for once his negative capability got in
     the way of his dramaturgy" (90, 94). G. Wilson Knight reserves his most
     elevated prose for *Timon of Athens*—no mean feat. Timon becomes "Christ-
     like, he suffers that their pain may cease" (236); Alcibiades is a "merciful
     bearer of the heavenly command" (238).
          Critics from earlier centuries are far less exercised about Timon's mood
     swings. William Hazlitt claims that Timon is no misanthrope, for the charac-
     ter "neither loves to abhor himself nor others. All his vehement misanthropy
     is forced, up-hill work" (55). Coleridge has little to say about the central char-
     acter, though he does find the starkly satirical aspects of the play more appro-
     priate to the age of Charles I than James I (*Shakespearean* I: 75). Samuel

Johnson tosses off the play as a "domestick tragedy" with a cautionary purpose (8: 745). Like G. Wilson Knight, he evaluates the protagonist via the servants' reactions: "Nothing contributes more to the exaltation of Timon's character than the zeal and fidelity of his servants" (8: 728).

CHAPTER 9
JULIUS CAESAR AND THE PUNISHMENT OF WAR CRIMES

1   Beginning in 1864, the Geneva Conventions addressed the humane treatment of POWs and war dead. The 1907 Hague Peace Conference instituted rules of war at land and sea with respect to neutrals. The 1919 Versailles Treaty assigned war guilt to Germany, assessed reparations, and sought to limit future German rearmament. The 1925 Locarno Conferences instituted reciprocal peace treaties between signatory nations. The 1928 Kellogg-Briand Pact of Paris made aggressive war between the 65 signatory nations illegal. Germany was a party to all these treaties.

    The chief allied prosecutors made opening statements memorable both for their legal sagacity and philosophical depth. Justice Robert Jackson's opening is still regarded as a high-water mark in twentieth century advocacy. The statements of Sir Hartley Shawcross of Great Britain, M. François de Menthon of France, and General R. A. Rudenko of the USSR were also effective. It is held by some observers that the able assistant prosecutors for each nation, notably but not limited to Sir David Maxwell-Fyfe, fared better as courtroom lawyers in cross-examination than their superiors, but such diversity of talent is to be expected in a collaborative effort.

2   The original indictment included 24 defendants. Martin Bormann was tried in absentia, Robert Ley committed suicide prior to the trial, and Gustav Krupp was evaluated as physically unfit to stand before the tribunal. The defendants were charged individually as conspirators, which afforded the prosecution more flexibility than would have been allowed in Renaissance English common law. In the 1599 (41 Eliz.) case of *Marsh versus Vauhan & Veal*, a reversal of conviction was granted because only one of two alleged conspirators was convicted:

> The Defendants pleaded *Not Guilty*. And the one was found *Guilty*, and the other not. And It was hereupon moved, That the Bill should Abate. For It ought to be against two, And the one cannot Conspire alone. And the one being acquitted, The other Sole cannot be attainted.   (1 *Croke* 701)

Count Three, the mistreatment and execution of POWs and civilians, finds no precise equivalent in the play. Caesar's mangled body was obviously ignobly used, while Brutus's discontented troops are on the verge of mutiny. Count Four, Crimes against Humanity, is one that Shakespeare could not anticipate in the sense of systematic genocide, or what U.S. prosecutor Col. Taylor calls a "criminal holocaust" involving the murder of over six million Jews, Gypsies, gays, and other so-called undesirables (*IMT* 4: 439).

3   Justice Jackson's analysis of modern Continental warfare theory is correct, but he conflates the work of the medieval church fathers with Grotius's book on the rules of war written in 1625:

> The imperialistic expansion during the eighteenth and nineteenth centuries added the foul doctrine, contrary to the teachings of early Christian and international law scholars such as Grotius, that all wars are to be regarded as legitimate wars. The sum of these two doctrines was to give warmaking a complete immunity from accountability to law.   (*IMT* 2: 145)

Though it had no legal standing, Grotius's *The Law of War and Peace* is a remarkably humane treatise on the treatment of innocents in war. It would protect prisoners, reject despoliation of waters and lands, and prohibit unchivalrous tactics like poisoning wells. Recent international treaties adopted many of the suggestions contained in Grotius's work.

4   *2 Institutes* 388. "Secret hatreds, juvenile deliberations, and private avarice" (my translation). James condoned a secret act of piracy undertaken by his predecessor, as Coke explains while invoking, perhaps unwittingly, a Shakespearean play title:

> By the express purview of that statute (28 H.8. cap. 15) about the end of the reign of Queen Eliz. certain English Pyrats that had robbed on the Sea Merchants of Venice in amity with the Queen being not known, obtained a Coronation Pardon, whereby amongst other things the King pardoned them all felonies.   (1 *Institutes* 391)

5   Corin Redgrave, interview, *The Charlie Rose Show*, PBS, KCET, Los Angeles 12 Feb. 1996.

CHAPTER 10
TITUS ANDRONICUS AND 'INCORPORATE' ROME

1   The OED lists two relevant senses of the term as used in the Renaissance. One relates to the action of "combining into one body," a meaning I do not need to force to include acts of absorption undertaken by this Roman commonwealth. Another denotes a formal company with a corporate hierarchy, a structure well entrenched in the statutes of England. Following Coke's description of incorporation quite closely, Blackstone makes this historical assessment: "The honour of originally inventing these political constitutions entirely belongs to the Romans" (1 *Bl. Comm.* 468).

2   17 U.S. 518, 636. Justice Washington quotes Blackstone at 2 *Bl. Comm.* 37 in his assenting remarks on the Dartmouth case: "It is likewise a franchise for a number of persons to be incorporated, and subsist as a body politic; with power to maintain perpetual succession, and do other corporate acts; and each individual member of such corporation is also said to have a franchise or freedom" (17 U.S. at 657). Blackstone lists the essential features of the corporation: "1. To have perpetual succession, . . . 2. To sue or be sued, . . . 3.

To purchase lands, ... 4. To have a common seal, . . . 5. To make by-laws or private statutes for the better government of the corporation" (1 *Bl. Comm.* 474-75). Item 4 deserves elaboration because of its remarks on the body vis-à-vis the corporation:

> For a corporation, being an invisible body, cannot manifest it's [sic] intentions by any personal act or oral discourse: it therefore acts and speaks only by it's common seal. For, though the particular members may express their private consents to any act, by words, or by signing their names, yet this does not bind the corporation: it is the fixing of the seal, and that only, which unites the several assents of the individuals who compose the community, and makes one joint assent of the whole.   (1 *Bl. Comm.* 475)

3   Derrida observes that Kant goes beyond merely railing against false philosophers by arguing that "their crime is properly political, it is a matter for [*releve d'*] a kind of police. Farther on Kant will speak of the 'police in the realm of the sciences' (*'die Polizei in Reiche der Wissenschaften'*)" ("Apocalyptic" 70). Derrida regards as exaggerated Kant's concerns about emotionalists who perpetually threaten to plunge philosophy into the abyss.

4   Heather Kerr takes up the issue of Saturninus's juridical competency in finding Titus's sons guilty on the slender evidence of Aaron's incriminating letter in addition to "his failure to ask who is its author" (3). She finds fault with the ruler's "curious logic" and his "forestalling of a judicial enquiry in the form of the trial Titus anticipates" (3).

5   Coke cites three primary sources of legal authority: "1. By Acts of Parliament. 2. By Judgements and judicial proceedings: and lastly, by Book-cases" (4 *Institutes* 134). Coke recognizes at least thirteen other authorities, ranging from the Law of Nature to Forest Law (1 *Institutes* 11a). The reader should feel free to apply case law and theory interchangeably among the plays.

6   At UCLA, Brian Gibbons spoke at length about the realistic accuracy of the RSC's representation of the shock associated with Lavinia's physical distress. I found his remarks persuasive and would expand the theoretical and legal context in which violence may be said to permeate the action.

7   For a detailed description of these wracked bodies, see Foucault on the historical progress of punishment in *Discipline and Punish*, from "the gloomy festival of punishment" surrounding Renaissance torture to punishment today wherein "physical pain, the pain of the body itself, is no longer the constituent element of the penalty" (11). Sara Hanna suggests that outsiders incite Romans to violence: "The Romans define their community by denying the humanity of aliens, only to find the aliens within Rome, magnifying their own savage impulses" (11). Eugene Waith regards the gory description in *Macbeth* of Duncan's violent end as theatrically effective, but he deems the physical presence of Lavinia accompanied by the description of her injuries to be poetically inappropriate: "A physical impersonation of the mutilated Lavinia should not block our vision" (47). D. J. Palmer finds a process of expiation in this scene of woe: "But in *Titus Andronicus*, with its reiterative imagery of

the devouring mouth, the revenge action itself is also a ritualized sequence of repetition through substitution" (335). Mary L. Fawcett treats the violence conceptually as a language "physically centered but profoundly destructive" (271). She notes particularly in Titus's banquet preparations the recitation of "parts of the bodies until we begin to think the world is made up of nothing but hands, tongues, bones, throats, blood, heads, and stumps" (270).

8   Hart defines five categories constituting legal punishment, none of which Shakespeare follows entirely. The first holds true for all but exceptional characters like Cleopatra and Timon: "It must involve pain or other consequences normally considered unpleasant" (*Punishment* 4). Hart's second category: "It must be for an offence against legal rules" (5), only marginally applies to *Antony and Cleopatra*. Third, for punishment to "be of an actual or supposed offender for his offence" would involve a symmetry rarely observed in the tragedies (5). Hart's fourth element: "It must be intentionally administered by human beings other than the offender" (5), is violated by revengers like Hamlet and Othello. Hart's fifth category: "It must be imposed and administered by an authority constituted by a legal system against which the offence is committed" (5), is not uniformly applicable to Shakespearean tragedy for obvious reasons.

Works Cited

Adelman, Janet. "'Anger's my Meat': Feeding, Dependency, and Aggression in *Coriolanus*." *Representing Shakespeare: New Psychoanalytic Essays*. Ed. Murray M. Schwartz and Coppélia Kahn. Baltimore: Johns Hopkins UP, 1980. 129–49.

————. "'Born of Women': Fantasies of Maternal Power." *Cannibals, Witches, and Divorce: Estranging the Renaissance*. Ed. Marjorie Garber. Baltimore: Johns Hopkins UP, 1987. 90–121.

American Jurisprudence. Ed. David P. Van Knapp, et al. 2nd ed. Vol. 18. Rochester: Lawyers Cooperative, 1985. 83 vols.

American Law Institute. *Model Penal Code and Commentaries, Part II, §§210.0 to 213.6*. Vol. I. Philadelphia: ALI, 1980. 3 vols.

————. *Restatement (Second) of Torts §283*. Vol. 2. St. Paul: ALI, 1965. 7 vols.

Aquinas, St. Thomas. *Summa Theologicæ*. Trans. Thomas Gilbey, O.P. 60 vols. New York: McGraw, 1963.

Arden of Feversham (1592). Prep. Hugh Macdonald. London: Oxford UP, 1947.

Arenella, Peter. "Convicting the Morally Blameless: Reassessing the Relationship Between Legal and Moral Accountability." *UCLA Law Review* 39, 6 (1992): 1511–1622.

Augustine, Aurelius. *The Works of Aurelius Augustine*. Ed. and trans. Marcus Dods. 15 vols. Edinburgh: Clark, 1871.

"Barings Collapse Inspires Opera." *Wall Street Journal* 20 Oct. 1995: A10.

Barton, Sir Dunbar Plunket. *Links Between Shakespeare and the Law*. London: Faber, n. d. [c. 1929].

Berger, Harry, Jr. "The Early Scenes of *Macbeth*: Preface to a New Edition." *English Literary History* 47, 1 (1980): 1–31.

———. "Text Against Performance in Shakespeare: The Example of *Macbeth*." *The Power of Forms in the English Renaissance*. Ed. Stephen Greenblatt. Norman, OK: Pilgrim, 1982. 49–79.

Bible, The Holy. King James Version. New York: American Bible, 1975.

Black's Law Dictionary. Ed. Henry Campbell Black, et al. 6th ed. St. Paul: West, 1991.

Blackstone, Sir William. *Commentaries on the Laws of England*. Ed. Edward Christian. 4 vols. London: A. Strahan, 1803.

———. *Commentaries on the Laws of England [The Student's Blackstone]*. Ed. Robert Malcolm Kerr. London: Murray, 1880.

Bracton on the Laws and Customs of England. Ed. George W. Woodbine. Trans. Samuel E. Thorne. Vol. 2. Cambridge, MA: Belknap, 1968. 2 vols.

Bradley, A. C. *Shakespearean Tragedy*. London: Macmillan, 1937.

Bradwell, Stephen. *Mary Glovers Late Woeful Case. Witchcraft and Hysteria in Elizabethan England*. Ed. Michael MacDonald. London: Routledge, 1991. 1–150.

Brand, C. E. *Roman Military Law*. Austin: U of Texas P, 1968.

Brook, Peter. *The Empty Space*. New York: Atheneum, 1968.

Brooks, Alexander. *Law, Psychiatry, and the Mental Health System*. Boston: Little, 1974.

Burke, Kenneth. "*Coriolanus*—and the Delights of Faction." *Hudson Review* 19, 2 (1966): 185–202.

Burton, Robert. *Anatomy of Melancholy*. Ed. Thomas C. Faulkner, et al. 2 vols. Oxford: Clarendon, 1989.

Busby, Karen. "LEAF and Pornography: Litigating on Equality and Sexual Representation." *Canadian Journal of Law and Society* 9, 1 (1994): 165–92.

Calendar of Close Rolls, Edward I. Vol. 1. London: HMSO, 1900. 2 vols.

Canada Supreme Court Reports [RCS]. Vol. 1. Ottawa: Queen's, 1992. 3 vols.

Chambers, E. K. *William Shakespeare: A Study of Facts and Problems.* Vol. 2. Oxford: Clarendon, 1930. 2 vols.

Charney, Maurice. *Shakespeare's Roman Plays: The Function of Imagery in Drama.* Cambridge, MA: Harvard UP, 1961.

Coke, Sir Edward. *The First Part of the Institutes of the Laws of England; or, a Commentary upon Littleton.* London: Streater, 1670.

———. *The Second Part of the Institutes of the Laws of England.* London: Streater, 1671.

———. *The Third Part of the Institutes of the Laws of England.* London: W. Clarke, 1809.

———. *The Fourth Part of the Institutes of the Lawes of England.* London: Crooke, 1669.

———. *The Reports of Sir Edward Coke [Coke's K.B. Reports].* Ed. John Henry Thomas and John Farquahar Fraser. 6 vols. London: Butterworth, 1826.

———. *The Twelfth Part of the Reports of Sir Edward Coke.* Ed. Hen. Tywford and Tho. Basset. London: Atkins, 1677.

Coleridge, Samuel Taylor. *Shakespearean Criticism.* Ed. Thomas Middleton Raysor. 2 vols. London: Dent, 1964.

Croke, Sir George. *The First Part of the Reports of Sir George Croke.* Ed. and trans. (from French to English) Sir Harbottle Grimston. London: A. Roper, 1669.

———. *The Second Part of the Reports of Sir George Croke.* Ed. and trans. Sir Harbottle Grimston. London: T. Newcomb, 1659.

Derrida, Jacques. "Of an Apocalyptic Tone Recently Adopted in Philosophy." *Semeia* 23 (1982): 63–97.

Devecmon, William C. *In Re Shakespeare's "Legal Acquirements."* New York: AMS, 1899.

Dryden, John. *All for Love: or, the World Well Lost.* Ed. N. J. Andrew. London: Benn, 1975.

Durkheim, Emile. *The Division of Labor in Society.* Trans. George Simpson. New York: Free, 1966.

Dworkin, Andrea. *Our Blood: Prophecies and Discourses on Sexual Politics.* New York: Harper, 1976.

————. Letter. *New York Times Book Review* 3 May 1992: 15.

Ellis-Fermor, Una. "*Timon of Athens*: An Unfinished Play." *Review of English Studies* 18 (1942): 270–83.

English Reports. Ed. John Farquhar Fraser, et al. 177 vols. Edinburgh: Green, 1907.

Fawcett, Mary L. "Arms/Words/Tears: Language and the Body in *Titus Andronicus.*" *English Literary History* 50, 2 (1983): 261–77.

Federal Reporter 2d [American Booksellers v. Hudnut]. 1,031 vols. to date. St. Paul: West, 1985–. Vol. 771. 323–34.

Fish, Stanley. "Dueling Pens: A Friendly Exchange About Unfriendly Words." Rejoinder to Franklyn S. Haimon. *Civil Liberties* 380 (Spring 1994): 18–20.

Foucault, Michel. *Discipline and Punish: The Birth of the Prison.* Trans. Alan Sheridan. New York: Vintage, 1979.

————. *Madness and Civilization: A History of Insanity in the Age of Reason.* Trans. Richard Howard. New York: Pantheon, 1965.

Freud, Sigmund. *The Standard Edition of the Complete Psychological Works of Sigmund Freud.* Gen. ed. James Strachey. 24 vols. London: Hogarth, 1966–73.

Gibbons, Brian. "The Verbal and the Visual in *Titus Andronicus.*" UCLA Center for Medieval and Renaissance Studies Conference: Shakespeare's Roman Plays. U of California, Los Angeles. 25 Feb. 1994.

Gielgud, Sir John. *Stage Directions.* New York: Random, 1963.

Greenblatt, Stephen. "Invisible Bullets: Renaissance Authority and Its Subversion." *Shakespeare's Rough Magic: Renaissance Essays in Honor of C. L. Barber*. Ed. Peter Erickson and Coppélia Kahn. Newark: U of Delaware P, 1985. 276–302.

Grennan, Eamon. "The Women's Voices in *Othello*: Speech, Silence, Song." *Shakespeare Quarterly* 38, 3 (1987): 275–92.

Gurr, Andrew. "Coriolanus and the Body Politic." *Shakespeare Survey 28*. Cambridge: Cambridge UP, 1975. 63–69.

Handelman, Susan. "*Timon of Athens*: The Rage of Disillusion." *American Imago* 1, 36 (1979): 45–68.

Hanna, Sara. "Raising Babel and Inferno in *Titus Andronicus*." *Shakespeare Yearbook*. Ed. Holgar Klein. Vol. 3. Lewiston, NY: Edwin Mellen, 1992. 11–29.

Hart, H. L. A. *Essays in Jurisprudence and Philosophy*. Oxford: Clarendon, 1983.

———. *Punishment and Responsibility: Essays in the Philosophy of Law*. New York: Oxford UP, 1968.

Hawley, William M. *Critical Hermeneutics and Shakespeare's History Plays*. New York: Peter Lang, 1992.

Hazlitt, William. *Characters of Shakespeare's Plays*. Intro. Sir Arthur Quiller-Couch. London: Oxford, 1934.

Hegel, G. W. F. *Hegel's Philosophy of Right*. Trans. and notes T. M. Knox. Oxford: Clarendon, 1953.

———. *The Philosophy of Fine Art*. Trans. and notes F. P. B. Osmaston. 4 vols. New York: Hacker, 1975.

Hobbes, Thomas. *Leviathan*. Ed. A. R. Waller. Cambridge: Cambridge UP, 1935.

Hofling, Charles K., M.D. "An Interpretation of Shakespeare's *Coriolanus*." *American Imago* 14, 4 (1957): 407–35.

Holdsworth, W. S. *A History of English Law*. 16 vols. Boston: Little, 1922.

Holinshed, Raphael. *Holinshed's Chronicles of England, Scotland, and Ireland*. Vol. 5. J. Johnson, 1808. 6 vols.

Holland, Norman N. *Psychoanalysis and Shakespeare*. New York: McGraw, 1964.

Hunter, G. K. "The Last Tragic Hero." *Later Shakespeare.* Ed. John Russell Brown and Bernard Harris. New York: St. Martin's, 1967. 11–28.

Hunter, Richard, and Ida Macalpine, eds. *Three Hundred Years of Psychiatry, 1535–1860.* London: Oxford, 1963.

James I. *Daemonology* (1597) and *Newes From Scotland* (1591). Ed. G. B. Harrison. London: Bodley, 1924.

Johnson, Samuel. *Johnson on Shakespeare. The Yale Edition of the Works of Samuel Johnson.* Ed. Arthur Sherbo, et al. Introd. Bertrand Bronson. Vols. 7–8. New Haven: Yale UP, 1968. 16 vols.

Jorden, Dr. Edward. *A Briefe Discourse of a Disease Called the Suffocation of the Mother.* London: Windet, 1603.

Justinian. *Corpus Juris Civilis.* Trans. S. P. Scott. Vols. 1–11. New York: AMS, 1973. 17 vols.

Kadish, Sanford H. *Blame and Punishment: Essays in the Criminal Law.* New York: Macmillan, 1987.

Kadish, Sanford H., Stephen J. Schulhofer, and Monrad G. Paulsen. *Criminal Law and Its Processes: Cases and Materials.* 4th ed. Boston: Little, 1983.

Kaminer, Wendy. "Feminists Against the First Amendment." *Atlantic Monthly* Nov. 1992: 111–18.

Kant, Immanuel. *The Fundamental Principles of the Metaphysics of Ethics.* Trans. Otto Manthey-Zorn. New York: Appleton, 1938.

———. *Kant's Critique of Judgement.* Trans. and introd. J. H. Bernard. 2nd ed. Rev. ed. London: Macmillan, 1914.

———. *The Metaphysical Elements of Justice.* Trans. John Ladd. Indianapolis: Bobbs, 1965.

———. *The Metaphysics of Ethics.* Trans. T. W. Semple. 3rd ed. Edinburgh: Clark, 1871.

———. *The Metaphysics of Morals.* Trans. Mary Gregor. Cambridge: Cambridge UP, 1991.

Kaplan, John, and Robert Weisberg. *Criminal Law: Cases and Materials.* 2nd ed. Boston: Little, 1986.

Kerr, Heather. "Aaron's Letter and Acts of Reading: The Text as Evidence in *Titus Andronicus*." *Australasian Universities Modern Language Association* 77 (1992): 1–19.

Kirsch, Arthur. "Macbeth's Suicide." *English Literary History* 51, 2 (1984): 269–96.

Knight, G. Wilson. *The Wheel of Fire: Interpretations of Shakespearean Tragedy with Three New Essays*. Rev. ed. London: Methuen, 1949.

Knights, L. C. *Some Shakespearean Themes*. London: Chatto, 1959.

Koffler, Judith Schenk. "Forged Alliance: Law and Literature." *Columbia Law Review* 89, 6 (1989): 1374–93.

Kornstein, Daniel J. *Kill All the Laywers? Shakespeare's Legal Appeal*. Princeton: Princeton UP, 1994.

Kyd, Thomas. *The First Part of Hieronimo and The Spanish Tragedy*. Ed. Andrew S. Cairncross. Lincoln: U of Nebraska P, 1967.

Lacan, Jacques. *The Four Fundamental Concepts of Psychoanalysis*. Ed. Jacques-Alain Miller. Trans. Alan Sheridan. New York: Norton, 1978.

Levin, Harry. "Shakespeare's Misanthrope." *Shakespeare Survey 26*. Ed. Kenneth Muir. Cambridge: Cambridge UP, 1973. 89–94.

Little, Arthur L., Jr. "'An essence that's not seen': The Primal Scene of Racism in *Othello*." *Shakespeare Quarterly* 44, 3 (1993): 304–24.

"Little Sister v. Big Brother." *Toronto Globe and Mail* 8 Oct. 1994: C1–2.

Lowe, Lisa. "'Say I play the man I am': Gender and Politics in *Coriolanus*." *Kenyon Review* 8, 4 (1986): 364–81.

MacDonald, Michael, and Terence R. Murphy. *Sleepless Souls: Suicide in Early Modern Britain*. Oxford: Clarendon, 1990.

MacKinnon, Catharine A. "Feminism, Marxism, Method, and the State: An Agenda for Theory." *Signs: Journal of Women in Culture and Society* 7, 3 (1982): 515–44.

———. *Toward a Feminist Theory of the State*. Cambridge, MA: Harvard UP, 1989.

Marowitz, Charles, and Simon Trussler, eds. *Theatre at Work: Play-wrights and Productions in the Modern British Theatre.* London: Methuen, 1967.

Mason, H. A. "*Anthony and Cleopatra*: Telling *versus* Shewing." *Cambridge Quarterly* 1, 4 (1966): 330–54.

Mitchell, John L., and David Ferrell. "Faal Emerging From Denny Case as Rising Legal Star." *Los Angeles Times* 20 Oct. 1993: A18.

North, Sir Thomas, trans. *Plutarch's Lives of the Noble Grecians and Romanes.* Vol. 6. Oxford: Blackwell, 1927. 8 vols.

Olivier, Laurence. *On Acting.* New York: Simon, 1986.

Orgel, Stephen. *The Illusion of Power: Political Theatre in the English Renaissance.* Berkeley: U of California P, 1975.

Palmer, D. J. "The Unspeakable in Pursuit of the Uneatable: Language and Action in *Titus Andronicus.*" *Critical Quarterly* 14, 4 (1972): 320–39.

Pillsbury, Samuel. "Emotional Justice: Moralizing the Passions of Criminal Punishment." *Cornell Law Review* 74, 4 (1989): 655–710.

Pitney, Rufus. "Coriolanus and his Mother." *Psychoanalytic Quarterly* 31, 3 (1962): 364–81.

Plowden's Reports. Ed. Edmund Plowden. 2 vols. London: Brooke, 1816.

Posner, Richard A. *Law and Literature: A Misunderstood Relation.* Cambridge, MA: Harvard UP, 1988.

———. *Overcoming Law.* Cambridge, MA: Harvard UP, 1995.

Rabkin, Norman. "*Coriolanus*: The Tragedy of Politics." *Shakespeare Quarterly* 17, 3 (1966): 195–212.

Rappold, Lee Ann. "*Hamlet* and the Elizabethan Common Law." *DAI* 53/12 (June 1993): 4337A. UC Santa Cruz.

Redgrave, Corin. Interview, *The Charlie Rose Show.* PBS. KCET. Los Angeles. 12 Feb. 1996.

Roberts, Peter. "King Lear." *Plays and Players* Feb. 1963: 53.

Robertson, J. M. *The Baconian Heresy: A Confutation.* London: Junkers, 1923.

Rodger, N. A. M., ed. *Articles of War: 1661, 1749, and 1866.* Emsworth, Eng.: Mason, 1982.

Rosenberg, Marvin. "In Defense of Iago." *Shakespeare Quarterly* 6, 2 (1955): 145–58.

Rushton, W. L. *Shakespeare a Lawyer.* London: Longman, 1858.

Rymer, Thomas. *A Short View of Tragedy.* London: Baldwin, 1693.

Schanzer, Ernest. "The Tragedy of Shakespeare's Brutus." *English Literary History* 21, 1 (1955): 1–15.

Schoenbaum, S. *William Shakespeare: A Documentary Life.* New York: Oxford UP, 1975.

Shakespeare, William. *The Riverside Shakespeare.* Gen. ed. Blakemore Evans and J. J. M. Tobin. 2nd ed. Boston: Houghton, 1997.

Sidney, Sir Philip. *A Defence of Poetry. Miscellaneous Prose of Sir Philip Sidney.* Ed. Katharine Duncan-Jones and Jan Van Dorsten. Oxford: Clarendon, 1973. 73–121.

Sommers, Alan. "'Wilderness of Tigers': Structure and Symbolism in *Titus Andronicus.*" *Essays in Criticism* 10, 3 (1960): 275–89.

State Trials [A Complete Collection of State Trials]. Ed. T. B. Howell. 34 vols. London: Longman, 1816.

Stephen, Sir James Fitzjames. *A History of the Criminal Law in England.* Vols. 2–3. London: Macmillan, 1883. 3 vols.

Stires, David B. "Beyond Crime and Punishment—Restitution." *Wall Street Journal* 20 Sept. 1995: A17.

Stockholder, Kay. *Dream Works: Lovers and Families in Shakespeare's Plays.* Toronto: U of Toronto P, 1987.

Tennenhouse, Leonard. *Power on Display: The Politics of Shakespeare's Genres.* New York: Methuen, 1986.

Toobin, Jeffrey. "X-Rated." *New Yorker* 3 Oct. 1994: 70–78.

Tourneur, Cyril. *The Revenger's Tragedy*. Ed. Lawrence J. Ross. Lincoln: U of Nebraska P, 1966.

"The Trial of Hamlet." Lawyers' Committee for the Shakespeare Theatre. U.S. Supreme Court West Conference Room. Presiding Judge Anthony Kennedy. *C-SPAN* 17 March 1994.

The Trial of the Major War Criminals Before the International Military Tribunal: Nuremberg [U.S. transcript]. Vols. 1–23. Nuremberg: Secretariat of the Tribunal, 1947–49. 40 vols.

Tribe, Laurence H. "Triangulating Hearsay." *Harvard Law Review* 87, 5 (1974): 957–74.

Tynan, Kenneth. *Curtains; Selections from the Drama: Criticism and Related Writings*. New York: Atheneum, 1961.

United States Code. 18 U.S.C. §3664a at 507. Supplement II 1988. Washington, D.C.: United States GPO, 1991.

United States Code Service, Lawyers Edition, Title 18. 18 USCS §1071–1690. Ed. Joseph E. Edwards, et al. Rochester: Lawyers Cooperative, 1994. 50 vols.

United States Reports. Ed. Henry Wheaton. Vol. 17. New York: Donaldson, 1819–. 518–715. 495 vols. to date.

United States Supreme Court Reports, Lawyers' Edition. 2nd series. [120 L Ed 2d 305–52]. Oct. 1991. Rochester: Lawyers Cooperative, 1992.

Waith, Eugene M. "The Metamorphosis of Violence in *Titus Andronicus*." *Shakespeare Survey 10*. Ed. Allardyce Nicholl. Cambridge: Cambridge UP, 1969. 39–49.

Walker, Ralph C. S. "What He Really Means." *Times Literary Supplement* 3 Jan. 1997: 10–11.

Wardle, Irving. "Complex Simplicity." *Plays and Players* Jan. 1963: 50–51.

Watson, Robert N. *Shakespeare and the Hazards of Ambition*. Cambridge, MA: Harvard UP, 1984.

Webster, John. *The Devil's Law Case*. Ed. Frances A. Shirley. Lincoln: U of Nebraska P, 1972.

Weisberg, Richard H. "Family Feud—A Response to Robert Weisberg on Law and Literature." *Yale Journal of Law & the Humanities* 1, 1 (1988): 69–79.

———. *Poethics: And Other Strategies of Law and Literature.* New York: Columbia UP, 1992.

West, Robin. "Economic Man and Literary Woman: One Contrast." *Mercer Law Review* 39, 3 (1988): 867–78.

———. "Submission, Choice, and Ethics: A Rejoinder to Judge Posner." *Harvard Law Review* 99, 7 (1986): 1449–56.

Wigmore, John Henry. *Evidence in Trials at Common Law.* Rev. by Peter Tillers. 11 vols. Boston: Little, 1983.

Willbern, David. "Phantasmagoric *Macbeth.*" *English Literary Renaissance* 16, 3 (1986): 520–49.

Windolf, F. Lyman. *Reflections of the Law in Literature.* Philadelphia: U of Pennsylvania P, 1956.

A Yorkshire Tragedy (c. 1605–08). Ed. A. C. Cawley and Barry Gaines. Manchester: Manchester UP, 1986.

TABLE OF CASES

High Court Sessions–English Renaissance
(approximate dates)

Hilary Term (Hil.)	11 Jan.–31 Jan.
Easter Term (Pasch.)	15 Apr.–8 May
Trinity Term (Trin.)	22 May–12 June
Michaelmas Term (Mich.)	2 Nov.–25 Nov.

INDEX